T0330457

SERVICES AND EMPLOYMENT

SERVICES AND EMPLOYMENT
Explaining the U.S.-European Gap

Edited by Mary Gregory, Wiemer Salverda,

and Ronald Schettkat

PRINCETON UNIVERSITY PRESS

PRINCETON AND OXFORD

Published by Princeton University Press, 41 William Street, Princeton, New Jersey 08540

In the United Kingdom: Princeton University Press, 3 Market Place, Woodstock, Oxfordshire OX20 1SY

LIBRARY OF CONGRESS CATALOGING-IN-PUBLICATION DATA
Services and employment : explaining the U.S.-European gap / edited by Mary Gregory, Wiemer Salverda, and Ronald Schettkat.
    p. cm.
  Includes bibliographical references and index.
  ISBN-13: 978-0-691-13086-6 (casebound : alk. paper)
  ISBN-10: 0-691-13086-8 (casebound : alk. paper)
    1. Service industries—United States.   2. Service industries—Europe.   3. Service industries workers—United States.   4. Service industries workers—Europe.
  I. Gregory, Mary (Mary B.)   II. Salverda, Wiemer.   III. Schettkat, Ronald.
    HD9981.5.S436   2007
    331.7′93094—dc22   2006037145

British Library Cataloging-in-Publication Data is available

This book has been composed in Sabon.

Printed on acid-free paper. ∞

press.princeton.edu

Printed in the United States of America

10 9 8 7 6 5 4 3 2 1

Contents

Preface

THIS VOLUME presents the results of a two-year international research project, Demand Patterns and Employment Growth: Consumption and Services in France, Germany, the Netherlands, Spain, the United Kingdom and the United States (abbreviated DEMPATEM). The project was coordinated by Wiemer Salverda and Ronald Schettkat and involved a substantial group of economists representing the various countries featuring in the research.

The DEMPATEM results are accompanied by invited contributions from four economists who have been leading analysts of the role of the service sector in employment and productivity growth: William J. Baumol, Richard B. Freeman, Victor R. Fuchs, and Robert J. Gordon. The editors are grateful to these distinguished economists for accepting our invitation to contribute to this volume.

We are also grateful to the many colleagues who attended the conference in Seville in October 2003 where the project findings were presented and who offered their comments and suggestions. None of them, or the invited contributors, should be taken as endorsing the conclusions of the DEMPATEM project.

We thank the European Commission for its generous funding of the research under the Fifth Framework Programme. We also wish to acknowledge the broader setting of the European Low-wage Employment Research Network (LoWER). The work undertaken within DEMPATEM aligns closely with the objectives and research agenda of the Network, and the two groups overlap significantly in membership (see http://www.uva-aias.net/lower.asp).

We thank our universities for their support, and in particular for hosting the workshops held in Oxford, Madrid, Paris, London, and Amsterdam.

We especially wish to thank the colleagues who cooperated so fruitfully in carrying through the project. Their contribution is only partially reflected in their authorships of the individual chapters. The full membership of the project team and the series of working papers that underlie the results are listed at the end of the book. The report to the European Commission can be found at http://www.uva-aias.net/files/lower/dempatemFinRep.pdf.

Mary Gregory
Wiemer Salverda
Ronald Schettkat

Contributors

William J. Baumol is Academic Director, Berkeley Center for Entrepreneurial Studies and Professor of Economics, New York University.

Richard B. Freeman is Herbert Ascherman Professor of Economics at Harvard University, Director of the Labor Studies Program at the National Bureau of Economic Research, and Senior Research Fellow in Labour Markets at the Centre for Economic Performance, London School of Economics.

Victor R. Fuchs is Henry J. Kaiser Jr. Professor Emeritus, Stanford University, and Research Associate, National Bureau of Economic Research.

Andrew Glyn is Fellow and Tutor in Economics at Corpus Christi College and the Department of Economics, Oxford University.

Robert J. Gordon is Stanley G. Harris Professor of the Social Sciences, Northwestern University.

Mary Gregory is Fellow and Tutor in Economics at St Hilda's College and the Department of Economics, Oxford University.

Adriaan S. Kalwij is Lecturer in Econometrics at Utrecht School of Economics, University of Utrecht.

Stephen Machin is Professor of Economics at University College, London and Research Director of the Centre for the Economics of Education at the Centre for Economic Performance, London School of Economics.

Joachim Möller is Professor of Empirical Macroeconomics and Regional Economics, Universität Regensburg, and Director of the Munich Institute of East European Studies (Osteuropainstitut München).

Giovanni Russo is an economist affiliated with the University of Trieste.

Wiemer Salverda is Director of the Amsterdam Institute for Advanced Labour Studies, University of Amsterdam, and Coordinator of the European Low-wage Employment Network, LoWER.

Ronald Schettkat is Professor of Economic Policy at Bergische Universität Wuppertal.

John Schmitt is an economist with the Center for Economic and Policy Research, Washington, D.C.

Michel Sollogoub is Professor of Microeconomics at the University of Paris-I Panthéon-Sorbonne and a member of the research laboratory Theory and Applications in Microeconomics and Macroeconomics TEAM.

SERVICES AND EMPLOYMENT

Introduction

Mary Gregory, Wiemer Salverda, and Ronald Schettkat

THE "JOBLESS GROWTH" experienced in the United States in the economic cycle of the first years of the 21st century brought to the fore an issue that has for some time been a major focus of political concern in Europe—the "missing jobs" or "employment gap." In the early 1970s the employment rate in the European Union economies[1] was marginally above the rate in the United States. Over the ensuing quarter-century the United States forged ahead in job creation while in Europe employment growth was at best sluggish. By the initial years of the new millennium the employment rate in the economies of the European Union averaged 65.3 percent of the population of working age, while in the United States it had risen to 74.4 percent. This gap of over nine percentage points represents around 25 million "missing jobs" in the EU. In response to this, and to the concomitant problems of higher unemployment rates, the prevalence of long-term unemployment, premature withdrawal from the labor force, and limited employment opportunities for women in many (but not all) EU countries, the EU Heads of Government at their Lisbon summit in 2000 adopted the objective of raising the employment rate across the European economies by almost ten percentage points within the following decade. If this ambitious objective is to be realized, even with some slippage beyond 2010, it is essential to gain an understanding of the factors that have given rise to the employment gap between the European Union and the United States.

There is no dearth of candidate explanations for Europe's poor employment performance. The most prominent have been those that center on labor market institutions of "social Europe" and the rigidities that they introduce: trade union power in wage bargaining, and the mandatory or conventional extension of bargaining outcomes to nonunionized workplaces; employment protection provisions; minimum wages; the generosity of unemployment benefit systems; the size of the tax wedge of payroll, income and consumption taxes between the wage cost to the

---

[1] We are referring to the relevant group of countries rather than the political entity. In 1970 the EU still comprised only the original six countries; the membership of 15 was reached in 1995. The enlarged EU of 25 members from 2005 lies outside our scope.

employer, influencing labor demand, and the take-home pay of the worker, affecting its supply. This view, given initial impetus by the OECD's *Jobs Study* of unemployment in the advanced economies in the early 1990s (OECD 1994), has a natural resonance with U.S. commentators but also has support within Europe.[2] Its influence can be seen in contemporary policy stances. In the United Kingdom the Labour government through Chancellor Gordon Brown has claimed a strong macroeconomic record in conjunction with its deregulated labor market. In the face of unemployment rates of 10 percent or above, Germany has attempted to seek major changes to its social insurance and unemployment benefit arrangements with the Hartz reforms, while France has retreated from the legislated 35-hour working week.

Even as these latter economies edge towards reform the argument on the centrality of labor market rigidities is losing its cohesion as the links between labor market institutions and employment performance are put under detailed scrutiny. The conjunction of labor market rigidities and high unemployment is increasingly accepted as involving only a minority of EU economies, albeit several of the major ones: Germany, France, Italy, and Spain. Rigidities in product and financial markets are coming under the spotlight, with restrictions to competition, innovation, and the creation of new firms all seen as inhibiting employment growth. Most tellingly, the emergence in the United States of jobless growth, more typical of European experience, is undermining the easy invocation of the job creation capability of the unregulated U.S. labor market.

The employment gap between the United States and Europe is not simply about jobs. Not only are more Americans in employment, but they work more hours per week and more weeks per year, mainly through shorter vacation entitlements and even shorter vacations actually taken. Per head of the working-age population Americans work an average of 25.1 hours each week of the year, the Germans 18.0 and the French 17.4. This implies that hours worked per person in France and Germany are around 70 percent of the U.S. level. As with the jobs gap, these differences are of recent origin. In the early 1970s hours worked per person of working age were approximately the same in the United States and Europe. Americans continue to work broadly the same hours as in 1970 but have raised their participation rate substantially. Europeans now work much shorter hours and have failed to compensate for this decline in hours by a rising participation rate. This poses the question: why does the population of the world's richest country work so much, while less wealthy continental Europeans take leisure?

If this reflects social and cultural attitudes between the two sides of

---

[2] Leading exponents include Siebert (1997), Nickell and Layard (1999), and Nickell (2003).

the Atlantic, why has this divergence emerged so dramatically since the early seventies? Frank (1999) argues in *Luxury Fever* that cultural attitudes are themselves shaped by the economic context of national life. The consumption patterns of the American income elite, whose incomes have been rising substantially in recent decades, stimulate consumption by less well-off Americans. In a book that has received widespread attention Warren and Tyagi (2003) make the argument that access to a public infrastructure that is increasingly diverging in quality, especially in the quality of schools, is pushing Americans into a spending race. To gain access to good schools, often located in the suburbs, households now require two incomes in order to be able to meet the higher housing and transport costs involved. As a result of these spending pressures, they argue, double-income families are in real terms no better off.

In a provocative recent contribution American Nobel laureate Prescott (2004) claims that "virtually all the large differences between the U.S. labor supply and those of Germany and France are due to differences in tax systems," particularly the higher income tax rates in Europe. This is a striking claim, as he acknowledges he had expected the major influences to be institutional constraints on the operation of labor markets and the nature of the unemployment benefit system.

Prescott's diagnosis has come under vigorous challenge from Alesina, Glaeser, and Sacerdote (2005), who also reject any appeal to deep cultural differences between a European approach to leisure and the workaholism of the United States. Instead they revert to the theme of labor market institutions, but with a new twist. Noting the sustained role of collective bargaining in continental Europe over the relevant time frame, they focus on the commitment by European labor unions to a policy of "work less, work all" in support of employment. Their argument is that, while this has failed to increase employment overall, it may have had a society-wide influence on leisure patterns through a "social multiplier" where the value of leisure is enhanced as more people participate. Alesina, Glaeser, and Sacerdote then raise the question whether union policies and regulations to which they have led, such as legally mandated holidays, are suboptimal in distorting labor supply decisions. Or are they in fact welfare-improving for the European countries, as Blanchard (2004) argues? General reductions in working hours achieved through collective bargaining may solve the coordination problem, allowing everyone to enjoy a lower-hours equilibrium than a competitive individualistic market would sustain (Schelling 1975).

The United States–Europe comparison can be taken a step further in a way that places the performance of the European economies in a more favorable light. Productivity growth has been much faster in Europe than in the United States over the last 30 years, such that productivity in Europe is now converging on the U.S. level. Since 1970 GDP per hour worked in the EU has risen from 65 to over 90 percent of its level in the United States, and in France it has even exceeded it in several recent years. This has occurred over a period in which the gap in GDP per head has remained virtually constant, with the European economies at 70 percent of the U.S. level. Just how dramatic these changes have been is shown in figure I.1, where the gap in GDP per head is decomposed among productivity per hour worked, mean hours of work per worker, the share of the working-age population in work (the employment rate), and the share of the working-age population in the total population.[3]

Until the mid-1970s the United States was the clear productivity leader with the EU countries partly compensating for the effect of their lower productivity on GDP per head through a higher employment rate and longer working hours. From the mid-1970s there was significant reversal in both these dimensions. U.S. labor input increased markedly through both the employment rate and hours of work, while in Europe employment rates remained stagnant and working hours fell sharply; these combined movements reversed the negative U.S. balance in labor input. At the same time the huge initial productivity lead of the United States was substantially eroded. By the 1990s the U.S. advantage in per capita income was being maintained largely through higher labor input supplementing its much reduced superiority in productivity.[4] The later years of the 1990s saw a partial reversal of this picture, sustained into the 2000s. Productivity growth in the United States recovered to rates last seen in the 1960s. This resurgence has, however, slowed down the "great American jobs machine," such that the U.S. growth pattern be-

---

[3] GDP per head of population can be written as

$$\frac{Y}{pop_{tot}} = \frac{Y}{hE} * \frac{hE}{E} * \frac{E}{pop_{15-65}} * \frac{pop_{15-65}}{pop_{tot}},$$

where Y denotes GDP, pop is population with subscripts tot for total and 15–65 for working age, h denotes hours of work, and E is persons employed. Using logs, the difference between the United States and Europe can be expressed as the sum of the differences in the components:

$$\Delta \ln \left(\frac{Y}{pop_{tot}} \right)^{US\text{-}EU} = \Delta \ln \left(\frac{Y}{hE} \right)^{US\text{-}EU} + \Delta \ln \left(\frac{hE}{E} \right)^{US\text{-}EU}$$

$$+ \Delta \ln \left(\frac{E}{pop_{15-65}} \right)^{US\text{-}EU} + \Delta \left(\frac{pop_{15-65}}{pop_{tot}} \right)^{US\text{-}EU}.$$

[4] For further detail and discussion of these developments see Blanchard 2004; Gordon 2004; Freeman and Schettkat 2002; and Baily and Solow 2001.

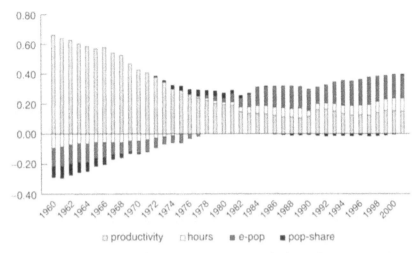

Fig. I.1. Contributions to the Gap in GDP per Head of Population, 1970–2001 (U.S. less EU at PPP prices)
Source: Computations are based on OECD data (Economic Outlook database, OECD PPP benchmarks [OECD 2002]).

gins to appear to parallel European experience (see Gordon, this volume; Schettkat 2004). In the succinct summary given by Blanchard (2004) the main difference in economic performance over the past 30 years is that Europe has used its higher rate of productivity growth to increase leisure as well as income, while the United States has forgone additional leisure in favor exclusively of higher income.[5]

The most direct route to higher income is the two-earner household, with high female labor market participation. The share of two-earner couples is some ten percentage points higher in the United States (and the United Kingdom) than in other European countries, and the shortfall in female employment in Europe is the largest single source of the U.S.-EU jobs gap (Salverda, Bazen, and Gregory 2001). Two-earner households and long-hours workers buy from the market goods and services that, at lower employment rates, would be provided within the house-

[5] This broad-brush description relates to the European countries as a group and ignores much cross-country variation. Employment rates are high in the Netherlands and the United Kingdom; hours of work declined dramatically in the Netherlands but not the United Kingdom; productivity differences with the United States are now minor except in the United Kingdom and Spain, with France in particular in some years exceeding U.S. levels of output per hour.

hold: child care and elder care, house maintenance and cleaning, ready meals and meals outside the home, valeting services for the income-rich and time-poor. This perspective has been further developed by Freeman and Schettkat (2005), who note that hours spent in market work have been declining for men while they have increased for women, especially in the United States, with the major difference in time spent in market work occurring among women in the core age group 25–54. In the 1990s overall working hours were remarkably similar for American and European women. However, the average American woman was allocating 50 percent of her working hours to the market and 50 percent to the household, while her European counterpart was spending two-thirds of her working hours on home production and only one-third in the market. This substitution of home production by market purchases of goods and services, a development that has been labeled *marketization*, has proceeded further in the United States than Europe. As Freeman and Schettkat further argue, this difference in marketization and the allocation of working time sustains a higher level of market demand, and one that comprises a different mix of purchases, with a particular orientation towards services (see also Freeman, this volume).

This insight on the role of marketization is a fruitful starting point for an alternative approach to the U.S.-EU employment gap, through demand differences. A striking feature of United States–Europe comparisons is that the gap in demand per head of population is considerably greater than the income gap, and has been widening over recent years as the employment gap has become established. A further, frequently neglected, fact is that the transatlantic employment gap is highly skewed, concentrated almost entirely in certain services. Although the industrialized economies are now all "service economies," this description applies with particular force to the United States. The share of services in U.S. final demand is around ten percentage points higher than in the European economies. While the shift of output and employment towards services continues everywhere, this "services gap" shows no sign of diminishing.

Two well-known explanations have been put forward for the increasing role of services in a modern economy. The "hierarchy of needs" postulates a shift into the consumption of services as income rises. More precisely, Fuchs (1980) has shown that the share of services in overall employment follows a logistic curve against income per capita, a relationship that continues to hold. Baumol's (1967) "cost disease," on the other hand, suggests that important areas of service provision are technologically stagnant and therefore experience rising relative prices, resulting in larger shares of expenditure and employment being concentrated in services. Both these approaches are directed to explaining the rising share of services within an economy over time. Our focus is the international comparative one. Why is the role of the service sector so much larger in the United States? In particular, how far do differences in levels and patterns of demand, including the marketization of household production, explain the United States–Europe differences in employment?

This major research agenda was addressed in the international project Demand Patterns and Employment Growth: Consumption and Services in France, Germany, the Netherlands, Spain, the United Kingdom and the United States (abbreviated DEMPATEM). The objective of the project was to examine how far differences in demand patterns, particularly for services by households, could account for the employment gap between the United States and these various EU economies. The analysis spans both the level and the structure of demand at the macroeconomic level and its detailed composition at the household level. To do this effectively required the assembly of a multinational research team to prepare comparable micro-level data on the expenditure patterns and characteristics of households, and on employment. The research program was constructed to be an integrated whole, while representing the range of European economic models and experiences. Together the five selected economies comprise 70 percent of the population of the EU-15. Germany and France are the major economies of the continental EU, and key representatives of the European "social model" and its current employment challenges. The United Kingdom and the Netherlands feature considerable success in employment growth, and dimensions of labor market flexibility, particularly in the substantial role of part-time work. Spain represents the new, fast-growing economies in the west and southern regions; it has its own approach to the employment problem through fixed-term contracts. The main economies not represented are the Scandinavian group, whose socioeconomic model is *sui generis* and, while widely respected, is not attracting imitators. The United States is taken as the benchmark throughout.

The framework for the DEMPATEM project combines micro-level analysis of demand and employment patterns with economy-wide multisectoral modeling of their linkages. Patterns of household consumption expenditure recorded in budget surveys are analyzed on a comparable basis across countries, with as much disaggregation, particularly of services, as the data allow. Differences in household composition and in the labor market participation of household members are incorporated. Harmonized input-output tables for each country trace the implications of demand patterns for the sectoral structure of production and levels and patterns of employment. The period analyzed, the 1970s to the late 1990s, brought significant structural change affecting consumption, production, and employment. In the EU economies the real incomes of households rose at historically high rates, bringing rising levels of consumption and living standards, a development that was more muted in the United States. On both sides of the Atlantic production patterns were increasingly characterized by deindustrialization and the continuing shift to services. Outsourcing, increasingly involving offshoring, was hollowing out manufacturing industry, in part replacing activities previously conducted within manufacturing by bought-in supplies, particularly of services. Business services, supplying to producers, became one of the fastest-growing sectors, as service-to-service supply chains in particular were developed. In employment, although each country experienced the shift to services, the striking characteristic was the divergence between the rising employment rates in the United States and their static record in the EU, giving rise to the employment gap.

The following chapters draw on the DEMPATEM analysis and the invited contributions to analyze a range of facets of the role of the service sector in the employment experience of the United States and the EU over recent decades.

In chapter 1 Wiemer Salverda and Ronald Schettkat introduce the analysis by highlighting the nature and source of the employment gap. In its emergence and persistence an association can be seen between the employment gap and the gap in expenditure per head (the "demand gap") between the United States and Europe. The employment gap is concentrated in the service sector, and within that in two areas, most importantly distribution, hotels, and catering, followed by community and personal services. Consumption dominates demand in both the United States and Europe, but particularly in the United States. Demand for services dominates in consumption, again particularly in the United States. The level and composition of private household expenditures are strongly influenced by institutional arrangements, with the public sector frequently an important provider of services for consumption in Europe that are provided privately in the United States. When services that are publicly provided for individual consumption, such as health care and education, are reallocated to private consumption, collective consumption emerges as taking a remarkably similar share of demand in the United States and in Europe. The rising relative price of services everywhere is confirmed. At purchasing power parity (PPP) dollars, however, services overall emerge as more expensive in the United States, although this relates heavily to education and health care rather than to marketed services such as hotels, restaurants, and recreational services. A final section reviews the main hypotheses that have been put forward to explain the rising share of services and indicates how these have been approached in the chapters that follow.

It was Victor Fuchs whose crucial contributions in the 1960s along-side those of William Baumol launched the debate on the reasons for the growing importance of the service sector. In chapter 2 Fuchs looks back at his own arguments in the light of the experience and enhanced knowledge gained over the intervening decades. He confirms with updated empirical support his famous finding on the rise in the employment share of services and its strong statistical relationship to GDP growth both across countries and over time within countries. Explaining this phenomenon, however, he still views as a difficult task. He endorses as the two main candidate explanations the differential growth in demand for services due to their higher income elasticity, on the one side, and low productivity growth in their production, on the other. He is, however, pessimistic about the possibility of successfully disentangling their relative contributions. The great stumbling block that he notes is the difficulty of achieving accurate measurement of service sector output (and therefore productivity). In health care, one of the largest service industries, developments in diagnosis and treatment bring not only longer lives but lives of higher quality. More subtly, part of the output of health care takes the form of caring—valued by the patient and properly a part of the industry's output, but again rarely measured. A further difficulty for the measurement of productivity, peculiar to services, is the contribution of the consumer as a cooperating agent in their production. In making her selections in the supermarket she contributes to productivity in retailing, while how well she follows her medication regime influences the productivity of her health care professionals. Fuchs concludes by indicating the pervasive implications of the growth of the "service economy": more employment opportunities for women, more self-employment, a greater role for small firms and nonprofit organizations, and, perhaps most fundamentally, the greater "personalization" of work.

William Baumol's seminal contribution in 1967 has caused his name to become inextricably bound up with the "cost disease" hypothesis, in which the growing share of services in the economy is attributed to the slow evolution of labor productivity in this sector. Baumol reminds us that he has always been happy to acknowledge that changing preferences in favor of services may also contribute to the growing employment share of services—this may even enhance the role of the cost-disease story, as he puts it. In his present contribution (chapter 3) he develops the cost disease approach a step further, probing within the service sector. He distinguishes three types of service, *stagnant*, *progressive*, and what he terms *asymptotically stagnant*. These are differentiated by their productivity characteristics. *Stagnant services*, of which health and education are leading instances, are characterized by the "handicraft attributes" of personal contact, preventing productivity gains and giving rise to cost disease. On the other hand, many of the services involved in the "new economy," such as telecommunications, where personal contact is not involved, achieve sometimes spectacular productivity growth. In an initially surprising and apparently paradoxical claim he then identifies a third set of services, *asymptotically stagnant sectors*, related to R&D and innovative activity. These services are not only subject to the cost disease themselves, but also "in some sense may be deemed the ultimate source of the problem." The contribution of R&D and innovation is the ultimate source of the remarkable growth of productivity achieved in agriculture and manufacturing. This productivity growth brings about these sectors' ever-diminishing share in employment. The "asymptotically stagnant" sectors themselves use inputs from both stagnant and progressive sources. Initially costs fall due to the progressive inputs, but then rise asymptotically as the inputs from stagnant sources take an ever-increasing share. R&D exemplifies the asymptotic stagnancy as stagnant mental work—we are no more proficient than Isaac Newton—is combined with equipment such as computers from progressive sources. In due course, Baumol suggests, the growing costs of R&D will lower demand for these services, slowing the pace of innovation everywhere including in goods production and mitigating the cost disease. He ends, however, in more upbeat mode, drawing on the conclusion from Oulton (2001) that, where asymptotically stagnant services, such as innovation, contribute intermediate inputs to other sectors, any nonzero productivity growth will contribute additively to productivity in the production of final output.

In chapter 4 Mary Gregory and Giovanni Russo address the DEMPATEM agenda directly, analyzing the impact of demand patterns on employment using an input-output framework applied to the United States and the five EU economies. The key concept that they use is the employment generated economy-wide in supplying each product or service to final demand; this encapsulates the employment created at all stages of the production process, reflecting technologies adopted throughout the supply chain. When employment intensity is measured on this basis, some striking results emerge that throw an important new light on the transatlantic employment comparison. The employment intensities of services and goods production emerge as approximately equal; the popular wisdom of the greater employment intensity of services emerges as an illusion, based on the final stage of delivery only. At the same time final demands originating in both services and "manufacturing" (i.e. nonservices) are increasingly generating jobs located in services. The final demand mixes of the European economies are *more* employment-friendly than the U.S. pattern; the demand mixes of all the European countries would raise U.S. employment, while the U.S. mix would result in lower employment in the European economies. On the other hand the European consumption patterns tend to be *less* employment-friendly than that of the United States. The consumption patterns of France and Germany would reduce U.S. employment by 3–5 percent respectively; conversely, if the U.S. consumption mix were adopted in the European economies, the level of employment there would be 2–4 percent higher. The most striking finding from Gregory and Russo's analysis is that demand growth has been the major source of employment growth, offset by job losses through labor productivity gains. Structural change along the supply chain, including outsourcing, both creates and destroys jobs, with only a small net effect. In the United States stronger demand growth has brought more job creation, while weaker productivity gains have been less job-destroying than in the European economies. These are the major factors that have opened up the employment gap.

This macro picture arising from the DEMPATEM research is complemented by the comparative analysis of household consumption patterns reported by Adriaan Kalwij and Stephen Machin in chapter 5. This rests on six detailed country contributions by John Schmitt for the United States, Laura Blow for the United Kingdom, Marijke van Deelen and Ronald Schettkat for Germany, François Gardes and Christophe Starzec for France, Adriaan Kalwij and Wiemer Salverda for the Netherlands, and Javier Ruiz-Castillo and María-José Luengo-Prado for Spain. The analysis is based on household budget surveys for each country. A major problem for the cross-country analysis of household expenditure patterns is the varying role of public provision, particularly in health care and education. The analysis here is restricted to those expenditures that are unaffected by the differing public/private split in provision across the six countries, giving coverage of between 55 and 75 percent of total average household expenditures in each country. Kalwij and Machin document the strong increase in expenditure on housing and other services, notably food and beverages away from home, private transportation, and communication services at the expense of the budget share of food and nonalcoholic beverages. In all countries the relative price of services has risen. The level of total household expenditure emerges as the most important influence on the rising budget share of services over time, with a further, smaller, impact from the changing demographic composition of households, including the rise of two-earner households. Overall the shift towards services runs parallel between the United States and Europe, but with the United States at a higher level. A wealth of further detail on consumption patterns is available in the individual country reports among the DEMPATEM working papers listed at the end of the book.

Following the theme of the importance of differences within the service sector, chapter 6 by Andrew Glyn, Joachim Möller, Wiemer Salverda, John Schmitt, and Michel Sollogoub takes as its focus retailing, along with hotels and catering. Within private services this sector makes the biggest single contribution to the transatlantic employment gap. It is the service sector most closely related to the consumption activities of households, and is exclusively in the market sector of the economy. In all countries these industries' workforce is biased towards women, young workers, and the low skilled, groups whose wage position would be at risk without the protection of collective bargaining or wage regulation. However, the authors' analysis of the wage structure in retailing relative to the rest of the economy shows that the retail sector in the United States is not able to exploit the higher wage flexibility often claimed and pay lower wages relative to regulated Europe. They conclude that differing wage patterns are not a dominant source of employment differences between the United States and Europe in these sectors. Examining relative productivity and its growth, the authors find that stronger productivity growth in the distributive services in the European economies contributed to the jobs gap in this sector only in the 1970s; in the two later decades this effect disappears. Labor market inflexibilities, prompting the substitution of capital for labor and forcing "excessive" labor productivity, do not appear to have been the fundamental restraint on European services, particularly in the 1990s. Their main finding is that the much higher volume of goods consumption per capita in the United States as compared to Europe—the "throughput" in distribution—is the main proximate factor behind the employment gap in retailing. Productivity is somewhat higher in European retailing but this plays only a subsidiary role.

In chapter 7 Robert Gordon also tackles the question of relative U.S. performance in retailing, but set in the context of the dramatic loss of ground by the European economies since 1995. This short span of years has seen Europe's growth rate of output per hour drop to only half the rate in the United States, wiping out fully one-fifth of the European productivity catch-up of the previous half-century (from 44 to 94 percent of the U.S. level, and then back to 85 percent). His main theme is that the discussion of policy reform in Europe has focused too narrowly on deregulation of labor and product markets when recent trends reflect much more fundamental lifestyle choices. Gordon notes that much of the acceleration of U.S. productivity growth in this period originates with distribution, particularly retailing, driven by the move to the "big box" retailing format on a large plot of land in a sprawling metropolitan area. He sees this as an example of "American exceptionalism," reflecting an attitude to urban growth that contrasts with the land-use planning and regulation found in Europe. A further area that Gordon addresses is the growing American dominance in many frontier areas of innovation. While this is fueled by information and communication technology (ICT), its roots lie deeper in many features contributing to the more favorable environment for innovation in the United States. While these institutions and lifestyle choices may not be universally admired on either side of the Atlantic, the rapid reopening of the productivity gap between Europe over the past few years is a sharp reminder of their fundamental importance.

Richard Freeman (chapter 8) examines the "marketization" hypothesis, that higher employment in the United States is due to the more extensive shift of traditional household production—food preparation, childcare, care of the elderly, domestic cleaning—to the market there than in Europe. Using time-use surveys and other sources, he shows that household production is lower in the United States than in Europe. As he notes, the marketization of household production is a powerful development as it works on both sides of the labor market to increase employment. On the supply side, when more women work in the market, taking the time from household production rather than leisure or the market time of other household members, household production is reduced. This increases market demand for replacement goods and services, either directly through the purchase of, for example, cleaning services, or indirectly through the nature of goods purchased, such as prepared meals in the supermarket, all of which generate additional employment. The differing extent of marketization affects the composition as well as the level of employment. Given the historical concentration of women in household production the marketization argument applies most readily to differences in women's employment, a major dimension of the United States–Europe employment gap. Increased engagement in paid work by more highly educated women, whose comparative advantage is likely to lie in market-based employment, will increase demand for lower-skilled workers to replace them in carrying out domestic jobs.

Chapter 9 brings together the insights into the role of services that emerge from the analyses in the earlier chapters, relating them to the various explanatory hypotheses to gauge their relative force. Unsurprisingly, given its widespread and complex roles, the growing prominence of the service sector is found to reflect a range of influences involving the behavior of households, firms, and governments. The greater orientation towards services of the U.S. economy can be seen as accounting for part of the United States–Europe employment gap. More strikingly, however, the period from the early 1970s to the mid-1990s appears to have been exceptional on both sides of the Atlantic. In the United States it featured remarkable expansion of employment but with only limited productivity gains; in the European economies it was characterized by strong productivity growth but sluggish employment. The emerging record of the decade since the mid-1990s suggests some reversal of these patterns. In the United States productivity growth has been remarkably strong relative to previous decades, while employment growth has slackened. In Europe, on the other hand, employment growth is becoming less sluggish, while productivity growth is faltering. Extrapolating these trends would suggest that the United States–Europe employment gap will start to narrow, while the productivity gap may again widen. We see the driving force behind the range of developments described in the individual chapters as the ongoing search for efficiency gains through specialization and the division of labor, implemented through the market. The growing role of the service sector epitomizes this process and carries it forward.

CHAPTER 1

The U.S.-European Gap in Service Employment and Demand: The Research Agenda

Wiemer Salverda and Ronald Schettkat

IN THIS CHAPTER we consider the evolution of the transatlantic gap in employment and relate it to the level and the structure of employment in services. This is followed by a discussion of the hypotheses found in the literature that aim to explain these from the level and structure of demand for goods and services (hierarchy of needs, marketization of household services), the production of services (cost disease), the structure of production (outsourcing), and the nature and evolution of the labor market (wage compression, female participation). Finally, we introduce the way the hypotheses are approached in the chapters that follow.

THE UNITED STATES–EUROPE EMPLOYMENT GAP

The past three decades have seen the patterns of employment in the European economies and the United States evolve in strikingly different ways. In the early 1970s the employment rate in Europe was higher than the rate in the United States, although the difference was small. The United States then forged ahead, expanding its labor force by 55 million between 1970 and 2000 in a development that led some commentators to talk of "the American jobs machine." At the same time employment growth in Europe[1] was at best sluggish. As a consequence, at the start of the new millennium the employment rate in the United States had risen to 75 percent, over 10 percentage points higher than in 1970, while in Europe it had declined by one percentage point to 66 percent. This

The authors are extremely grateful to Mary Gregory for her invaluable help.
[1] In this study *Europe* normally refers to the group of countries involved in the DEMPATEM project: France, Germany, the Netherlands, Spain, and the United Kingdom. Together these comprise almost 70 percent of the population of EU 15.

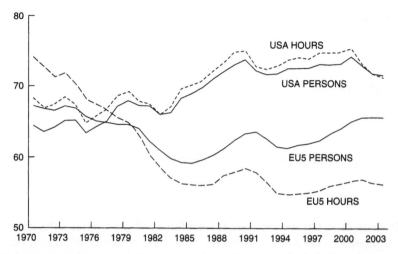

Fig. 1.1. The U.S.-Europe Employment Gap: Employment Rates, Measured as Persons in Work and Hours Worked, Percentage of Working-Age Population
Note: Hours worked are converted to full-time equivalents of 1,840 hours per year.
Source: OECD Labour Force Surveys Database; OECD Annual Hours Worked per Person Database.

gap of nine percentage points represents around 25 million "missing jobs" in the EU. Measured in hours worked, the divergence is even more striking. Average hours of American workers declined by 5 percent over this period, while those of European workers fell by 21 percent. Americans now spend an average of 1,350 hours annually in paid work per head of the adult population compared to only 1,030 hours for a European adult.

Figure 1.1 shows this evolution of the employment gap between Europe and the United States. From the mid-1970s until the end of the 1990s the employment rate (the number of persons employed as a proportion of the working-age population) in the United States shows a clear upward trend with only minor cyclical setbacks, until the "jobless growth" cycle at the turn of the century. In Europe, on the other hand, the employment rate shows a steady decline until the mid-1980s, which the subsequent recovery, with its strong cyclical pattern, has not fully offset. The jobs gap began to open up as the employment rate in Europe fell sharply during the recession of the early 1980s, and has remained relatively constant thereafter. For hours worked[2] the difference in pattern

---

[2] Annual hours worked are based on OECD statistics , with additional estimates by the authors for Spain before 1977. The figures used here for employment differ somewhat

is even starker. The United States has been characterized by an upward trend in hours worked closely paralleling the growth of employment. In Europe, on the other hand, hours worked fell steeply and continuously from 1970 through to the mid-1980s. This downwards trend was checked in the later 1980s, and since then has fluctuated cyclically around an essentially flat trend, although, as with employment, some narrowing of the gap in hours can be detected in the last years of the period.

Differential employment growth in the United States and in Europe coincides with many other transatlantic differences, for example, in the role of the public sector, welfare state provisions, wage and income inequality, and labor market regulation. Not surprisingly, many efforts have been made to explain the employment gap in terms of these differences in the economic and social "models" favored on the two sides of the Atlantic. The most frequent line of argument, of which the OECD's *Jobs Study* (OECD 1994) is one of the earliest and most prominent exponents, attributes the sluggish European record on employment growth to differences in labor market regulations. Employment protection in Europe, it is argued, causes employers to be reluctant to hire, while high unemployment benefits slow job search by the unemployed, reducing wage pressure and preventing labor markets from shifting to a higher employment equilibrium.

A large volume of literature compares European labor market institutions with the perfect market model and discovers inefficiencies; it then equates the actual U.S. labor market to the perfect market model and concludes that European labor market institutions need to be reshaped in accordance with the U.S. model (for a prototype paper along these lines see Siebert 1997; a comprehensive critical discussion is given in Freeman and Schettkat 2002, 2005). However, no actual institutional arrangement can win the beauty contest with the theoretical model. It is also clear that the actual U.S. labor market cannot be equated to the perfect model; clearly it contains imperfections. Further, it is not obvious how far European labor market institutions should be classified as imperfections; on an alternative view they can be regarded as measures to overcome imperfections rather than just as impediments to otherwise smoothly functioning labor markets (Blanchard 2004).

Moreover, the links between employment protection and employment performance, between unemployment compensation and employment,

---

from those given by the OECD because of differences in sources and methods. For example, the labor force surveys tend to produce higher estimates for European employment than National Accounts figures. Although the estimated employment rates may differ between countries on the different estimates, the trends are similar (see Schettkat and Damen 2004).

and between wage inequality and employment that the OECD inferred have proved difficult to substantiate empirically (for overviews see OECD's *Employment Outlook,* annual issues; Bertola 1999; Nickell and Layard 1999; Machin and Manning 1999; Freeman, this volume). In addition, the results of many studies exploiting time-series information have been found to be very sensitive to the periods covered and the specification of key variables (see Baker et al. 2004). On the other hand, assessments of U.S. employment growth indicate that it cannot be reduced to the expansion of low-wage industries; rather it has occurred independently of the industry's initial wage position (Freeman and Schettkat 1999, 2001b; Krueger and Pischke 1999). Consequently more recent studies investigating the transatlantic employment gap have brought a shift of emphasis. Institutional heterogeneity within the European Union has become a central feature (Blanchard and Wolfers 2000). The OECD itself has led the way in replacing the exclusive focus on labor market institutions by a major role for product market regulation as a further source of the diverging trends observed in employment.

A common feature of these approaches is that high European unemployment and sluggish employment growth are regarded as equilibrium outcomes, that is, as the employment rates compatible with stable inflation. To shift the economy to an equilibrium with lower unemployment and higher employment requires institutional reforms, especially a reshaping of the incentive structure in labor markets to make low-wage employment more attractive in Europe. In other words, the focus is on improving the performance of the EU economies from a supply-side perspective (Blanchard 2004). This approach can be summarized as "Get supply right and demand takes care of itself."

Where the general equilibrium approach gives primacy to the supply side in determining income and output, with demand in the subordinate role, our approach makes the level and pattern of demand its central focus. It can be argued that differentiating between demand and supply is immaterial. As Alfred Marshall pointed out a century ago, demand and supply cut as the two blades of scissors. However, which is the better focus is relevant to the issue at hand. Demand does not necessarily exactly reflect income or GDP. Relative to Europe, the United States has low rates of household saving and taxation, supporting high private consumption relative to income. Moreover, higher income may be spent in different ways, creating different levels and patterns of employment. These are the aspects on which we now focus.

The Demand Gap and Services Employment

Two striking, but neglected, features of the economic situation between Europe and the United States over the past 30 years have been that the emergence of the employment gap has been paralleled by a significant and growing demand gap, and that the employment gap is not economy-wide but is heavily, indeed almost exclusively, concentrated in the service sector. The conjunction of these two features prompts the hypothesis that the employment gap may be linked with the level, and possibly the associated pattern, of demand through the relative role of services in the United States and Europe. We consider these two aspects in turn, linking them through the role of services.

It is well known that income per capita is higher in the United States than in Europe, so that differences in the level of demand per capita between the two sides of the Atlantic are also to be expected (e.g., Blanchard 2004). The concept of the demand gap captures the differences in domestic demand relative to GDP in the United States and Europe, with its evolution over time reflecting the development of demand relative to production on the two sides of the Atlantic. The demand gap is thus analogous to the employment gap, capturing United States–Europe differences in employment relative to population. The demand gap between the United States and Europe is shown in figure 1.2. The United States has had a higher level of demand throughout the period. The margin was relatively narrow for some years until the mid-1980s, when it widened sharply, at the same time as the employment gap became established. The demand gap then increased strongly through the 1990s, substantially exceeding the gap in GDP per head as the United States trade deficit grew while Europe recorded a persistent export sur-

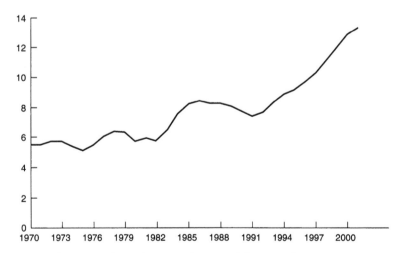

Fig. 1.2. The Demand Gap between the United States and Europe
Standardized demand = domestic demand / GDP
Source: Authors' calculations based OECD Economic Outlook Database.

plus. This demand gap has shown no tendency to diminish in the most recent cycle. While the demand gap and the employment gap do not track each other throughout, the similarities in the timing of their emergence, and their persistence, are suggestive. The demand gap appears too important as a macroeconomic phenomenon to be ignored in the search for explanations of the employment gap.

The demand gap can be seen to derive from household consumption and particularly from consumption of services. Table 1.1 shows the employment gap together with the gaps in demand and consumption, for agriculture, manufacturing, and services, and for the five European economies individually relative to the United States. All are expressed as lev-

TABLE 1.1

Employment, Final Demand, and Private Household Consumption per Head of Population 15–64 Years (US $ PPPs, US = 100, 1995)

	US[a]	UK[b]	FR	GER	NL	ESP
Employment (FTEs)[c]						
Overall	100	86.4	78.6	87.6	77.6	69.8
Agriculture	100	73.7	143.3	94.3	105.6	189.9
Manufacturing	100	109.1	93.3	137.4	88.6	94.3
Services	100	81.9	71.9	70.7	73.4	58.1
Final Demand						
Overall	100	78.3	70.7	65.2	82.9	50.1
Agriculture[d]	100	112.8	91.0	56.3	234.9	94.8
Manufacturing	100	94.8	92.8	88.9	99.9	62.4
Services	100	67.6	59.8	54.1	72.0	43.4
Consumption						
Overall	100	70.3	63.3	54.8	56.8	42.6
Agriculture[d]	100	141.9	150.6	93.8	47.5	129.0
Manufacturing	100	90.1	83.7	59.1	38.2	49.8
Services	100	63.0	58.2	53.6	60.9	40.5

Source: Computations based on OECD Input-Output Database for demand and OECD STAN Database for employment.
[a] Data refer to 1998.
[b] Data refer to 1997.
[c] Employment is measured as persons adjusted to a full-time equivalent basis.
[d] The international comparable input-output tables of the OECD are based on an industry, not a commodity, classification. Consumption of "agriculture" is therefore not identical to the consumption of food.

els per head of adult population. Overall, the demand shortfall in Europe exceeds the employment shortfall, while the consumption shortfall is greater again. In agriculture the European economies often exceed U.S. levels of employment, demand, and consumption. They are fairly close in employment and demand for manufactures, although rather less so in consumption of manufactures. The major and systematic disparities occur for services, where the shortfalls in demand and particularly in the consumption of services in the European economies are very pronounced.

Figure 1.3 charts the evolution of the employment gap for services against its level for the whole economy. A substantial gap in services employment between the United States and Europe is long-standing; the U.S. employment rate in services has consistently been 10 percentage points or more above its level in Europe. Until the mid-1970s the shortfall in service employment in Europe was more than offset by higher rates of manufacturing and agricultural employment. Between then and the mid-1980s rapid productivity growth and concomitant deindustrialization in Europe eliminated that advantage, and by the end of the 1990s the jobs gap can be seen as virtually entirely concentrated in services. On this dynamic perspective the decline in agricultural and then manufacturing employment in Europe has made the key contribution to the rising jobs gap with the United States—in that it has brought into the

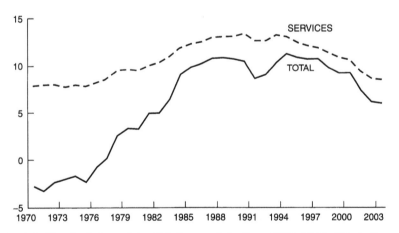

Fig. 1.3. The Evolution of the U.S.-Europe Jobs Gap, 1970–2003, Whole Economy and Services (difference in employment/population rates, percentage points) Services are defined as community and personal services, finance and business services, retail and wholesale trade and hotels, transport, and communications. *Source:* Computations are based on data in the Economic Outlook Database of OECD.

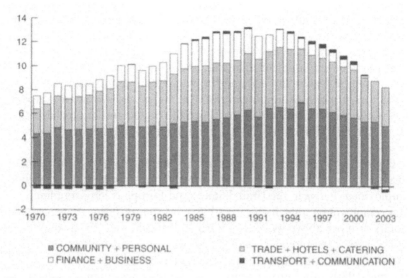

Fig. 1.4. The Composition of the Employment Gap in Services, 1970–2003
Employment-to-population (aged 15–64) ratios for the U.S. minus France, Germany, Netherlands, Spain, and UK
Source: Authors' calculations based on OECD Labour Force Statistics Database.

open the large and continuing difference in service-industry employment.

The service sector is, however, a very broad and heterogeneous category that includes widely diverging activities. Figure 1.4 therefore disaggregates the employment gap in services by the main service industries. The two biggest sources of the employment gap between the United States and Europe emerge as the retailing, hotels, and catering sector, and community and personal services (which include education, health care, and public administration as well as private sector services such as hairdressing). These sectors are all characterized by a strong orientation towards consumer demand. Transportation and communication are very similar in size in the United States and Europe. The finance and business services sector had a higher share in 1970 and grew much more rapidly in the United States in the 1980s, more than doubling its employment share in a very few years. However, Europe caught up shortly afterwards, and by the end of the period the employment gap in this sector was turning in its favor. Thus services to business play a very similar role in the United States and in Europe (Greenhalgh and Gregory 2000, 2001; Russo and Schettkat 1999). The main source of the employment gap thus emerges as being in services that predominantly supply the consumer. At the same time it is clear that the growth of services employment (head count) in Europe on balance matched that of the United States.

The jobs gap question can therefore be redefined: why does the United States employ about 10 percentage points more of its adult population in the provision of consumer services than the average European country?

SERVICE DEMAND IN EUROPE AND THE UNITED STATES

The United States and the European economies are all now service economies, in that demand for services makes up half or more of overall final demand. The share of services has undergone a systematic and sustained rise since 1970, shown in table 1.2. In many cases the increase in the service share can be seen even within a five-year period. The transatlantic difference is very evident. For the most part, the service-sector share in final demand in the United States has been around 10 percentage points higher than in the United Kingdom, France, and the Netherlands, rather more in Germany. In the 1990s the service share in the European countries was close to, sometimes still below, the level it had already reached in the United States in the 1970s.

TABLE 1.2
The Share of Services in Final Demand (current prices)

	Share (%)			*Share (%)*	
United States	1972	55.2	Germany	1972	
	1977	55.0		1978	41.4
	1985	58.1		1986	42.8
	1990	60.9		1990	41.8
	1997	63.0		1995	51.4
United Kingdom	1968	43.4	Netherlands	1972	41.5
	1979	44.2		1977	43.6
	1984	48.2		1986	44.1
	1990	50.4		1990	
	1995	57.9		1995	48.0
France	1972	33.8	Spain	1972	
	1977	42.8		1977	
	1985	47.2		1986	50.6
	1990	48.2		1990	55.9
	1995	53.7		1995	54.7

Source: Authors' calculations from OECD Input-Output Database.
Note: Blank cells indicate data not available.

For each economy the overall share of services depends on both the composition of national aggregate demand (between private consumption, government consumption, investment, imports, exports) and the relative share of services within these components. Exports, for example, consist mainly of manufactured goods, so that countries with a strong export orientation will tend, ceteris paribus, to have a lower service share in final demand. As is illustrated in figure 1.5, top panel, consumption is everywhere the dominant component of aggregate demand, accounting for 70 percent or more. Moreover, the consumption share is for the most part markedly higher in the United States than in the European countries, often by around five percentage points, although the gap is nine percentage points in the Netherlands, a small open economy with high shares of exports and imports. The United Kingdom, however, is a notable exception, with the consumption share exceeding the U.S. level.

Services in Consumption

In the same way that consumption dominates in aggregate demand, services dominate in consumption, comprising over 70 percent of consumption against one-third or less for exports and under one-quarter for investment (table 1.3). The result of this combination of dominant roles is that between 80 and 94 percent of final demand for services arises from consumption.

Private and Public Consumption

The level and composition of private household expenditures are strongly influenced by institutional arrangements involving public against private provision, for example in the health and education sectors. When a household purchases a product, this is classified as household consumption. If the government buys or provides the same product, this is classified as government or public consumption. In Europe the public sector is frequently an important provider of services for consumption that are provided privately in the United States (see also the further discussion in Kalwij and Machin, this volume). Differing institutional arrangements are most prominent in health care, where public provision is the norm in Europe while private purchase has a major role in the United States. Other sectors where public provision is more commonly found in Europe than in the United States include child and elder care, parts of education and housing, and income insurance, including pensions. In countries where public provision is strongest, notably France and Germany, government consumption is typically between 25 and 35 percent of final consumption, while in the United States it is only 17 percent.

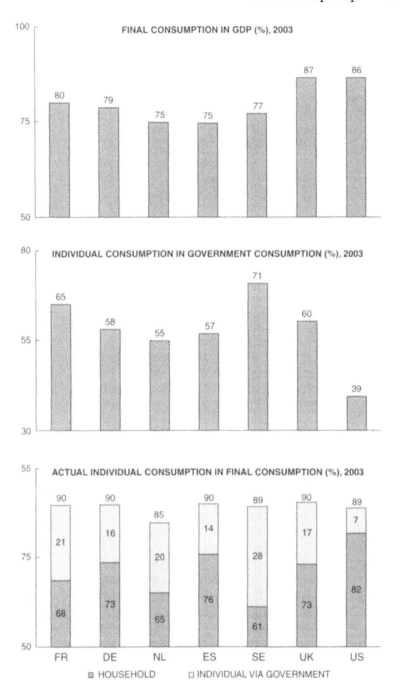

Fig. 1.5. Consumption and Individual Consumption, 2003
Source: Authors' calculations based on OECD National Accounts Statistics.

TABLE 1.3
The Share of Services in Components of Final Demand (current prices)

| | | Final Demand | Consumption | | | Investment | Exports | Imports |
	Year	Overall	Overall	Private	Public			
United States	1997	63.7	78.5	77.8	81.7	21.0	30.5	14.6
United Kingdom	1995	57.9	75.0	67.9	100.0	15.9	33.0	17.1
France	1995	53.7	71.6	60.7	97.2	19.6	16.6	9.3
Germany	1995	51.4	75.5	65.9	99.6	13.4	14.3	10.8
Netherlands	1995	48.7	80.8	71.9	95.9	22.1	21.7	12.9
Spain	1995	54.7	74.5	67.8	96.0	15.8	18.3	10.2

Source: Authors' calculations based on OECD National Accounts Statistics

This differing role of public provision of health and other services is reflected in the higher share of services in public consumption in the European economies shown in table 1.3.

To circumvent the impact of differing institutional arrangements for providing the same service, the categories of "individual" and "collective" consumption, distinguishing the ultimate beneficiary, can be used in place of private and public consumption, based on the purchaser of the service.[3] Public consumption is thus divided into the part provided directly to the individual consumer, which includes education and health care, and the part that is true collective consumption, such as defense or public administration. Individual consumption then comprises private household expenditures plus the individual consumption that is publicly provided; public consumption is identified with collective consumption. For the European economies about 60 percent of public consumption is classified as individual and only 40 percent as collective; for the United States, where public consumption is already smaller due to greater role of private purchase, only 40 percent is classified as private, and the proportion of collective consumption rises to 60 percent (figure 1.5, center panel).

This poses the interesting question: how big is the collective sector in the United States relative to Europe, once the public provision of individual services is removed? As shown in the bottom panel of figure 1.5 a surprising degree of equalization emerges. In all countries collective consumption takes a very similar proportion of overall final consumption, around 10 percent (higher in the Netherlands). Even Sweden, included as potentially an extreme example of collective provision, conforms to this pattern. Collective consumption in the United States is neither larger (in spite of the greater expenditure on defense) nor smaller (in spite of the ethos against collectivism) than in the European economies. Government consumption is higher in Europe because governments provide more services direct to individual consumers; "true" collective consumption is no higher in Europe than in the United States.

The Price of Services

Services have been absorbing an increasing share of demand everywhere as incomes have grown, and take a higher share in the United States where incomes and expenditure are higher. How far do these developments reflect "real" changes over time and differences across countries? Or does the rising share of services reflect their increasing relative price, leading them to take an ever larger share of expenditure? In other words,

---

[3] This approach is applied in the present UN System of National Accounts (SNA).

do service prices rise more than the prices of goods? If they do, is this because demand is increasingly oriented towards services, putting upward pressure on their prices, as Fuchs and others have suggested? Or does slow productivity growth put upward pressure from the cost side, as Baumol's "cost disease" would indicate? On the international comparison, there is a widely held belief that services are relatively cheaper in the United States, leading to higher demand there. More specifically, it is argued that low wages in service industries employing low-skilled labor in the United States lead to low prices for these services, inducing Americans to substitute consumption of services for consumption of goods. We first review the relative trends in service prices within each country, in terms of national prices. We then compare price structures across countries.

The share of services in final demand at constant national prices is shown in table 1.4, which can be compared with table 1.3. The upward trend in the share of services is again evident, but is much more muted than at current prices, indicating the contribution of the rising relative price of services (see below).

The relative price trends for individual categories of household consumption are shown in table 1.5. In order to identify them while ab-

TABLE 1.4
The Share of Services in Final Demand at Constant (National) Prices

		Share (%)			Share (%)
United States	1972	51.4	Germany	1972	
	1977	54.0		1978	41.0
	1985	54.0		1986	41.6
	1990	55.6		1990	40.5
	1997			1995	
United Kingdom	1968	40.3	Netherlands	1972	43.2
	1979	42.9		1977	43.1
	1984	47.1		1986	43.0
	1990	44.7		1990	
	1995			1995	
France	1972	42.5	Spain		
	1977	43.5			
	1985	46.5			
	1990	45.1			
	1995				

Source: Authors' calculation from OECD Input-Output Database.
Note: Blank cells indicate data not available.

TABLE 1.5
Implicit Price Trends in Individual Categories of Private Household
Consumption Deviation from Overall Price Trends of Final Consumption
(percentage points, 1980–latest available years)

	US	UK	FR	W GER	NL	SP	SE
Food	0.03	0.04	−0.06	−0.58	−0.4	−0.15	−0.59
Clothing	1.43	1.65	2.65	1.67	0.47	3.79	2.52
Furnishing	0.33	1.16	−0.05	0.22	0.88	−0.13	0.46
Housing	0.17	0.31	0.49	1.02	0.97	0.07	1.15
Restaurants and hotels	−0.18	0.38	0.70	−0.85	−0.07	−1.90	0.74
Transport and communication	0.32	0.35	−0.08	0.29	0.48	0.25	0.73
Recreation	−2.20	−1.44	−0.20	−0.63	−0.63	0.06	−0.30
Education	2.05	1.60	1.55	2.65	2.28	1.12	0.74
Health	0.67	0.36	−1.09	−0.04	−0.93	−0.19	−0.78
Miscellaneous	1.01	0.44	0.13	0.56	0.56	0.33	−0.57
Total goods	−0.76	−0.92	0.05		−1.65		−0.87
Total services	3.21	3.68	3.05		−2.22		4.84

Source: Authors' computations based on OECD National Accounts (OECD 2000b)

stracting from the varying national rates of price inflation,[4] the change
for each individual category is expressed as a deviation from the overall
trend in national prices. In each country the generalization about faster
rises in service prices is confirmed; inflation in services has outstripped
the rise in goods prices by a significant margin (table 1.5, final row).
Since 1980 service prices have risen by more than 3 percent annually
relative to the overall price trend, while the prices of goods have lagged
behind it by about 0.8 percent annually (unweighted average across
countries). The individual expenditure categories within both goods and
services, however, show diverse patterns. In particular, within services
these range from a falling price of recreation to steep increases in the
costs of education, both relative to trend inflation. (While the distinction
between goods and services prices is insightful, it is acknowledged that
the expenditure categories themselves are all to a degree composite;

[4] Overall price inflation was computed as the trend in the implicit price deflator, derived
as the ratio of current to constant prices. The time series were taken from the OECD
National Accounts, volume 2. These run from 1980 to slightly varying dates in the 1990s,
as available. The expenditure categories for the 1990s follow the 1993 SNA classification.
They are not strictly comparable with the earlier data, but at the level of the major categories used here, the differences are small.

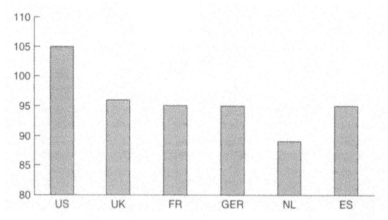

Fig. 1.6. Prices for Consumer Services Relative to Goods Prices in the U.S. and in EU Countries
Source: Authors' calculations based on OECD National Accounts.

health care includes the cost of medications, while the services provided by restaurants and hotels involve the provision of food and the use of furnishings.) While the rising relative price of services is unambiguous, it is nonetheless clear that this differential in price inflation has not been sufficiently strong or systematic to be more than a part of the explanation for the rising share of services in expenditure.

Turning to the international perspective, are relative price structures similar in Europe and the United States, or what differences does the consumer face? The price of consumer services relative to goods in purchasing power parity (PPP) dollars[5] is shown in figure 1.6, based on a detailed EU-OECD analysis (OECD 2002). This reveals that it is goods rather than services that are relatively cheaper in the United States. The European consumer in each of the five countries faces a lower cost of services than the U.S. consumer; one dollar buys more services but fewer goods in Europe. By contradicting the conventional wisdom that services are cheaper in the United States, this result also undermines the hypothesis that the U.S. service sector is bigger than its European counterpart because of a more service-friendly price structure in the United States.

[5] PPPs (usually expressed in U.S. dollars) give the quantity of goods or services one dollar could buy in another country at a common set of relative prices. PPPs have the advantage over standard nominal exchange rates of taking the local price structure into account, allowing for the comparison of the "quantities" consumed of various products. PPPs are sometimes also labeled *(international) constant prices*, though *international comparable prices*—for a number of countries at a certain point in time—would be a better label.

While overall the relative price of services is higher in the United States, systematic differences emerge between the United States and Europe in the price structure for individual services. Services traded in markets, including hotels, restaurants, and recreational and cultural services, have a markedly higher relative price in Europe. The two European "low-price service industries" are health and education. Both are characterized by a mix of public and private provision and financing so that prices are cost indicators rather than actual market prices. Nevertheless, government involvement in the provision of health and education, which especially in health is stronger in Europe than in the United States, does seem to be associated with a lower price level in these industries.[6]

The overview preceding has indicated a number of aspects in which the empirical evidence challenges conventional wisdom on both the sources of the employment gap and the role of services. The next section introduces the various hypotheses that have been put forward to link the role of services with labor market outcomes.

LINKING INCOME/DEMAND AND SERVICE EMPLOYMENT: THEORETICAL HYPOTHESES

Service Employment and the Growth of GDP: A Striking Regularity

A striking empirical regularity has been identified by Victor Fuchs (1980): across time and across countries the share of service industry employment in total employment is closely related to the level of income (GDP) per head, a relationship that holds with an "astonishing" degree of predictability "seldom observed in economics." The Fuchs relationship is displayed in figure 1.7[7], where the solid line represents the relationship for the United States based on time-series estimates for the years 1960 to 2001, when U.S. real per capita incomes grew from US$13,800 to 36,700. The curve is fitted within the assumption that the share of service employment in total employment tends to zero at very low levels of GDP per capita and grows with income asymptotically towards unity. The actual positions of the five countries that represent Europe for the various years are located relative to this line.

At higher levels of income per capita, the Netherlands, France, and the United Kingdom tend to reach even higher shares of service-industry employment than the predicted American shares, while Germany tends

---

[6] Whether lower prices (costs) of public provision in Europe result from quality or efficiency differences cannot be discussed here.

[7] The data presented in figure 1.7 relate to persons; data limitations preclude adjustment for hours of work.

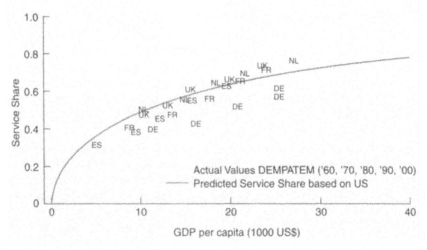

Fig. 1.7. Predicted Service Share in U.S. Employment, and Actual Shares for France, Germany, Netherlands, Spain, and UK (1960, 1970, 1980, 1990, 2000) *Source:* Authors' calculations.

to be below the predicted values. These deviations of observed from predicted values of the Fuchs curve are, however, minor. The correlation between predicted and actual values is remarkable. In particular, the United States does not appear to be an exceptional case in terms of the relation between the share of services and income (see also Fuchs, this volume).

As impressive as the regularity between service-industry employment share and income per capita is, it leaves open the question of causality and why this pattern is so persistent. Fuchs himself explicitly notes that these results are "not tests of theoretically grounded hypotheses" and that no appropriate economic theory has been developed to explain this phenomenon. A number of hypotheses have, however, been advanced aimed at explaining the association between GDP per head and the employment share of services. We distinguish five separate, although not mutually exclusive, hypotheses covering demand, supply, the boundaries of the market, wage-setting institutions, and production structures (for a comprehensive discussion see Schettkat and Yocarini 2003).

DEMAND: THE HIERARCHY OF NEEDS

The earliest hypothesis on the growth of the service share in employment is the "hierarchy of needs" approach, a demand-side approach based on income elasticities. Fisher (1935) and Clark (1951) argue that countries will demand more services as incomes rise because services are luxuries, that is, have an income-elasticity greater than one, whereas the demand for goods has an income-elasticity less than one. Services satisfy higher needs than goods, ranking above them in the hierarchy of needs. As income grows, a larger share is allocated to the purchase of services, raising the share of services in employment.

SUPPLY: THE COST DISEASE

William Baumol (1967, 2001, this volume) challenges the hierarchy-of-needs hypothesis with the argument that the shift to service employment results not from an evolving demand pattern but from differential productivity growth between sectors. He formally eliminates any effect from demand by assuming that, at constant prices, goods and services each receive a constant share of real income. If services lag behind in productivity growth because of technological stagnation, rising real income and therefore overall demand will require a higher growth rate of service employment. If, further, it is assumed that wages in services must increase in tandem with the technologically progressive nonservice part of the economy, then the prices of service outputs must rise more than proportionally. Income per capita grows because of the productivity growth in technologically progressive goods production, while relative productivity in the service sector declines over time. The rise in the service share in employment in Baumol's "cost disease" model derives not from any shift in demand in favor of services but from their technological stagnancy (or asymptotic stagnancy, see Baumol, this volume).

Thus, according to Baumol's model the higher share of service industry employment in the United States than in Europe should result from higher per capita income in the United States caused by the higher level of productivity in U.S. goods production. This model is very much in line with the observed situation up to the 1970s, when the United States and Europe were on similar employment levels but at different productivity levels with the U.S. economy being technologically the more advanced. From the mid-1970 until the late 1990s, however, U.S. per-capita income grew largely because of rising labor inputs rather than productivity gains. For this period of the 1980s and 1990s, the cost-disease hypothesis seems to fit less well as an explanation for rising U.S. service employment. Moreover, the recent recovery of U.S. productivity growth has been related to a rise of productivity in services. Explanations for, and therefore sustainability of, these productivity improvements range from a "cure of Baumol's disease" (Triplett and Bosworth 2003) to a onetime "Walmart-Effect" (Wolff 2005; see also the appendix to this chapter).

INCOME GENERATION AND MARKETIZATION

In his seminal studies, Fuchs (1968, 1980, this volume) confirms that demand for services is relatively constant when measured in constant prices, but he adds complexity by arguing that not only the level of income per capita but also the way in which that income level is achieved can affect the structure of demand. For example, a high degree of female labor force participation will necessarily reduce household production, which then may be substituted by market-produced services and goods. The outsourcing of productive activities from the household to the market has been labeled "marketization" (Freeman and Schettkat 2002). (This consequence for relative United States–Europe employment of the differing degree of marketization parallels the impact on GDP comparisons of the exclusion from national accounts of household production and the welfare contribution of possible leisure time, as noted by Ironmonger 2000). If, as is claimed, marketization is more advanced in the United States than in European countries, with American households outsourcing production to a greater extent than those in Europe, one should observe higher employment in the United States, particularly of women, higher per capita income in the United States, and higher spending levels by American households. Furthermore, in terms of the distribution of household time American households should be observed as allocating more hours to market activities, substituting them for hours in household production. Evidence on the observed patterns of domestic time-use appears to confirm this (see Freeman and Schettkat 2005; Freeman, this volume). In 1970 this was of little relevance as Europe (EU4) had a slightly higher employment rate for women than the United States, but this situation has changed markedly over the past three decades.

OUTSOURCING OF SERVICE ACTIVITIES TO SPECIALIZED SERVICE FIRMS

A further explanation frequently offered for the rapid growth of services (and as source of deindustrialization) is the phenomenon of outsourcing (Schettkat and Russo 2001; Greenhalgh and Gregory 2001; Gregory, Zissimos, and Greenhalgh 2001). It is a common observation that manufacturing and service firms increasingly focus on core activities and outsource noncore activities to specialist suppliers. Much of the outsourcing involves services, notably recruitment, marketing, information technology (IT), and financial services, but also cleaning and security. This process supports, and is supported by, differentially rapid growth of these "business to business" services. In one sense nothing "real" changes with outsourcing. Activities previously carried out in-house are now purchased from external suppliers. When the outsourcing is of services by manufacturers, the fall in manufacturing employment and shift to services (deindustrialization) are merely a statistical artifact, generated by the national accounting convention that employees are classified to the sector of their employer's main activity. However, outsourcing is undertaken in order to achieve lower costs or efficiency gains through specialization and economies of scale among suppliers. Outsourcing relocates but also eliminates jobs; the overall result is improvements to productivity (Ten Raa and Wolff 2001). If less regulation of new firm formation and greater entrepreneurial spirit encourage the more intensive development of specialist service suppliers to business in the United States, this will be a further source of the lagging service share in employment in Europe, particularly in business services.

THE WAGE-COMPRESSION HYPOTHESIS

Politically the most influential view in recent decades has been that employment growth in services in Europe has been constrained by over-compressed wage structures, which fail to reflect differences in productivity levels between individual workers or between sectors of the economy. A range of labor market institutions is held to contribute to this equality in wages. Collective bargaining compresses the wage structure, reducing differentials and imposing rigidities. Minimum wages and generous unemployment benefits keep the wages of the low skilled too high to allow their profitable engagement by employers. On this view strongly differentiated wages in the United States support expansion of low-skill, low-wage service industries there, while compressed wage structures in Europe restrict the development of these services. This leads to the policy stance that more flexible wage structures, including a widening of earnings dispersion, could provide a cure for Europe's stagnant employment record.

In terms of the wage-compression hypothesis, an increase in wage inequality can be seen as a cure for Baumol's cost disease, if it allows wage growth to be constrained to the lagging productivity growth of services. In Baumol's model, wages in goods and service production rise at the same rate under the assumption of competitive labor markets. However, in imperfect labor markets wage differentiation in accordance with industry-specific productivity growth rates may reduce or even cure the cost disease. The "rising wage-differential hypothesis" thus shares many aspects with Baumol's original model but, crucially, relaxes Baumol's assumption of competitive labor markets by allowing wages to be differentiated according to industry productivity. Ironically, for this mechanism to work, imperfect rather than competitive labor markets are required, whereas the usual rhetoric is that European labor markets need to become more competitive.[8] While basically a supply-side perspective, wage compression may also potentially have an impact through demand; low-skilled services are importantly purchased by consumers, and these demands will be curtailed by high relative prices.

EXPLORING THESE THEMES

These various hypotheses on the sources of the growing service share provide the connecting themes across the contributions that follow.

The demand-side hypothesis, that the demand for services is income elastic, driving up their share in expenditure as incomes rise, is of longest standing. As services become increasingly the dominant sector in the advanced economies, how far can this generalization continue to be maintained? This was the key theme of the research by the international group coordinated by Kalwij and Machin as part of the DEMPATEM project (chapter 5 in this volume). Using consumer budget surveys, patterns of household expenditure are analyzed within and across the six selected economies (France, Germany, the Netherlands, Spain, the United Kingdom, and the United States) based on a detailed commodity breakdown constructed to give like-for-like comparisons as far as possible. The changing role of services in household budgets leads to the identification of luxury and losing categories, in terms of rising and declining expenditure shares, within goods and services purchases. These patterns are then related to a range of potential determinants including household structure and demographic characteristics, and relative prices, to identify the role of changing preferences.

Discrimination between the respective impacts of demand and the cost disease as sources of the rising share of services can be achieved through the role of relative prices. To the extent that shifting preferences bring an increase in relative demand for services, their relative price will rise, and their increasing share in expenditure should be evident when measured at constant prices. On the other hand, to the extent that services are affected by the cost disease of relatively low productivity growth, the shift to services, at unchanged preferences, will be visible in nominal expenditure shares and in employment but not in expenditure shares at constant prices. The harmonized data for the six countries are utilized by Kalwij and Machin to examine both the trend in the relative price of services within each country and its role in accounting for the rising share of services.

[8] For empirical challenges to the "wage-compression hypothesis" see Krueger and Pischke 1997; Card, Kramarz, and Lemieux 1999; Freeman and Schettkat 1999, 2001b; Möller 2004; and chapter 6 this volume.

How far do the rising share of services in consumption demand and the greater service orientation in the expenditure patterns of U.S. households explain the higher levels of employment there? An appropriate framework for this is a multisector input-output table. Each category of household consumption requires, in addition to the final output, intermediate outputs from many sectors of the economy, both goods and services. At each of these stages employment is created, arising ultimately from, and therefore attributable to, the household's consumption. Using this framework Gregory and Russo (chapter 4) estimate the extent to which the growing service-orientation of household consumption has affected employment in each of the countries individually. They then simulate the employment that would result in the United States were each of the European consumption patterns, with their lower service shares, to apply, and conversely the level of employment that would result were the U.S. pattern to be adopted in the European economies.

The "marketization" hypothesis offers a related approach for analyzing the United States–Europe employment gap through the role of services. It provides a powerful framework because the shift from household to market work raises both the supply and the demand for labor, impelling greater employment from both sides of the market. The increase in time supplied to the market, particularly by women, requires market purchases of goods and services in replacement of household production; this in turn generates demand for labor for their production. The marketization hypothesis subsumes three separate but related elements. First is the division of household time between market work and household work, particularly by women. The second element is that households that supply more market work demand additional market goods and services to substitute for foregone household production— "less time spent in meal preparation at home should produce greater expenditures on food in restaurants" (Freeman, this volume). The third element is that spending patterns associated with the outsourcing to the market of household activities should be reflected in differences in employment patterns in activities such as catering, day care for children, and private services to households (see Freeman, this volume).

The first subhypothesis, on the division of household time between the market and home production, is explored by Freeman using comparative household time-use surveys. The changing pattern of household purchases with the increase in market work is examined as a further theme in the Kalwij-Machin analysis, through the impact on spending patterns of a dual-earner household structure. The third strand, on relative employment patterns, is taken up by Glyn et al. (chapter 6 in this volume). In line with the marketization hypothesis the key sectors contributing to the United States–Europe employment gap are identified as community and personal services, and retailing, hotels, and catering. Retailing then provides the context for a meso-level analysis of the impact of consumption behavior on employment in the United States relative to the European economies.

An alternative focus on marketization emphasizes the potential productivity gains from outsourcing and specialization. Part of the shift from household to market production can be seen as deriving from scale effects that accompany economic growth: "As demand increases, it becomes more efficient to produce goods and services in specialized firms instead of unspecialized households" (Fuchs, this volume). A parallel instance is the development of outsourcing by firms, a structural change in the organization of production that will also have implications for measured service employment. As the scale of the economy expands, new service firms and industries emerge, supplying services to goods-producing firms—services that might previously have been produced within the goods-producing firm itself. This theme of structural change and the outsourcing of intermediate services to business-to-business suppliers is addressed empirically for the six economies by Gregory and Russo.

To the extent that wage compression and regulated markets are a source of the lower employment levels in the European economies, the effect should be observable through greater wage dispersion, particularly in low pay, in the United States. Further, inflexible labor markets should raise labor costs, encouraging capital-labor substitution and restraining the growth of employment in favor of productivity gains. Both of these hypotheses are examined by Glyn et al. (chapter 6), again for retailing as a sector that should bring these features to the fore.

Labor productivity, as the obverse of employment, provides a natural alternative focus for comparison of the European record relative to the United States. This is the perspective adopted by Gordon (chapter 7). He too selects retailing as a key sector, noting the differing patterns of urban growth between the United States and European countries conditioned by the role of regulatory barriers and land-use restrictions. He then broadens the analysis to reflect on the environment towards innovation as the key ingredient for relative performance in productivity growth. A much less buoyant view of productivity is, however, put forward by Baumol (chapter 3). He highlights one key set of services, those related to R&D and innovative activities, that are not only subject to cost disease themselves but may be deemed the ultimate source of the cost-disease problem. They are the ultimate source of the productivity growth in agriculture and manufacturing and therefore of these sectors' continuing fall in employment requirements, but are themselves stagnant sectors, subject to cost disease. As a consequence the high productivity growth in these other sectors may in due course decline.

Both Baumol and Fuchs draw attention to the major problem for the analysis of the role of services that arises from issues of measurement. In many services the quality of the service is poorly reflected in measured output and productivity. Innovations in medical treatment or pedagogy, for example, are frequently not labor-saving but may be strongly output-enhancing. In addition to the standard problem of adjusting measured output for quality, Fuchs particularly emphasizes the role of the consumer's input into the productivity of services. The issue of the measurement of output and productivity in services is reviewed in the appendix to this chapter.

As this overview demonstrates, a wide range of themes is potentially relevant to the analysis of the role of the service sector in the modern economy. We concur with Baumol that acceptance of any one hypothesis does not imply that the others must be rejected. In complex modern economies it is doubtful whether any major occurrence or systematic relationship, such as the growth of the service sector, can be explained by a single simple hypothesis. The chapters that follow explore a number of facets of the diversity.

Appendix: Measurement of Service Output and Productivity

The treatment of service industries in economic statistics, long neglected even when acknowledged as less than satisfactory, has begun to receive considerable attention in recent years, in recognition of the fact that the advanced "industrialized" countries are now service economies. Tripplett and Bosworth (2004) report improvements in the recognition and measurement of service activities in the U.S. statistics, although many conceptual and measurement problems remain.[9] In the United Kingdom the recent Atkinson Review (2005) makes many recommendations for improving the measurement of the output of the public sector.

An initial difficulty is that "service" is an amorphous concept, often lacking a clear-cut definition, as noted by the late Zvi Griliches (1992). Often, negative definitions are applied, merely defining what a service is not: services cannot be stored; they cannot be dropped on your foot (Harker 1995). Production and consumption of services may occur simultaneously. A service may require the input of time by both its pro-

---

[9] Tripplett and Bosworth (2004) mention, for example, that the Bureau of Labor Statistics (BLS) has greatly expanded the coverage of the producer price index (PPI) program to cover a large proportion of services. Not so long ago the PPI was restricted to goods alone. The Census Bureau now produces annual surveys of most services-producing industries.

ducer and its consumer (Petit 2000).[10] Service industries are very hetero-geneous with respect to skill levels and wages, as exemplified by the contrast between fast-food and financial services, between McDonalds and McKinsey. Service activities can be found in every sector of the economy, making the range of skill requirements and wages in service occupations as heterogeneous as the economy itself (Freeman and Schet-tkat 1998, 1999).

In some services the professional provider has a productivity advan-tage over self-provision, as in many professional services; in other ser-vices, where no particular expertise is required, productivity in the two modes of production, market provision and self-provision, can be rea-sonably similar. The former are often identified as business services, whereas the latter are classified as consumer services. Consumer services have developed the image of being technologically stagnant; this fits some but not all of these services. The production of many services has undergone substantial changes in organization, sometimes towards pro-vision partly involving the time participation of the buyer. Self-service in supermarkets now begins to include even the activities of the cashier; retail banking is increasingly done by the customer through teller ma-chines and Internet banking. Here the market is clearly outsourcing to the household.

Professional services, including legal advice, tax, and accounting, are bought in the market because specialization creates economies of scale. It is difficult for smaller firms and impossible for private households to gain the necessary expertise in these areas. The concentration of exper-tise in service providers within professions creates economies of scale, allowing the fixed investment in human capital to be spread over many users. As a result of these economies of scale, services requiring profes-sional expertise can be acquired at lower cost from external providers than through internal provision, but the process may be hampered by the extraction of rents. This explains why firms outsource some services rather than producing them in-house. Again, however, if one digs deeper, the distinction between business and consumer services becomes blurred. Most services are intermediate and final at the same time. In addition, almost all products are composite products, that is, the production of final manufactures requires the input of intermediate services and the production of final services requires the input of goods. Thus differences in the degree and nature of vertical integration within activities affect the measured shares of industries (see Gregory and Russo, this volume).

---

[10] Time can be seen as a constraint on consumption (Petit 2000). Scarcity of leisure may therefore result in more "efficient consumption" as Linder (1970) has pointed out with respect to the "American way of leisure."

It is often thought that the measurement of output is more straightforward in manufacturing than in the service sector because manufacturing output is more homogeneous (Grilliches 1992, 7). The measurement of changes in quality, however, is a problem that the National Income and Product Accounts statistics has never fully solved.[11] If the price of a car increases by 10 percent, how much of that increase is caused by improvements in the car, and how much just reflects inflation? (Oi and Rosen 1992; Gordon 1990, 1998). New deflation methods such as the chain index improve measurement, but as the example of computers shows, the measurement problem affects both goods and services. But in services quality not only depends on the service provider but also on the participation of the consumer (Grilliches 1992, 5). Victor Fuchs (this volume) mentions that the right medical diagnosis may critically depend on correct information provided by the patient. In education a tutor will achieve nothing without her student's cooperation. Does a shop provide a better service if it has longer opening hours or if it arranges its goods nicely? "What is the productivity of a milkman?," is a famous question asked by Nicolas Kaldor (1966). Does the milkman double his productivity if he drops off two bottles of milk instead of one? (see also Glyn et al. in this volume).

Some authors are optimistic that the cost disease has been overcome with the use of information technology (e.g., Triplett and Bosworth 2003; van Ark and de Jong 2004). Other work, however, indicates that the recent productivity improvements in the United States are concentrated in very few service industries, where substantial changes in the organization of the industry have taken place. In retail trade, for example, the concentration of businesses may have led to onetime productivity improvements, the so-called Wal-Mart effect (see Basker 2005; Wolff 2005).

In the DEMPATEM study major efforts were made to improve the international comparability of the statistics used, based on initial information provided by the national statistical offices and improved towards international comparability by the OECD. In the micro study of household expenditures, a lot of effort has been put into securing the international comparability of the individual spending components. This also shows that improvements in international comparability come at the cost of comprehensiveness since items such as medical services are heavily influenced by the national institutional framework (see Kalwij and Machin, this volume). Inevitably, international comparative studies lack the precision and detail of specialized national industry studies.

---

[11] The OECD (1996) gives an overview of various methods used to estimate real value added in services ranging from double deflation—regarded as preferable (1996, 7)—to direct deflation by a wage rate index.

CHAPTER 2

Reflections on the Rise of
Service Sector Employment

Victor R. Fuchs

"THE MOST important concomitant of economic progress," wrote Colin
Clark in 1940, is "the movement of labor from agriculture to manufacture, and from manufacture to commerce and services." This prediction
has proven to be one of the most accurate in the history of economic
thought. In country after country, decade after decade, the service sector's share of employment has grown inexorably along with the growth
of gross domestic product per capita.

Because the service sector is the principal source of employment in all
high-income countries, policy analysts and government officials now pay
it more attention than in the past, but often for the wrong reasons.
When a country has high unemployment, expansion of the service sector
is often touted as a possible solution. In some other countries, service
employment is viewed with suspicion, as less desirable than employment
in agriculture or manufacturing. In my judgment there is little merit in
either point of view. Unless impeded by government controls, labor and
capital tend to find their way to their most productive uses. After more
than 40 years of study and reflection about the growth of service employment, I conclude that attempts to control the sectoral distribution
of employment will be relatively ineffective or counterproductive. This
chapter emphasizes the pervasiveness and regularity of the growth of
service sector employment, discusses the reasons for its growth, and con-
siders its implications for the economy, economic analysis, and society
as a whole.

THE GROWTH OF THE SERVICE SECTOR'S SHARE

The two most striking features of the growth of the service sector's share
of employment are its pervasiveness and predictability. In the United
States, the country I am most familiar with, there has not been a single

decade when the share has not been greater at the end of the decade than at the beginning. All modern societies, whether in Europe, Asia, Oceania, or North America, are "service economies" in the sense that more than half of all employed persons are working in the service industries. In many countries the share now exceeds 70 percent and is still growing.

Not only does the service sector's share grow over time, but its level at any given time in each country is highly predictable by a single variable—the level of GDP per capita. I first demonstrated this regularity using U.S. time series for 1870 through 1978 and cross-section data for 24 OECD countries in 1960, 1970, and 1976.

In order to develop a realistic, estimable form that relates each sector's share of employment to the level of GDP, I assume that

1. Agriculture's share is 1.0 at zero GDP and approaches zero asymptotically as GDP rises:

$$A = e^{\beta(GDP^{\alpha})}$$

2. Service's share is zero at zero GDP per capita and approaches 1.0 asymptotically as GDP rises:

$$S = 1 - e^{\delta(GDP^{\gamma})}$$

These equations are transformed to logarithms and estimated as a system using a maximum likelihood iterative procedure

$$\ln A = \beta \, GDP^{\alpha} \text{ and } \ln(1 - S) = \delta GDP^{\gamma}.$$

Inasmuch as Industry's share equals one minus the shares of Agriculture and Service by definition, the Industry equation is obtained as the residual:

$$I = e^{\delta(GDP^{\gamma})} - e^{\beta(GDP^{\alpha})}.$$

These regressions were run for the U.S. historical data and for OECD cross-sections in 1960, 1970, and 1976. For the OECD countries in 1970, GDP per capita in 1970 U.S. dollars was obtained from Kravis, Heston, and Summers (1978) using the International Comparison Project direct estimates for the eight countries and indirect estimates for the remainder. Real GDP per capita in 1960 (or 1976) was estimated in U.S. 1970 dollars by fixing the 1970 purchasing power parity estimate as the base and extrapolating back to 1960 (or forward to 1976) using each country's own estimated rate of change of real GDP per capita.

The results, presented in table 2.1, show similar parameter values for all four sets of estimates. Moreover, as shown in table 2.2, the correlation between the shares predicted by the regressions and the actual

TABLE 2.1

Regression Results: Sector Shares of Civilian Employment as a Function of Gross Domestic Product per Capita, U.S. Time Series and OECD Cross-Sections

	U.S. 1870–1978	OECD		
		1960	1970	1976
N	12	23	24	23
Agriculture				
β	−0.787	−0.895	−0.716	−0.722
	(0.044)	(0.131)	(0.147)	(0.158)
α	0.861	0.831	0.945	0.904
	(0.040)	(0.159)	(0.166)	(0.158)
Service				
δ	−0.306	−0.263	−0.232	−0.242
	(0.011)	(0.029)	(0.033)	(0.037)
γ	0.633	0.634	0.714	0.720
	(0.028)	(0.119)	(0.118)	(0.113)

Equations: $A = e^{\beta(GDP^{\alpha})}$ $S = 1 - e^{\delta(GDP^{\gamma})}$

Note: Standard errors are in parentheses. GDP per capita is in thousands of 1970 U.S. dollars. Currency conversions are based on direct price comparisons for 1970.

shares is very high in all cases (the median coefficient is .88). Most striking of all, the coefficients of correlation between cross predictions (using equations estimated from other series) and actual values are, on average, about as high as the coefficients between the predicted and actual shares of the same series.

The similarity of the patterns and goodness of fit are also revealed in the graphs of the U.S. and 1970 OECD equations presented in figure 2.1. The time-series and cross-section curves for Agriculture are virtually identical. The curves for Industry and those for Service also reveal a close correspondence between the shape of the U.S. time series and the OECD cross-section, but there are noticeable differences in levels. For any given real GDP per capita, the United States has had a larger fraction of employment in Service and a smaller fraction in Industry than the other OECD countries. This may be explained by differences in composition of exports, with Industry playing a larger role in the other OECD countries and Agriculture playing a larger role in the United States. It is particularly interesting to note that both the U.S. and the OECD equations predict a peak in Industry's share of employment at approximately the same level of real GDP per capita—somewhere between $3,000 and $3,500 in 1970 dollars (between $21,130 and

TABLE 2.2

Coefficients of Correlation between Actual and Predicted Sector Shares of Employment, U.S. Time Series and OECD Cross-Sections

	Actual Share			
	U.S.	OECD		
Predicted Share	1870–1976	1960	1970	1976
Agriculture				
U.S. 1870–1978	.986	.891	.924	.948
OECD 1960	.984	.893	.926	.952
OECD 1970	.986	.890	.923	.949
OECD 1976	.986	.890	.923	.947
Industry				
U.S. 1870–1978	.900	.832	.832	.754
OECD 1960	.886	.836	.820	.698
OECD 1970	.902	.830	.833	.766
OECD 1976	.901	.832	.833	.758
Service				
U.S. 1870–1978	.987	.796	.842	.871
OECD 1960	.987	.796	.842	.870
OECD 1970	.987	.796	.842	.869
OECD 1976	.987	.796	.842	.869

$24,640 in 2001 dollars). Given the functional forms imposed on Agriculture and Service, the Industry curve must first rise and then fall, regardless of whether the data fit such a pattern or not. Indeed, the distribution of Industry shares in the 1970 OECD cross-section (figure 1b) does not clearly suggest a parabolic shape for the function. It is, therefore, all the more striking that of 11 OECD countries with less than $3,250 per capita GDP in 1970, 10 showed an increase in Industry's share of employment between 1960 and 1976, while 10 of the 12 countries with more than $3,250 GDP per capita showed a decrease. This difference is statistically significant (by the Chi-squared test) at $p < .001$.

Inspection of the actual shares (also plotted on figure 2.1) shows that most observations fall very close to the estimated curves. For the U.S. time series, the median residual (absolute) is approximately 0.01 in each sector. As might be expected, 1930 and 1940 show negative residuals for Industry (−0.03) because of the depression.

For the OECD series the median residuals (absolute) are Agriculture 0.03, Industry 0.03, and Service 0.04. Most countries conform well to the predictions, but there are a few notably large residuals, some of

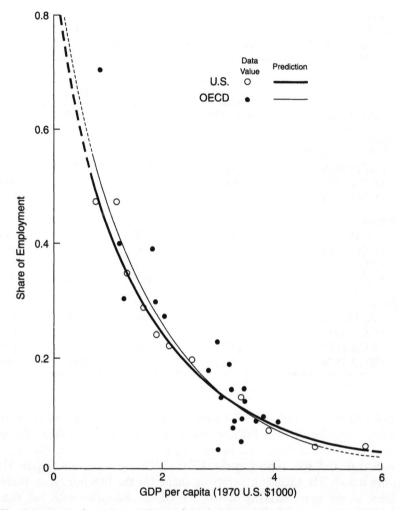

Fig. 2.1a. Agriculture Sector Share of Civilian Employment versus Real GDP per Capita, U.S. Time Series and OECD Cross-Section, 1970

which are also observed in 1960 and 1976 (not plotted). Turkey and Greece consistently have a larger than predicted share of employment in Agriculture and have large negative residuals in Industry. This may be related to the employment of many Greek and Turkish nationals in other OECD countries. The United Kingdom shows a large negative residual in Agriculture in 1960 and 1976 as well as 1970. The United Kingdom had a large positive residual in Industry in 1960; this was smaller in 1970 and had virtually disappeared in 1976.

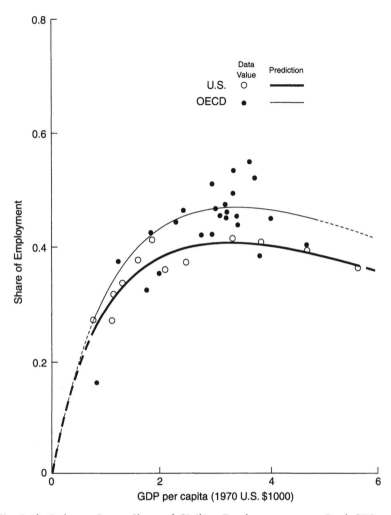

Fig. 2.1b. Industry Sector Share of Civilian Employment versus Real GDP per Capita, U.S. Time Series and OECD Cross-Section, 1970

West Germany shows an interesting pattern with substantially more employment in Industry in 1970 and 1976 than would be expected given its real GDP per capita. This excess is exactly offset by a negative residual in Service. The growth of industrial exports from Germany may account for some of this pattern.

One of the most demanding tests of an alleged economic relationship is to see how well a cross-section regression predicts change over time. Another test is to see if a time-series regression for one period in one

48 • Victor R. Fuchs

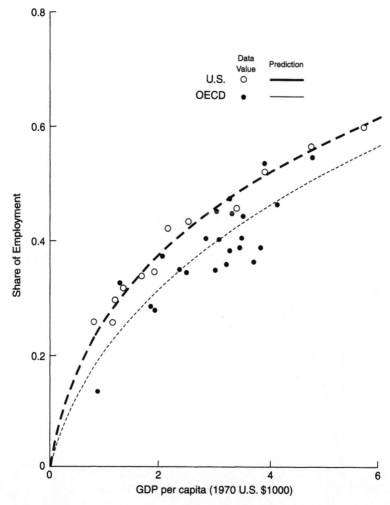

Fig. 2.1c. Service Sector Share of Civilian Employment versus Real GDP per Capita, U.S. Time Series and OECD Cross-Section, 1970

country predicts changes in other countries over a different time period. By this standard, the functions portrayed in figure 2.1 stand up rather well (see table 2.3). The actual changes in sector shares in the OECD countries between 1960 and 1976 are positively correlated with predicted changes based on either the 1970s OECD regression or the U.S. 1870–1978 regression.

The correlation coefficient between actual and predicted change is much lower for Service than for Industry or Agriculture, but this is be-

TABLE 2.3
Correlation Coefficients and Residuals of Actual and Predicted
Changes in Sector Shares of Employment in OECD Countries, 1960–76

	Agriculture	Industry	Service
Coefficient of correlation between actual change and predicted change, based on:			
OECD 1970 regression	.760	.786	.356
U.S. 1870–1978 regression	.757	.785	.324
Median change (absolute)	.90	.05	.12
Median residual (absolute)	.04	.06	.02

[a] Absolute residual = $(X_{76} - X_{60}) - (\hat{X}_{76} - \hat{X}_{60})$ where X = actual sector share, and $\hat{X}$ = share predicted by 1970 OECD regression.

cause the variance in change is small. Between 1960 and 1976 every country showed an increase in the share of employment in Service; the mean change was 0.12, but the standard deviation was only 0.04. Despite the large change in the Service share in most countries, the difference between the actual and predicted change (median absolute residual) was less than 0.02 for half the countries, and only two countries had absolute residuals larger than 0.06.

Although the correlation coefficient for Industry is higher than for Service, the median absolute residual is actually higher also. During the period 1960–76 many of the OECD countries were at levels of GDP per capita that put them on the flat portion of the Industry employment share curve. For those countries, changes in that share between 1960 and 1976 were affected relatively more by cyclical phenomena and country-specific transitory factors in either 1960 or 1976 than by movement along the long-run function.

Application of this model to more recent data (U.S. time series and pooled OECD time series for 1960–2001 and OECD cross-section for 1980, 1990, and 2001) by Ronald Schettkat shows that the regularity found for early periods continues to the present. His results are reported in detail in chapter 1 of this volume.

Of particular interest to me because so much of my research has focused on the United States is Schettkat's conclusion that the "U.S. does not seem to be an exceptional case." Not only is there generally a close correspondence between sector shares and those predicted by the model for any given level of GDP per capita, but those discrepancies that do appear can often be explained by differences in hours worked per employee. For example, hours per employed person in Germany are almost the same in the service sector as in the rest of the economy, but in the U.S. hours per employed person in services are 19 percent less than in the rest of the economy. This makes a big difference when comparing sector shares of employment in the two countries.

The regularity in the relationship between sector shares of employment and GDP per capita in many time periods and many countries, and the close correspondence between the coefficients derived from time series and those from cross-section regressions is unusual. It is tempting to think that there must be some fundamental proposition that can be derived from economic theory to explain these results. Unfortunately I do not believe that this is the case. Economics does, however, provide a framework for considering several possible explanations for the rise of service sector employment, as discussed in the next section.

WHY THE RISE?

Documenting the rise of service sector employment is an easy task. Demonstrating its relationship to the growth of GDP per capita is also relatively straightforward. But *explaining* this relationship is more difficult, and, in my judgment, much hard work remains to be done. The key obstacle continues to be the measurement of service sector output, despite considerable improvement in the measures for particular service industries.

By definition, service sector employment is identical to service sector output divided by labor productivity in the sector.

$$E \equiv O \div O/E$$

Changes in sector shares are the result of sector differences in changes in output and/or labor productivity.

If we had good measures of service sector output, and if we understood the exogenous determinants of changes in sector shares of output, the determinants of sector differences in rates of change of labor productivity, and the endogenous interactions between changes in output and changes in productivity, we could explain the rise of service sector employment. The broad outline of these interrelationships is sketched in figure 2.2.

Consider first the determinants of sector shares of output. One possibility is a higher income elasticity of demand for services than for goods. Thus, as GDP per capita rises, demand for services will grow faster than the demand for goods. This explanation received some support from Colin Clark and Allan G. B. Fisher, but in *The Service Economy* I ex-

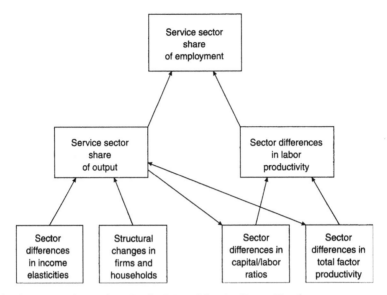

Fig. 2.2. Interrelationships in the Rise of Service Sector Employment

pressed some skepticism that this was an important explanation: "Examination of cross-sectional buying patterns and of trends in output over time, suggests that the growth of income and a consequent shift in demand has not been a major source of the relative growth of service employment" (1968, 3). My current view is that this conclusion will have to be modified if better measures of service sector output reveal that we have been underestimating its growth relative to the growth of goods output. I will return to this question later.

Structural changes in the way firms organize production can also affect measured service employment. In particular, the growth in the scale of the economy that accompanies a rise in GDP per capita may result in the formation of new service firms and industries that supply services to goods producing firms—services that might previously have been produced within the goods-producing firm itself. There is some evidence of shifts of this kind, but it probably does not involve a sufficient number of employees to account for a major share of the rise of service employment.

Probably more important has been the shift of many services out of *households* into market production as a "concomitant" (to use Clark's phrase) of economic growth. Health care, child care, education, and personal, repair, and professional services have all tended to gravitate from the household to the market economy. To be sure, there has also been a shift of goods production from households to the market: food and clothing are important examples. I believe the shift has been greater for services than goods in modern times, but the precise contribution of this shift to the rise of service sector employment remains to be determined.

Some of the shift from household to market production is undoubtedly related to scale effects that accompany economic growth. As demand increases, it becomes more efficient to produce goods and services in specialized firms instead of unspecialized households. Another related phenomenon is the increase in female labor force participation. It seems to me that the relationship between service sector employment and female labor force participation is both important and complex, as shown in figure 2.3.

Most of the increase in service sector employment probably results from exogenous factors that are unrelated to the growth of female labor force participation. Most of the latter growth is attributable to exogenous social, economic, and technological changes that are unrelated to the increase in service sector employment. But in addition, these two major trends have reinforced and amplified each other. The increase in the availability of service sector jobs has made it easier for women to find paid employment, and as more women enter the labor force, demand grows for market-produced services to replace those formerly produced in the home.

Turning from the determinants of output to those that influence sector differences in changes in labor productivity, let us consider first changes in capital/labor ratios. By capital I include both physical objects such as plant and equipment but also human capital reflecting education, formal on-the-job training, and work experience. If the capital/labor ratio has been increasing more rapidly in firms that produce goods than in firms that produce services, the share of employment in the service sector will increase, ceteris paribus. Sector capital/labor ratios may be influenced by exogenous technological change, by union wage effects, and by changes in scale of output (hence the connection in figure 2.3 to output shares).

Even if capital/labor ratios do not change at different rates in the goods and services sectors, it is certainly possible that total factor productivity has grown more rapidly in goods production, and this would

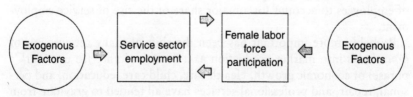

Fig. 2.3. The Relationship between Service Sector Employment and Female Labor Force Participation

tend to shift employment to services unless the fall in the price of goods relative to services induced a more than offsetting shift in demand to goods.

The slower growth of productivity in services is the explanation favored by many observers. The extreme position, advanced by William Baumol, is that there is little possibility of improvement in service industry productivity. This is surely not correct. Consider Baumol's strongest example, the productivity of a string quartet. It is true that it takes 30 minutes to play a 30-minute piece today, just as it did hundreds of years ago. This example, however, neglects the effect of recordings and television, the enlargement of concert halls and improvements in acoustics, and the speed of jet travel, which enables the same quartet to perform in one country on one day and in another one on the next. Looked at from the point of view of economic activity and the creation of utility, who can doubt that the output and productivity of string quartets has improved immensely?

Or consider one of the largest service industries, the production of health services. There is currently a burgeoning literature suggesting that official measures of output (and productivity) in this industry have been greatly understated. New drugs, new diagnostic techniques, and new surgical procedures have enabled physicians and other health care workers to make significant advances in the production of health for their patients. The results of these advances typically never make it into measures of the real GDP. Banking and finance is another sector where I suspect the growth of output has been badly understated.

To be sure, producing more accurate measures of output for the service industries will not be easy. (If it were, someone would have won a Nobel Prize for this long ago.) Take health as an example. Increased output sometimes takes the form of extending years of life, but it can also take the form of improving the quality of life through reductions in disability and pain. A comprehensive measure must combine these various dimensions of health. Econometricians, psychometricians, and biometricians are currently addressing this challenge.

The problem of measuring improvements in health in terms of length and quality of life is formidable, but measuring the output of health services is even more complex. There are certain outputs that take the form of caring or validation services that do not show up in health outcomes, but are nevertheless valued by patients and ought to be considered as part of the output of this industry.

Translating measures of output into measures of productivity is much more difficult for many service industries than it is for the goods-producing sector because the consumer is often a cooperating agent in the production process. Sometimes, as in the barber's chair, the role is essentially passive, but in the supermarket, the Laundromat, the self-serve gas station, and at the automatic teller, the consumer actually works. Conventional measures of total factor productivity that ignore the consumer input can be misleading. Not only may the consumer's time be a significant input, but the quality of that input needs to be considered. Whether or not the patient gives an accurate medical history and complies with physician instructions regarding drugs and diet can significantly influence the physician's productivity. In education, as every teacher knows, productivity is determined to a large extent by what the student contributes.

The unfortunate fact is that until we have more accurate measures of output and productivity, we will not be able to decompose the rise in service employment into the portion attributable to sector differences in growth of output and that attributable to sector differences in changes in total factor productivity. In saying this, I am retreating somewhat from the position I took in *The Service Economy*. At that time I believed that a difference in productivity change was clearly the more important explanation. Currently, I am more uncertain because the problem of measuring output tends to be more severe for services than goods and the downward bias in measuring output growth is probably more severe for services than for goods.

IMPLICATIONS OF THE RISE OF SERVICE SECTOR EMPLOYMENT

Regardless of which explanations prove to be more important, I believe the rise of service sector employment has profound implications for the economy, for economics, and for society as a whole. The transition from agriculture to industry is usually characterized as a "revolution." The shift from industrial to service employment, which advanced first and furthest in the United States but is evident in all modern economies, has proceeded more quietly, but it too has implications of "revolutionary" proportions.

Implications for the Economy

Differences between the Industry and service sectors are most noticeable with respect to labor force characteristics. I shall discuss these differences with respect to the United States, where labor markets are less influenced by unions and government regulations than in other modern economies. Thus, what we observe in the United States can also serve as an indication of tendencies that are probably present in other countries, but may be blunted by labor market curbs of one kind or another.

Probably the most significant difference is that many occupations in the service sector do not make special demands for characteristically male qualities, such as size and physical strength. This means that women can compete on more nearly equal terms with men. We find women holding down a much larger proportion of jobs in the service sector than in goods production.

There are also more older workers in services, despite the fact that this is the more rapidly growing sector and would, *ceteris paribus*, tend to have a disproportionately large number of young workers. One reason why women and older workers are attracted to the service sector is that it provides greater opportunities for part-time employment, especially in retail trade and services. If data were available on those working fewer than 35 hours per week *voluntarily*, the difference between the sectors would probably be even greater. I also believe that there is a considerable amount of service work that is performed "off-the-books," that is, in the so-called gray economy. Opportunities for unrecorded personal and repair services are probably much greater than for the production of goods because barriers to entry (capital requirements and economies of scale) are usually smaller in services. Thus the true difference in sector work is probably greater than that indicated by official statistics.

Self-employment is also much more important in the service sector than in Industry. Moreover, the census of population probably understates the number of self-employed in Services relative to Industry because corporate employees are classified as wage and salary workers regardless of the size of the corporation. The officers of small, owner-managed corporations are, for analytical purposes, similar to partners or individual proprietors, and should be considered self-employed. Most of the small corporations are in the service industries.

Given the importance of females, part-time employment, and self-employment in the service sector, it is not surprising to find a difference in the importance of unions in the two sectors. This difference was greater a few decades ago when many U.S. goods-producing industries were highly unionized and most service-producing industries were not. The difference has diminished but not disappeared as a result of the dramatic decline of unions in manufacturing and the rise of unions among government employees. In 2000, the rate of unionization was 50 percent higher in Industry than in Service, but low in both sectors.

Although unionization is not widespread in services, strikes in that sector attract considerable attention. Walkouts by teachers, sanitation workers, and hospital employees provoke more comment and intervention than much longer strikes by workers in mining, manufacturing, and construction. This is undoubtedly related in part to the perishable nature of service output. When no care is available for the sick, when children must stay home from school, or when garbage rots in the street, the disruption to modern life is much greater than when consumers of goods use up inventories or must delay purchase. New approaches to dealing with labor disputes and strikes are probably needed.

The shift of employment to the service sector carries with it important implications for industrial organization in the United States because the size of the "firm" and the nature of ownership and control are often different in Services than Industry. In Industry, with some notable exceptions, such as construction, most of the output is accounted for by large corporations. Ownership is frequently separate from management, and significant market power held by a few firms in each industry is not uncommon.

In the service sector, on the other hand, and again with some exceptions, firms are typically small, usually owner-managed and often noncorporate. Furthermore, nearly all firms in the Industry sector are organized for profit, whereas nonprofit operations, public and private, account for one-third of the service sector's employment. Although Wal-Mart is the largest employer in the United States, it is still true that most persons employed in trade and services work in small companies. Also, a substantial fraction of service sector employment is accounted for by self-employed professionals and domestic servants, who represent the extreme in small size of employer. Because most service firms are small, they offer more entrepreneurial opportunities for women and ethnic minorities who have more difficulty raising the large amounts of capital needed for many goods-producing industries.

Government, which is often referred to as a "huge bureaucracy," actually includes many small employers in the United States. Employment at the local level of government exceeds that of state and federal (civilian) government combined by 67 percent. About half of local government jobs are in relatively small units.

Although the shift to services tends to increase the relative importance of small firms in the economy, there are forces *within* many industries that tend to increase the size of the average "firm." The pressure for consolidation of school districts and other local government units is a notable example. Bank mergers is another.

Industries in which small firms account for the bulk of the output typically do not present control problems of the "trust-busting" variety. On the other hand, the growth of such industries may increase the need to guard against the restrictive practices of trade associations and professional organizations. Small firms may pose another problem for the economy because it is alleged that they do not allocate sufficient resources to research and other activities with large external benefits.

The growing importance of the nonprofit sector will probably pose some disturbing questions about how to promote efficiency and equity in such organizations. Some economists argue that nonprofit organizations tend to continue operating even when they are losing money, and the capital invested in them could be put to more efficient use. Others argue that nonprofit firms serve consumers better than for-profit firms when it is difficult for the consumer to judge the quality of the output (e.g., nursing homes). When nonprofit operations dominate many industries, there may be a need for new kinds of analyses and new instruments of regulation and control.

Implications for Economics

In my judgment, the growth of the service sector has important implications for economics analogous in some respects to the shift from agriculture to industry. With some delay, it is now apparent that the earlier transition had considerable influence on economic analysis: land became less important as an input in production and distribution models, and physical capital became much more important. The need for theories of imperfect competition became more apparent. Short-run supply curves could no longer be thought of as completely inelastic, and the possibility of constant or increasing returns had to be examined with greater rigor.

Although most of the necessary theoretical tools can be found in one form or another in the writings of the earliest economists, the development and refinement of concepts are often related to changes in the economy itself. Analytical work requires compromises with reality. The compromises that may be appropriate, or the second-order effects that may be neglected, in an economy dominated by agriculture and manufacturing may turn out to be inappropriate, or too important to be neglected, in an economy dominated by the service industries. I shall try to illustrate this point by reference to the analysis of productivity and growth.

One lesson that studies of productivity in the service industries should force upon us is the importance of the consumer as a cooperating agent in the production process. To the best of my knowledge, this point is neglected in the analysis of productivity in goods-producing industries, as well it might be. After all, productivity in the automobile industry is not much affected by whether the ultimate drivers are bright or stupid, or whether they drive carefully or carelessly. By contrast, productivity in many service industries is dependent in part on the knowledge, experience, and motivation of the consumer. Consider, for instance, what would happen to service-industry productivity in the United States if technology and capital and labor inputs remained as they are, but U.S. consumers were exchanged for ones from Bangladesh.

In a similar vein, productivity can be and often is affected by the level of honesty of the consumer. If, for example, consumers can be trusted to refrain from stealing merchandise, to report prices and costs properly at checkout counters, and to honor verbal commitments for purchases and other contracts, there can be tremendous savings in personnel on the part of producers of services. These savings are probably important when comparisons are made with productivity in other countries or with the same country at different points in time. It may be that qualities such as honesty are themselves functions of the general level of productivity and income. A full analysis of productivity, therefore, requires consideration of these interrelations.

A second example of an analytical implication of the growth of service-industry employment concerns the labor embodiment of technological change. This refers to a situation where technological change or an advance in knowledge affects productivity through new additions to the labor force. For example, if newly trained doctors, after receiving the same amount of schooling as their predecessors, know more about disease and are more effective in treating sick people, we should attribute the increase in output to labor-embodied technological change.

Most previous discussions of embodiment have concentrated on physical capital, where it has typically been assumed that capital is a fixed factor and that labor is variable. W.E.G. Salter, for example, notes that by investing in fixed capital equipment an entrepreneur gives "hostages to fortune"; a decision to employ fixed capital equipment is irrevocable in contrast to labor, which can be discharged at will (1960). This may be a reasonably satisfactory description of the situation in manufacturing (though probably less so now than formerly), but it will not do for much of the service sector. In fact, given the growing opportunity to rent capital equipment, the reverse is sometimes closer to the truth. If one argues that rented capital equipment represents an irrevocable commitment for society, if not for the particular firm or industry using it, the same can be said for the supply of labor, and the distinction loses all force.

Let us imagine, for instance, a technological change in some government activity—a change that requires new labor skills. Civil service rules may prohibit the firing of old employees, and it may be difficult to train them in the new techniques. The full benefits of the advance, therefore, will not be realized immediately. If this type of technological change occurs at an even rate, the rate of change in productivity in government will be unaffected even though the level will be less than optimal. But such changes probably do not occur at a smooth rate. If the output of the government agency is accelerating rapidly, it is likely that new additions of capital and labor are being made and that they can incorporate the latest technological change, thus raising the average level of productivity. But if the level of output is falling, the reverse will be true. This may be one reason that changes in output and changes in productivity are frequently found to be positively correlated.

The argument applies not only to government but to all industries in which individuals are attached to specific organizations for long periods of time (through contract, moral commitment, or high hiring costs) and cannot easily be replaced by others. Such long-term attachments are common in many service industries. To be sure, sometimes the existing labor force can be trained or adapted to take advantage of technological change, but in many cases this is not easy to accomplish, for example, economics professors who lack knowledge of modern mathematical techniques.

The question may be raised why, if technological change is embodied in new entrants to the labor force, do we usually find that older workers earn more than do new entrants with the same number of years of schooling? The answer is, of course, that employers place a value on the experience and maturity of the older worker that more than offsets the value of the labor-embodied technological change. If one could compare two workers of equal experience and maturity, one with the education of twenty years ago and the other with the current model, there is little doubt that the latter would command higher earnings. This is particularly evident in fields experiencing rapid technological change, such as electrical engineering and computers, where recent graduates often earn as much as old-timers do despite the maturity and experience of the latter. The concept of labor embodiment is likely to be most relevant when formal schooling and job security are important, as in the professional and technical occupations.

Another area where the growth of services may require some refinement of concepts is the analysis of the relation between changes in demand and changes in productivity. In many service industries it is not enough to know by *how much* demand has changed in order to predict the effect on productivity. At least two other dimensions of demand in addition to quantity must be specified.

One source of variation arises because demand is frequently uneven, with peaks coming at particular hours of the day, particular days of the week, and even particular weeks of the month. Such fluctuations are important for retailing, banking, barber and beauty shops, places of amusement, and some local government services. During nonpeak times there is usually idle capacity. An increase in demand, if it occurs at these times, may result in very substantial gains in productivity. On the other hand, an increase in demand at times of peak demand will probably not result in any increase in productivity.

A second source of variation is the "size of transaction." This refers to the volume of business done with a single customer at a single purchase. David Schwartzman and Jean Wilburn have found examples of service industries where increased demand that takes the form of increases in the average size of transaction results in greater increases in measured productivity than does an equivalent increase in demand that takes the form of more transactions. George Benston has reported a similar finding for banking, and I suspect that this is true of many service industries.

My final example of how the growth of services may affect economic analysis concerns the gross domestic product in constant dollars. This statistic is the keystone of many studies of productivity and economic growth. Unfortunately, it is probably becoming less and less useful for such purposes. The reason is simple. Measures of real output in the service sector have always been unsatisfactory; as this sector becomes more important, the aggregate measure must become less satisfactory in the absence of significant improvements in the measures for individual industries.

Economists have long been aware that the value of real GDP per capita as a measure of output and economic well-being differs depending upon the level of economic development. There has been a presumption that the measure becomes more useful the more highly developed the economy. Up to a point it is probably true that the higher GDP is, the more reliable it is as a measure of economic welfare. But the trend may now be in the other direction, because at high levels of GDP per capita a large fraction of productive effort is devoted to services, where real output is very difficult to measure.

One example of the difficulty of measuring productivity and economic welfare at high levels of GDP per capita can be found in mortality statistics. At low or moderate levels of economic development, there is usually a negative correlation between real GDP per capita and death rates. However, currently there is very weak correlation across high-income countries between life expectancy and GDP per capita.

Implications for Society

The rise of service sector employment has obvious implications for the economy. The implications for economics are less obvious, but with a lag they will eventually make their impact on textbooks, just as the proverbial "widget manufacturer" took pride of place from the "wheat farmer" only long after the Industrial Revolution had relegated agriculture to a subordinate role in the economy. Least obvious of all, and somewhat speculative, are the implications for society as a whole.

Does the industrial distribution of employment matter? I believe it does. A hypothetical example may help to clarify the point. Suppose we had an economy in which inputs of physical capital and human labor were roughly equal in economic importance; that is, the annual value of the services flowing from each was approximately the same. Suppose further that 90 percent of the physical capital and 10 percent of the labor were employed in Industry, and 10 percent of the capital and 90 per cent of the labor in the production of services. Although the sectors would be equal in economic importance, it seems reasonable to expect that the dominant tone of the society would be set by the service component. The kind of work people do, the kinds of organizations they work for, the location of the work, the education they need, the health hazards they face, and many other critical aspects of their lives would be different than if capital and labor were equally divided between the two sectors. Indeed, the theologian Harvey Cox has written, "When man changes his tools and his techniques, his ways of producing and distributing the goods of life, he also changes his gods."

Consider the question of location. Mines and factories and the like tend to require large number of workers gathered at concentrated sites. Many, probably most services are produced in dispersed locations, frequently in or near residential areas. Not a few service workers can now, thanks to computers, work from home, much as artisans did in the era before factories took over.

Or consider the relation between workers and their work. For many decades social critics have argued that industrialization has alienated workers from their work, that the individual has no contact with the final fruit of his or her labor, and that the transfer from a craft society to one of mass production has resulted in work no longer being a source of pride and satisfaction.

Whatever validity such statements may have had in the past, it is questionable whether they now accord with reality. The advent of a service economy may imply a reversal of these trends. Employees in many service industries are closely related to their work and often render a highly personalized service that offers ample scope for the development and exercise of personal skills. This is true of some goods-producing occupations as well, but the direct interaction between consumer and worker that occurs frequently in services creates the possibility of a more completely human and satisfying work experience. To be sure, within many service industries there is some tendency for work to become less personalized (e.g., teaching machines in education, self-service counters in retailing, and laboratory tests in medicine); but with more and more people engaged in service occupations, the net effect for the labor force as a whole is probably in the direction of the *personalization* of work.

It should be stressed that deriving satisfaction from a job well done and taking pride in one's work are only possibilities, not certainties.

62 • Victor R. Fuchs

Teachers can ignore their pupils; doctors can think more of their bank balances than of their patients. The salesman who must go through life with an artificial smile on his face while caring little for his customers and less for what he sells is often held in low regard. But at their best many service occupations are extremely rewarding, and the line between "work" and "leisure" activity is often difficult to draw.

To test this proposition I recently presented a prominent young economics professor with the following hypothetical. "The XYZ Foundation offers to pay your current and all projected future income on condition that you stop all research and teaching, write no more papers or books, give no more speeches or lectures, and attend no more conferences." Without hesitation, the professor rejected this arrangement. He said it would mean a significant loss of utility to him.

CONCLUDING COMMENTS

In the 1960s, when I was describing the rise of service sector employment, there were economists who thought this might be a temporary phenomenon, the result of some cyclical downturn in the demand for manufactured goods. Subsequent decades have demonstrated that the predominance of service employment is here to stay. Furthermore, there can be little doubt that the service sector's share of employment is highly correlated with GDP per capita, both across countries and within each country over time.

What remains elusive, however, is a robust, quantitative explanation for the pervasiveness and predictability of the shift of employment to services. Sector differentials in the growth of labor productivity or sector shifts in demand are the chief contenders, but it must be emphasized that resolution of this question requires better measures of output, especially for services.

Such measures are a necessary, but not sufficient, ingredient for measuring changes in service productivity because it will also be necessary to take account of those heretofore unmeasured inputs provided by consumers of many services. Also, more is at stake than explaining the rise of service employment. Given the large and growing importance of the service sector in modern economies, it is not possible to obtain a satisfactory understanding of these economies without a much more comprehensive effort to measure and analyze changes in output and productivity in the service industries.

Finally, I strongly suggest that the full range of social science, not just economics, needs to focus more attention on the service sector, and the implications for society of the shifts discussed in this chapter.

CHAPTER 3

On Mechanisms Underlying the Growing Share of Service Employment in the Industrialized Economies

William J. Baumol

THE THEME OF this book is the search for explanations of the growing share of jobs found in the services, a trend that has persisted for more than half a century, and one that pervades all of the world's industrialized countries. As laid out in the introduction, (at least) three hypotheses have been offered to account for this remarkably enduring phenomenon. As the apparent author of one of them, it seems to me essential to make clear that if the hypothesis with which I am associated proves valid, it does not follow that others must be rejected. In an economy as complex as ours, I doubt whether any major occurrence or systematic relationship can be fully explained by any single and simple hypothesis. Thus, there is some intuitive plausibility, as part of the story, to another of these proposed explanations: the hypothesized intertemporal trajectory of preferences in which, it is said, consumers tend to focus on food and other agricultural products when society is poor; then turn toward manufactures as wealth increases; and, finally, having grown sated with these, begin increasingly to favor the services. The fact that some data may cast some doubt upon this conjecture is hardly conclusive. It is true, Robert Summers's calculations (1985) suggest, that, properly deflated, real service purchases, approximately, have only kept up with the purchases of other outputs. Moreover, some services, such as those supplied by household servants, have tended to disappear, rather than staying ahead of GDP as a whole. But there are other services whose purchases have risen dramatically, and I believe the material at hand is insufficient to reject the hypothesis that predictable demand patterns play a role in the growing share of service employment, though it may justify suspicion about the strength of the relationship. Turning to a related matter, my alternative approach to explanation of the employment trends, I would note that while some of my writing has evidently misled readers to conclude that I believe the share of services in the total output of the economy can be expected to remain unchanged, I may protest that this was meant only as an assumption adopted for expository purposes, as a way to simplify the story. For I said, or at least intended to say, merely that the story is most straightforward if the proportion between the output of the services and that of the other components of GDP remains constant, because in that case it is mere tautology to observe that the economic sectors with the lowest labor productivity growth *must*, ceteris paribus, attract a growing share of the economy's total labor force in order for its output to stay abreast of other product outputs.

Yet, imperfect though the evidence may be, there is one tentative conclusion to which one must surely grant plausibility. First, the shift to the services has been so marked, so persistent, and so pervasive that one can almost certainly reject the notion that is the fortuitous result of a number of unrelated and more or less randomly occurring influences. Acceptance of such a view would be like concluding that 20 coin flips all of which come out "heads" is very likely to be sheer accident. However, it may require much more accumulation and analysis of data before one can conclude with confidence that the share of the services in the purchases of the world's economies is approximately constant. Moreover, if the share of real service output does turn out to be growing significantly, as the demand hypothesis asserts, the role of the cost-disease story will surely be enhanced. For if there is marked growth in the real output share of the sectors whose labor productivity grows slowly, then their portion of the economy's labor force will have to expand even more swiftly than if the output shares remain roughly unchanging.

But the central argument of this chapter is not mere reiteration of the story in the cost-disease model and its use in explaining the share of services in employment. Rather, I propose here to go one step further and argue that there is one set of key services—those related to R&D and innovative activity generally—that are not only subject to the cost disease themselves, but also in some sense may be deemed the ultimate source of the problem, because it is from them that the astonishing relative and absolute growth of productivity in manufacturing and agriculture ultimately stems, and that is one reason why manufacturing and agriculture are demanding an ever-smaller share of the labor forces in the industrial economies. Thus there is a subset of the services that are apparently both the locus and the origin of this development. The story will, I believe, almost seem obvious once described more fully, but with some surprising features. To explain all this, some review of the cost-disease story will be helpful.

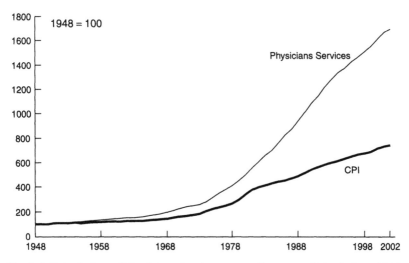

Fig. 3.1. Price Index of Physicians Services versus Consumer Price Index, 1948–2002 (1948 = 100).
Source: U.S. Department of Labor, Bureau of Labor Statistics, http://data .bls.gov.

THE COST-DISEASE SCENARIO ILLUSTRATED BY HEALTH CARE AND EDUCATION

Pertinent U.S. government data document a startlingly persistent and dramatic rise in the *cost* of personal services such as education, health care, and a variety of others. The public is painfully aware of the speed at which general medical costs in the United States have been increasing. The cost of a hospital stay has been going up even more rapidly. These cost increases have been replicated in other countries, as will be shown presently, and have made health care a prime subject of debate in political contests, not only in the United States but in virtually every industrialized country.

Between 1948 and 2002, the U.S. Consumer Price Index increased at an average rate of about 3.7 percent per year, whereas the price of physicians' services rose 5.2 percent per year.[1] This difference seems tiny, but compounded over those 54 years it had the effect of increasing the price of a doctor visit nearly 130 percent, measured in dollars of constant purchasing power. Figure 3.1 shows the history over the entire period

[1] U.S. Department of Labor, Bureau of Labor Statistics, http://data.bls.gov.

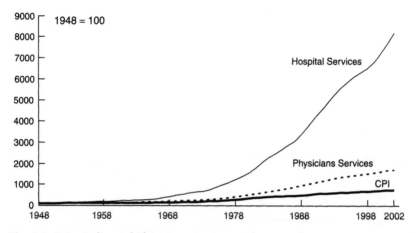

Fig. 3.2. Price Indices of Physicians Services and Hospital Services versus Consumer Price Index, 1948–2002 (1948 = 100)
Source: U.S. Department of Labor, Bureau of Labor Statistics, http://data .bls.gov.

of both the CPI and the price of physician services. What is noteworthy is not only how much more rapidly the latter increased, but also the length of time, more than half a century, over which the phenomenon has endured, and the absence of any protracted exceptional periods in which the rise of physician service prices fell behind. These are remarkable statistics, particularly because doctors' earnings barely kept up with the economy's overall inflation rate during this period. Evidently, the entire phenomenon requires some explanation that cannot be expected to be obvious.

But this record of rising cost of doctors' services is surpassed by the performance of hospital costs, as shown in figure 3.2. As the graph shows, in comparison even with the price of physician services, during the post–World War II period, the price of hospital care skyrocketed: the average price of a hospital room increased at an annual rate of 8.2 percent compounded. This amounts to a 1,000 percent increase since 1948, measured in constant dollars. To make graphic comparison possible, in figure 3.2 it was necessary to suppress severely the vertical calibration of the graph, to make it feasible to accommodate the spectacular rise in hospital costs. What is striking is that compared to the hospital cost explosion, the rise in the price of physician services now looks like the modest slope of an exceedingly gentle hillside. As for the hospital cost figures, we note again that it is persistent, cumulative, and of very long duration. Indeed, for reasons that will soon emerge, there are solid grounds from which to infer that the trend has been under way very much longer than the available data demonstrate.

Despite a great variety of government programs entailing many different approaches, including different forms of price ceilings, inhibition of doctor incomes, special medical purchase arrangements, and so on, virtually every major industrial nation has failed in its attempt to prevent health care costs from rising faster than its economy's rate of inflation, as panel (a) of figure 3.3 shows. In this graph the bar for each country shows its average yearly rate of increase in real (inflation-adjusted) health care costs per person between 1970 and 1998. We see that the phenomenon is nearly universal among the industrial countries. One simply does not have to invent a tale about greedy physicians, incompetent managements, or monopolization and anticompetitive programs by hospital equipment suppliers or pharmaceutical firms with unconstrained pricing to account for the phenomenon, for the problem is evidently widespread, indeed probably universal among industrialized countries, despite a variety of government controls instituted to contain rising costs.

It is significant that the cost of education has a similar record. Real education costs per pupil in the United States have increased an average of 7.2 percent per year in the past 50 years or so. And during the approximately 30-year period 1965–94, U.S. increases in education costs have been *lower* than education cost increases for four of the six top industrial countries, as shown in panel (b) of figure 3.3.

Why Are Health Care and Education Costs So Persistently Rising?

What accounts for the ever-increasing health care costs? There are probably a number of contributory factors. But there is a particularly significant reason—one that cannot be avoided by any hospital administration no matter how pure its motives and efficient its operations and that must play a primary role in the persistence and universality of the phenomenon. The common influence underlying all of these problems of rising cost, which is *economic* in character, and has no implications of either inefficiency or wrongdoing, has been called the *cost disease of the personal services.*

This "cost disease" stems from the basic nature of many personal services. Most such services, notably health care services, have indispensable *handicraft attributes:* they require direct contact between those who provide the service and those who consume it. Doctors and nurses engage in activities that require direct, person-to-person contact. Moreover, the quality of the service deteriorates if less time is provided to the patients by the medical personnel.

In contrast, in other parts of the economy such as manufacturing, no

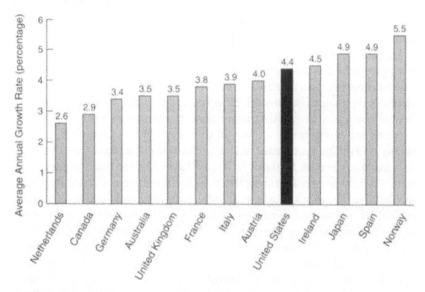

Fig. 3.3a. International Comparison: Growth Rates of Real per Capita Health Care Expenditures, 1970–98
Source: OECD "Health At a Glance, 2001," 2001, www.sourceoecd.org.

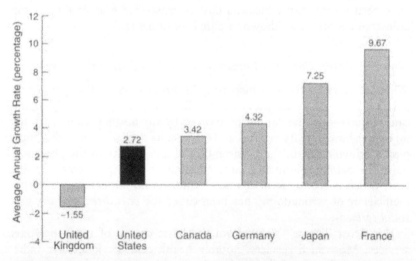

Fig. 3.3b. International Comparison: Growth Rates of Real Per-Pupil Education Costs, 1965–94
Source: U.S. Department of Education, "Digest of Education Statistics," http://nces.ed.gov.

direct personal contact between the consumer and the producer is required. For instance, the buyer of an automobile usually has no idea who worked on it and does not care how much labor time went into its production. A labor-saving innovation in auto production need not imply a reduction in product quality. As a result, over the years it has proved far easier for technological change to save labor in manufacturing than to save labor in providing services. Labor productivity (output per worker) in U.S. manufacturing and agriculture has increased at an average rate of something like 2 percent a year since World War II, but the productivity of college teaching (crudely measured by number of students taught per teacher) has increased at a rate of only 1 percent per year during that period. And, in elementary and secondary education, labor productivity has actually *declined*. The average number of pupils per teacher has fallen from about 27 pupils per teacher in 1955 to 17 pupils per teacher in 1994, partly because classes have become smaller.

These disparate productivity performances have grave consequences for prices. When manufacturing wages rise 2 percent, the cost of manufactured products need not rise because increased output per worker approximately makes up for the rise in wages. But the nature of many services makes it very difficult to introduce labor-saving devices in those parts of the service sector. A 2 percent wage increase for doctors and nurses is not offset by a corresponding increase in labor-saving productivity and must lead to an equivalent rise in hospital budgets. Of course, spectacular advances in medical technology have occurred and have meant that today's patient gets far more for his money in terms of contribution to his health than he would have obtained at a hospital 50 years ago. But the medical innovations are, *with some noteworthy exceptions*, not *labor saving* in character. That is why such innovations, invaluable as they are, do not stem the hospitals' vulnerability to the cost disease.

In the long run, wages for all workers throughout the economy tend to go up and down together, for otherwise the activity whose wage rate falls seriously behind will tend to lose its labor force. So autoworkers and doctors will eventually see their wages rise at roughly the same rate in the long run. But if productivity on the assembly line advances, even though productivity in the hospital does not, then a stay in the hospital must grow ever more expensive, relative to manufacturing, as time goes on.

Because labor-saving productivity improvements are very difficult for most personal services such as hospital care, their costs can be expected to rise faster, year in and year out, than the cost of manufactured products. Over a period of several decades, this difference in the growth rate of costs of the two sectors adds up, making services enormously more expensive compared with manufactured goods. In this way, hospital services and other services with handicraft characteristics have grown steadily more expensive compared to goods, and they are likely to continue to do so.

The Cost Disease and the Share of Jobs in the Affected Sectors

The material in the preceding sections was provided merely to recapitulate the cost-disease story and to suggest the type of evidence that has been cited to argue its validity. We come now, at last, to the portion of the cost-disease story that is pertinent to the matter at issue here—why employment in the industrialized economies has for roughly half a century been shifting from agriculture and manufacturing to the service sectors. As we know, this is no minor shift. In the United States, agricultural employment has fallen from some 90 percent of the nation's labor force in the beginning of the 19th century to something under 2 percent today, and manufacturing accounts for less than 15 percent of the remainder. Thus, the United States, along with the remainder of the "industrial" world, has really become a service economy. Now, if as overall productivity has grown, tastes had shifted overwhelmingly to the services, this could evidently account for the phenomenon. And it may very well prove to be a valid part of the story, but the evidence seems clearly to indicate that by itself such an income-induced shift in demand has hardly been sufficient in magnitude to constitute the mainstay of the explanation. And, as asserted, the cost-disease analysis can, in principle, easily account for much of the remainder.

The argument is straightforward. The elementary mathematics of the cost-disease story tells us directly of the relationship. In the deliberately oversimplified cost-disease model, the economy is taken to be composed of two sectors: a progressive sector, 1, in which productivity grows exponentially, and a stagnant sector, 2, in which productivity remains constant. There is a single input, labor, with quantities L_1 and L_2 used by the respective sectors, and whose outputs in the simplified model are given by

$$y_1 = cL_1e^{rt}, \ y_2 = bL_2. \tag{1}$$

Letting w represent the common wage rate, we have the unit-cost figures

$$AC_1 = wL_1/y_1 = w/ce^{rt}, \ AC_2 = wL_2/y_2 = w/b. \tag{2}$$

This yields for the stagnant sector a relative cost that grows exponentially with time:

$$AC_2/AC_1 = ce^{rt}/b. \tag{3}$$

Thus we have:

Proposition 1. In the cost-disease model, the per-unit cost of the output of the stagnant sector will rise without limit relative to that of the progressive sector.

Next, we obtain directly from (1):

Proposition 2. If $y_1 = ky_2$, that is, if the proportion between the outputs of the two sectors remains absolutely constant, then the labor force will shift ever more toward the stagnant sector, and if the total labor force is fixed, that of the stagnant sector will rise and that of the progressive sector will fall absolutely. For (1) gives us immediately

$$y_1 = cL_1e^{rt} = ky_2 = bkL_2, \text{ or } L_1 = kbL_2/ce^r. \tag{4}$$

That is the result on which this chapter focuses.

ALL SERVICES OR JUST THE "STAGNANT SERVICES?"

It should be made clear at once that the two propositions do not hold for the entire set of services, but for that subset to which coauthors and I have referred as the "stagnant services." A moment's thought will make it clear that there are a number of very significant services that are hardly laggard in their productivity growth. Thus, telecommunications, a hallmark of the "new economy" and evidently one of the leading revenue sources in the service sector, has a productivity growth record that, computer manufacture apart, is at the forefront in the modern economy. Thus, it is all too easy to examine aggregated data for the entire service sector of an industrial economy and conclude that the productivity lag of the services is a thing of the past. The cost-disease story, as well as the labor-shift scenario, should, according to our model, hold only for those services whose productivity growth is comparatively slow, those that we have dubbed the "stagnant services." The logic of our analysis makes no distinction between services and manufactures as such, but only between products whose productivity growth is slow and those for which it is rapid. It is true that virtually all the slow growers are services, but the converse emphatically is untrue, as has just been illustrated via telecommunications. But it is also evident that many of the other high-tech services are characterized by rapid productivity growth, and for them we should expect neither constantly rising costs nor a rising proportion of the labor force.

Moreover, this is not suggested by the theory alone. Some years ago Edward Wolff carried out a carefully disaggregated study of these matters, and the results were strikingly consistent with these conclusions (see Baumol, Blackman, and Wolff 1989, 130–33). When services were divided into those that were progressive and those that were stagnant in terms of productivity growth rates, the data showed that rising real prices (in the sense to be made clear next) and a rising share of the labor force were, at least in the United States in the decades after World War II, characteristics only of the stagnant services. Indeed, the progressive services accounted for virtually none of the increase in the employment share of the service sector.

This observation, incidentally, suggests, though it does not prove, that the cost disease, rather than the shift in demands induced by rising income, is plausibly the primary influence that has led to the rise in service sector employment. For one will surely surmise that the high-tech services are among the products whose demand will keep pace as incomes rise. Yet, probably, just because their productivity has risen so rapidly, their share of employment has not grown significantly. This pattern is surely more readily reconciled with the cost-disease model and its roots in the relative productivity growth of the different outputs, than with the income rise/demand response hypothesis.

Nominal Costs, Labor Costs, and "Real Costs"

Though it is a digression, it is well to pause for a moment and point out a misunderstanding of the cost-disease analysis that has more than once led the discussion on a path irrelevant to issues such as those in question here. There is an important sense in which the notion that the model entails rising cost of the stagnant services is an absurdity. If, as is entirely reasonable, we choose to measure the true cost of an item in terms of the labor time that is required to obtain it, then evidently, as can be seen directly from equations (1) and (4), the cost-disease model implies that the progressive services will be *falling* in cost at a continuing and perhaps an exponential rate. And the labor price of the stagnant services instead of rising, can in a competitive market be expected to remain constant, since their productivity in the model is assumed unchanging. Moreover, in reality, because many of the stagnant services are characterized by growth rates that are small but positive, even their exchange rate with labor can also be expected to be declining.

Then, in what sense are the costs ostensibly rising in this model? The obvious answer is that if nominal wages grow at a rate somewhere in between the rates of productivity growth of the two services, then the nominal cost and price of the progressive output should be falling and that of the stagnant output should be rising. But that is not quite all there is to the story. It is clear that in this model we can expect the cost and nominal price of the stagnant services to be rising faster or falling more slowly than those of the progressive outputs. But since the price level for the economy is defined and calculated as some weighted average of the prices of all the commodities in that economy, in our model the price index must rise at a rate somewhere in between those of the stagnant and the progressive outputs. It follows tautologically that the stagnant outputs must rise in price faster than a general price index. That is, as conventionally defined, it must be rising in *real* terms.

Economists will have good reason to respond to this that the standard measure of real price or real cost as just employed is inappropriate, and that it is the labor value that really tells us whether commodities are growing more or less expensive, that is, easier or harder for an average consumer to afford. That is true, and it is the sense in which one bright observer was driven to remark that the cost-disease model provides a profoundly optimistic view of the trends in question. Obviously, if productivity is rising everywhere, even if not at the same pace, then goods must be growing ever more affordable, not less so. So, is there a cost disease?

The answer is that there emphatically is one and that it can be a source of serious social damage, particularly if it leads to what has been called "fiscal illusion." Governments that provide education and health care do not pay for them in labor units. They pay for them in money that ultimately must be acquired by means such as taxes. The political problem of covering education and health care costs that are rising persistently and cumulatively at a rate faster than inflation should be evident. Moreover, if as has been happening, these payments constitute a continually rising share of GDP, the problem is exacerbated. Two unfortunate consequences may follow. First, if politicians do not understand what is going on, they may well (and often do) conclude that their public simply cannot afford the rising "real" costs of the products, and therefore the politicians will be tempted to cut back severely on such outputs even when the public wants them badly and even though rising productivity must make it easier, not harder, for them to afford those items, despite their rising prices. This is the damage that can be caused by the fiscal illusion that society cannot afford the requisite payments.

But there is, as a matter of fact, also a very *real* cost. We know that when a rising share of GDP is produced via government financing and taxation the incentive effects can be serious. This, apparently, is the most damaging consequence threatened by the cost disease.

QUALITY ADJUSTMENT OF PRODUCTIVITY DATA:
SHOULD WE OR SHOULDN'T WE?

Having provided one pertinent digression, let me offer a second that will also shed some light on what is at stake here. Economists generally agree that when measuring productivity growth it would be better to make corrections in the calculation to take account of rising quality of the output. Thus, suppose there were a medical procedure that over the course of a decade had doubled the labor time requirements because of the changing technology, but whose result had been a doubling of share of cases with full patient recovery. It is reasonable to argue that there would have been no net change in labor productivity, with a doubling of both input and output. But often, and usually apologetically, no adjustments for quality improvements are undertaken in productivity growth calculations, normally because there is no good way in which to measure the change in quality.

However, I will argue that there is nothing inherently erroneous about data on productivity in which there has been no quality adjustment. Rather, a quality-adjusted productivity index and one that is unadjusted are *both* legitimate measures, but which of these indexes is pertinent in a particular use depends on the purpose for which it is being employed. More specifically, if the purpose is to study how the change in productivity affects what consumers are getting for their money, then only the quality-adjusted index is fully defensible. In the case of health care, for example, such a calculation would probably show that, despite the rising price of a day at the hospital, many if not most patients are now receiving a greater benefit per dollar than they were, say, half a century ago. What patients are receiving now is a product very superior to what they were given at that earlier date, and because quality is the heart of the matter it must be taken into account in the construction of the productivity growth index.

On the other hand, if budgeting is the issue, it is the unadjusted productivity figure that, arguably, gives the right answer. If city X has a 2 million annual attendance at its public schools, and last year the cost per pupil was $2,000, then a 10 percent growth in unadjusted productivity (presumably meaning an increase in average class size) can be expected to bring that cost down by $200, regardless of whether the quality of the teaching has improved or deteriorated, and no matter what the reason. An improved approach to teaching may result, for example, in a striking improvement in average scores on standard tests, but that will not ease the community's budget pressures.

Moreover, and that is to the point here, it is the unadjusted productivity growth trajectory that will tell us how many people will be dropped from manufacturing jobs and will be driven to seek entry into the information sector of the economy, including the teaching staff of the city, which perhaps had not been able to fill all the teaching positions it had hoped to staff. In other words, for some purposes, it is a productivity index *unadjusted* for changes in product quality that seems the pertinent variant for our purposes, and there is nothing illegitimate about use of such an index here.

ON ASYMPTOTICALLY STAGNANT PRODUCTS: THE CASE OF RESEARCH AND DEVELOPMENT (R&D) ACTIVITY

Some years after the cost-disease model was introduced, it was extended to include a hybrid sector—the asymptotically stagnant sector—defined to employ in relatively fixed proportions some inputs supplied by the progressive sector and some by the stagnant sector (see, for example, Baumol, Blackman, and Wolff 1989, chap. 6). Two industries that seem to fit the description of asymptotic stagnancy rather closely are television broadcasting (whose primary inputs are electronic equipment and live performance) and computer usage (whose main inputs are sophisticated hardware and human labor devoted to software creation,[2] data gathering, etc.). Since the story is important for the argument of this chapter I will summarize it very briefly.

The "asymptotically stagnant" sector is a simplified representation of a third type of sector of the economy, in addition to the progressive and the stagnant sector. I will argue that this third sort of sector includes R&D activity. An asymptotically stagnant product is defined to be one whose activities that use in (more or less) fixed proportions two different types of input, one produced by progressive sector 1, and one that either is obtained from stagnant sector 2 or is composed of pure labor (or some combination of the two). An asymptotically stagnant product's cost is characterized by a distinctive intertemporal cost pattern. Initially, its cost tends to fall rapidly. But after some time this is reversed and the trajectory of the unit cost of the output of the asymptotically stagnant sector approaches closer and closer to that of its stagnant input. The intuitive explanation is simple. The falling cost of the progressive sector input accounts for the initial fall in the real unit cost of the asymptotically stagnant sector. But the very fall in the cost of that input reduces its *share* in the total costs of the asymptotically stagnant sector, leaving the behavior of those costs to be determined largely by the course of the stagnant sector input. Hence, an initial period of decline in the cost of the asymptotically stagnant sector is followed by a future of rising relative cost.[3] It is noteworthy that this sector appears to include some of the economy's most high-tech activities.

[2] However, productivity in software creation has been rising rapidly, even if not as quickly as in hardware. Thus, it is surely incorrect to characterize all nonhardware inputs into the computation process as stagnant in terms of productivity growth.

[3] For some empirical evidence on the cost behavior of the sectors used here as illustrations of asymptotic stagnancy, see Baumol, Blackman, and Wolff 1989, 131–40.

For a somewhat more formal discussion of the behavior just described, assume for simplicity that input-output proportions are absolutely fixed. Let y_3 represent the output of the sector and y_{13} and y_{23} be the inputs of the other two sectors used in the production of y_3. We can then write

$$y_{13}/y_3 = k_1, \quad y_{23}/y_3 = k_2, \tag{5}$$

where by appropriate choice of units we can set $k_2 = 1$. We then obtain for the average cost of sector 3

$$AC_3 = k_1 AC_1 + k_2 AC_2 = k_1 w/ce^{rt} + AC_2. \tag{6}$$

Measured in terms of labor units, that is, holding w constant, the first term of (6) must approach zero asymptotically. Consequently, the behavior of AC_3 over time will approach that of the stagnant sector, 2.

Thus, we have:

> Proposition 3. The behavior of the average cost of an asymptotically stagnant sector will approach, asymptotically, that of the stagnant sector from which the former obtains some of its inputs.

The presence of asymptotically stagnant outputs does not disturb the sectoral job proportion results of proposition 2 or its derivation, since sector 3 is assumed to use the sector 1 and sector 2 inputs in fixed proportion, with the production functions of those two sectors also directly applicable to supply of the sector 3 inputs they provide. Again considering the case of fixed output proportions, but this time with all three products, all that happens now is that some portion of the outputs of sectors 1 and 2 now go to sector 3 rather than to final consumers, so nothing in (4) changes. Consequently, proposition 2 continues to hold, essentially unmodified. The one new observation that emerges is that, even in sector 3 production, the share of labor used to supply its progressive input will decline with the passage of time, toward zero, while the labor embodied in the stagnant input will continue to rise without pause. The intuitive reasons for this result should be obvious.

The only surprising observation about the phenomenon we are discussing is that the sectors of the economy suffering from the asymptotic stagnation problem in its most extreme form include, in reality, some of those providing the most high-tech activities—those in the vanguard of innovation and change. That this is predicted by the theory should be clear from (6), which shows that the more rapid the rate of productivity growth of the sector 1 input—that is, the greater the value of r—the more rapidly will the intertemporal behavior of AC_3 approach that of the stagnant sector.

R&D as Asymptotically Stagnant Activity

There is reason to presume that the cost trajectory of R&D activity falls somewhere between those of a sector that is purely stagnant and one that is asymptotically stagnant. R&D may, itself, be thought of as using, preponderantly, two types of input—mental labor (that is, human time) and technological equipment such as computers—making it an activity approximating the characteristics of asymptotic stagnancy, though one with some intertemporal variation in input proportions. Innovation is such an activity. The act of thinking is a crucial input for the research process, but have we become more proficient at this handicraft activity than Isaac Newton, Gottfried Leibniz, or Christian Huygens? Probably not. The productivity of labor has risen at an annual rate of slightly less than 2 percent compounded since roughly 1830, when the Industrial Revolution really took off, so that the real product of an hour of labor has multiplied by a factor of perhaps 20 since that time. This means that the opportunity cost of an hour devoted to the technologically stagnant process of thinking must have risen by about 1,900 percent!

A Complication: Demand Effects of the Rising Cost of R&D Services

There is one last observation that may be of interest here. I have asserted that the R&D services are plausibly considered the primary source of the economy's productivity growth, and hence, to lie at the root of the cost disease. But R&D can conceivably be the source of a countervailing influence that can ultimately inhibit its contribution to productivity growth in the economy and can thereby serve to slow the virulence of the cost disease. If R&D is interpreted as just another input in the production process, such a rise in its relative price must have cut back its derived demand—inducing some substitution away from this input and toward other inputs whose real cost was reduced by technical change. The cost disease of the stagnant component of research, then, may conceivably serve to mitigate the cost disease, at least intermittently and temporarily, since it can be shown that the relationships can lead to an oscillatory time path, and it can even, ultimately, constitute an impediment to innovation.

One can easily confirm this possibility with the aid of a simple model of the feedback relationship between the production and dissemination of information and the rate of growth of productivity in industry. Here the growth rate of productivity is no longer taken to be a constant but, as in reality, is taken to be an increasing function of R&D. Thus, R&D is considered to be the sector of the economy that is engaged in the production of new technical information, that is, of invention. The magnitude of its information production clearly influences the rate of productivity growth. However, a rise in that growth rate in turn can depress the output of information by making asymptotically stagnant R&D more expensive relative to other output-increasing inputs, thereby closing the feedback loop, with effects on the trajectory of innovation that may not be obvious without a formal model.

In brief, the analysis has three elements:

1. Production of new information through R&D activity increases productivity growth in industry.
2. As a result, the price (real cost) of information production and dissemination rises because these activities are asymptotically stagnant.
3. As information grows relatively more costly, other inputs tend to be substituted for information in the production process. For example, when R&D costs have risen, a firm that wants to increase its output may decide not to invest more in R&D designed to raise the productivity of its machines but, instead, to buy additional machines of the current type. Thus, the rising cost of the innovation process can cut the derived demand for innovative activity. That, in turn, impedes productivity growth, thus reversing the first of the three steps of the intertemporal process in its next iteration.

One of the immediate implications is that, depending upon the price (and income) elasticity of the (derived) demand for R&D, it is possible that its rising relative cost will reduce its use relative to other inputs with the passage of time. Moreover, it can be shown that, with time, in this model: (a) output of R&D may decline, (b) total expenditure on R&D may rise, both absolutely and as a share of GDP, and (c) the amount of R&D labor time may fall relative to GDP.

STAGNANT-SECTOR OUTPUTS AS BUSINESS-SECTOR INPUTS: THE OULTON GROWTH THEOREM

It may be thought, as I once did, that in the cost-disease-beset economy, there must arise another impediment to growth—the slowing of average productivity growth in the economy, as increasing innovative activity leads to a transfer of labor from the (productivity) progressive final-product sector to the asymptotically stagnant innovation sector. For then, the average productivity of the two sectors, weighted by the sizes of their labor inputs, must ultimately decline. However, Nicholas Oulton (2001) of the Bank of England has contributed an important new theorem that entails very different productivity behavior in the economy when, as is true of innovation, this (ultimately) more-stagnant activity supplies an *intermediate product* that is used as an input elsewhere in the economy, rather than being used directly by consumers. Oulton shows that when the allocation of inputs is efficient and entails a shift of primary input from the progressive final-product sector to the stagnant or asymptotically stagnant intermediate-product sector, then the economy's overall productivity can, in rather general circumstances, actually be expected to grow faster. That is, the shift of labor to the stagnant sector can in this case be expected to increase overall productivity growth rather than depress it. It does so because in this case productivity growth in the two sectors is *additive*, with growth of labor productivity in innovation, however limited, indirectly adding to the given total factor productivity growth in the final-product sector, thereby enhancing productivity growth in the final product of the given labor force of the economy. As Oulton explains, the seemingly "very paradoxical" result (assuming, for simplicity that innovation is produced by labor alone, while the final product uses both labor and innovation as inputs, as in our model here):

> There are two ways in which the economy can obtain more final product, given that total employment is fixed. One is if TFP rises in final product supply, the other is if TFP rises in innovation. . . . TFP growth in innovation raises the productivity of labor employed there. . . . Hence TFP growth in innovation causes higher final-product output, since the final-product sector buys in the output of the innovation sector. The higher the proportion of the labor force employed in innovation, the bigger the impact on TFP growth in the final-product sector [given the rate of TFP growth in the final-product sector's utilization of its two inputs]. . . . The reason is that such a shift will raise the contribution to the aggregate coming from innovation without reducing the contribution coming from the final-product sector. (2001, 14–15)[4]

CONCLUDING COMMENT

It does not seem appropriate here to carry the description of the model any further (for a full discussion, see Baumol 2002, chap. 15). What is relevant for the issue at hand is that to the extent that the cost disease,

---

[4] Throughout the quotation, for more direct applicability to the current discussion, I have substituted *final-product output* for *car output* and *innovation* for *business services*.

or rather the inequality of the productivity growth rates of the different economic sectors, is responsible for the shift of labor toward the services, we should not be surprised to find that there is a cyclical or oscillatory element in the process rather than a steady force that drives labor in that direction monotonically and without letup.

CHAPTER 4

Do Demand Differences Cause the U.S.-European Employment Gap?

Mary Gregory and Giovanni Russo

IT IS FREQUENTLY remarked that services are more labor-intensive than manufactured goods, and that the growth of labor productivity in the production of services is less rapid than in manufacturing. To the extent that the first of these statements is true, higher levels of employment may be expected when demand patterns are oriented towards services. To the extent that the second is true, the economy will be characterized by lower productivity growth overall as the services sector becomes more important.

However, both of these generalizations are based on the final stage of production only—in the case of services at the point of delivery. While the travel agent or pharmacist provides a face-to-face service that itself is labor-intensive, it involves accessing databases collated and maintained elsewhere, using software developed in other service sectors, and communications links and electronic equipment bought in from manufacturing and construction. Production in these sectors in turn requires a further range of purchased inputs, again drawn from both manufacturing and services. While economic analysis tends to concentrate on final output and the use of primary factors, much of the economy's output and employment are involved in intermediate stages of the production process. Although productivity gains may be difficult to achieve in the face-to-face delivery of services, developments in information and communications technology impacting back through the supply chain are now transforming the overall efficiency of delivery in a number of areas of

We thank Sarah Voitchovsky and Justin van de Ven for excellent research assistance. We are grateful to Gavin Cameron for providing us with the UK sectoral price deflators and to Nadim Ahmad for providing the input-output tables. We received many valuable comments during DEMPATEM meetings and a seminar at Oxford University. In particular we would like to thank Thijs Ten Raa, Pascal Petit, Ronald Schettkat, and Andrew Glyn.

services. It is the implications of these processes for employment and productivity that we wish to capture.

The central concept that we use is the total employment generated for product supply, involving each stage in the supply chain through to delivery of the final product. Similarly, productivity gains incorporate those achieved throughout the supply chain, as well as those at the final stage of production.[1] Measuring employment on a product supply basis, therefore, is complex, requiring information on input purchases and associated employment at all stages in the supply chain. The resulting measure, reflecting the structure of the entire supply chain, typically diverges significantly from conventional perceptions. An extreme example is the business services sector, one of the areas of most rapid employment growth in recent years. On a final output basis this sector does not feature directly, as it supplies only to the business market and not to final demand. Business service jobs are, however, included pervasively on a product supply basis, with their employment attributed to the final activities of the clients who commissioned them, even when they are many stages removed in the supply chain.

Reattributing employment on the product supply basis in the six selected countries reveals a number of important, and possibly counterintuitive, results. The number of jobs generated in the production of all final outputs has been falling in each country. This reflects the productivity gains of the period, those achieved through the supply chain as well as at final production/delivery, and confirms the importance of looking beyond a single stage of production where employment may have expanded. Measured on the product supply basis, the employment-intensities of services and manufacturing emerge as broadly equal. Each group contains more and less employment-intensive sectors, and the familiar generalization about the higher labor-intensity of services finds little empirical support. Looking within the structure of the supply chain reveals that final demands, whether originating in manufacturing or in services, are increasingly generating jobs located in services.

On the central question of the employment-friendliness of the more service-oriented American consumption pattern, the consumption patterns of the European economies are confirmed as tending to be less employment-friendly than that of the United States. This difference, however, accounts for only a minor part of the employment gap. The largest employment gaps are for France, at 14 percentage points, and Germany, at 8 points. If the United States were to follow the consumption patterns of these economies, its employment would fall by 5.0 per-

---

[1] This perspective on product supply incorporating the supply chain was formally developed by Pasinetti (1973), who named it the "vertically integrated sector."

cent and 3.6 percent respectively. This would reduce the gap to the United States by one-fourth for France, and one-third for Germany. Conversely, if the European economies were to adopt a U.S.-type consumption mix, employment would again be higher, by around 3 percent in the United Kingdom, Germany, and the Netherlands, and 4.5 percent in France; only in Spain would it be reduced. This would reduce the employment gaps for France and Germany each by one-fifth, and for the Netherlands marginally; the gap for the United Kingdom, already small, would be halved; but for Spain the gap would widen.

The final stage of the analysis extends the focus to productivity and the structure of the supply chain. The employment change that occurred within each of the six economies is decomposed across three proximate sources: the growth of final demand, the changing use of inputs, and the growth of labor productivity. This reveals striking empirical regularities. Demand growth has been the major source of employment growth everywhere. But this is heavily offset by job losses resulting from labor productivity gains. Structural change along the supply chain is on occasion job-creating, on occasion job-destroying, and on occasion job-transferring, for example through outsourcing; but its overall contribution to employment change is small. The trend in employment within each economy is therefore largely determined as the outcome of the race between the two opposing forces of the growth of final demand, generating employment, and labor productivity growth, which is job-saving. In the United States stronger demand growth has brought more job creation, while weaker productivity gains (until the most recent years) have been less job-destroying than in the European economies. These are the major factors that have given rise to the development of the United States–Europe employment gap.

Deriving Employment in Product Supply

The product supply approach, attributing to final products the employment generated throughout the supply chain, can be succinctly shown in an input-output framework. Total employment can be expressed as

$$N = n'X$$
$$= n'(I - A)^{-1}F, \tag{1}$$

where N is the level of total employment, X and F are vectors of gross output and final demand for domestic outputs by sector, $(I - A)^{-1}$ is the Leontief inverse matrix, and n' the vector of labor requirements per unit of sectoral gross output. To attribute employment on a product supply basis (1) is expanded as

$$N = \hat{n}(I - A)^{-1} \hat{F}, \qquad (2)$$

where $\hat{n}$ and $\hat{F}$ express n and F as diagonal matrices. N is now the square sector-by-sector matrix where N_{ij} is employment in (row) sector i generated by final demand in sector j. The i-th row-sum of N gives the employment generated within sector i to supply its output for final use and to all intermediate users. This is the sectoral allocation of employment as conventionally measured. Each j-th column-sum of N gives the employment generated economy-wide for the production of the j-th sector's final demand. This is the product supply allocation, attributing employment to the sector of the final demand that it serves, independent of the sector in which the employment takes place.

As (2) shows, the employment generated economy-wide by the production of a sector's final output depends on the entire set of interindustry relationships encapsulated in the inverse coefficient matrix, and on the employment-intensity n, of every sector. The resulting employment generated in the production of the sector's final output may be (much) greater or smaller than the number of jobs located within the sector itself. No simple relation such as a correlation between a sector's relative ranking on the two measures can be expected.

The allocation of employment across product supply is illustrated by a numerical example in appendix B.

JOB CREATION IN PRODUCT SUPPLY: EVIDENCE FROM SIX COUNTRIES

We now apply this approach to the six selected economies (United States, United Kingdom, Germany, France, the Netherlands, Spain) for the period from the late 1970s to the late 1990s. The United States is taken as the benchmark. The five European economies together account for 70 percent of the population of the EU-15. Germany and France are the major economies of the continental EU, and key representatives of the "European social model" and its current employment challenges. The United Kingdom and the Netherlands both have relatively successful records in terms of employment growth; in both part-time work has been a strong feature, contributing flexibility to the labor market but reducing employment and its growth when standardized in FTE terms. Spain represents the new, fast-growing economies in the west and southern regions of the EU.

The main data that we use are the standardized domestic-use input-output tables prepared by the OECD.[2] To allow for the differing inci-

---

[2] The domestic-use tables record on the final demand side the demand for domestic goods, and in the table itself the transactions between industries in domestically produced

dence of part-time work across the six economies, employment is measured as far as possible on a full-time equivalent (FTE) basis, again from the OECD. More detail on the data is given in appendix A.

For each country we first present the product supply measure of employment-intensity for the individual sector. This is calculated as the employment generated economy-wide by the injection of one unit of new final demand to the sector (in practice, 1 million units in the country's own currency), notionally holding final demands for all other sectors at zero. This expenditure stimulus is repeated sequentially for each sector.[3] Figure 4.1, panels (a)–(f), shows the employment-intensities of individual sectors in each of the six economies for three years as available in the late 1970s, late 1980s, and the second half of the 1990s. The sectors are arranged in the conventional sequence, with primary industries to the left, followed by manufactures and then the various service sectors.

The number of jobs generated/required (at the final stage and through the supply chain) to produce each unit of the sector's output has been falling over time. Equivalently, labor productivity has been increasing in the production of all products, when efficiency gains throughout the supply chain are incorporated. There is considerable heterogeneity across sectors, with the most employment-intensive sectors generating twice, even three or four times, the number of jobs of the least employment-friendly. From the productivity side, the production of certain outputs is achieved at three or four times the efficiency, in terms of economy-wide labor use, of the least efficient. When employment required is measured on the product supply basis, a manufacturing/services divide in either productivity levels or productivity gains is by no means evident. Some manufacturing industries generate high numbers of jobs, as do some services; on the other hand some service industries generate surprisingly few jobs. Spectacular productivity gains have been achieved within manufacturing, notably in the production of electronic goods and medical equipment, while some services, including posts and communications, also show major gains. The laggards likewise are not exclusively the preserve of the service sector. Comparing the patterns across countries, the strength of the productivity gains in France and Spain is conspicuous, while in the Netherlands the counterpart to its record of strong employment growth has been weak productivity gains.

---

intermediate goods. The exclusion of purchases of imported intermediate goods implies that industry-level value added cannot be computed (cf. total-use tables that include intermediate purchases of imports).

[3] We use the terms *sector*, *product*, and *industry* interchangeably; while each sector/industry clearly produces a vast range of individual products, for the purpose of the analysis it is treated as a single entity.

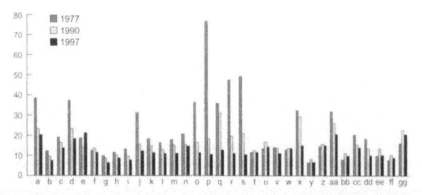

Fig. 4.1. Total Job Creation from an Expenditure Stimulus Targeted on Individual Sectors.
(a) United States. 1 Million U.S. (1997) Dollars. a. Agriculture, forestry & fishing. b. Mining & quarrying. c. Food, beverages & tobacco. d. Textiles, apparel & leather. e. Wood products & furniture. f. Paper, paper products & printing. g. Petroleum & coal products. h. Industrial chemicals. i. Drugs & medicines. j. Rubber & plastic products. k. Non-metallic mineral products. l. Iron & steel. m. Non-ferrous metals. n. Metal products. o. Non-electrical machinery. p. Office & computing machinery. q. Electrical apparatus, not elsewhere classified. r. Radio, TV & communication equipment. s. Professional goods. t. Motor vehicles. u. Shipbuilding & repairing. v. Aircraft. w. Other transport. x. Other manufacturing. y. Electricity, gas & water. z. Construction. aa. Wholesale & retail trade. bb. Restaurants & hotels. cc. Transport & storage. dd. Communication. ee. Finance & insurance. ff. Real estate & business services. gg. Community, social & personal services. hh. Producers of government services

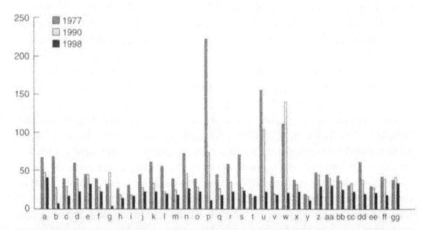

(b) United Kingdom. 1 Million (1998) Pounds. a. Agriculture, forestry & fishing. b. Mining & quarrying. c. Food, beverages & tobacco. d. Textiles, apparel & leather. e. Wood products & furniture. f. Paper, paper products & printing. g. Petroleum & coal products. h. Industrial chemicals. i. Drugs & medicines. j. Rubber & plastic products. k. Non-metallic mineral products. l. Iron & steel. m. Non-ferrous metals. n. Metal products. o. Non-electrical machinery. p. Office & computing machinery. q. Electrical apparatus, not elsewhere classified. r. Radio, TV & communication equipment. s. Professional goods. t. Motor vehicles. u. Shipbuilding & repairing. v. Aircraft. w. Other transport. x. Other manufacturing. y. Electricity, gas & water. z. .Construction. aa. Wholesale & retail trade. bb. Restaurants & hotels. cc. Transport & storage. dd. Communication. ee. Finance & insurance. ff. Real estate & business services. gg. Community, social & personal services. hh. Producers of government services

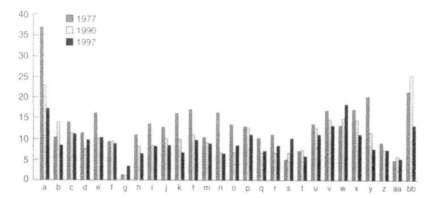

Fig. 4.1. Continued.

(c) Germany. 1 Million (1995) DM. a. Agriculture, forestry & fishing. b. Mining & quarrying. c. Food, beverages & tobacco. d. Textiles, apparel & leather. e. Wood products & furniture. f. Paper, paper products & printing. g. & coal products. h. Industrial chemicals. i. Rubber & plastic products. j. Non-metallic mineral products. k. Basic Metal Industries. l. Metal products. m. Non-electrical machinery. n. Office & computing machinery. o. Electrical apparatus, not elsewhere classified. p. Professional goods. q. Motor vehicles. r. Other Transport, Ships, Aircraft. s. Other manufacturing. t. Electricity, gas & water. u. Construction. v. Wholesale & retail trade. w. Restaurants & hotels. x. Transport & storage. y. Communication. z. Finance & insurance. aa. Real estate & business services. bb. Community, social & personal services. cc. Producers of government services

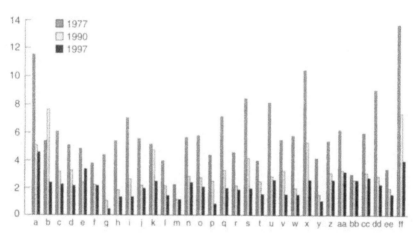

(d) France. 1 Million (1995) FF. a. Agriculture, forestry & fishing. b. Mining & quarrying. c. Food, beverages & tobacco. d. Textiles, apparel & leather. e. Wood products & furniture. f. Paper, paper products & printing. g. Petroleum & coal products. h. Industrial chemicals. i. Drugs & medicines. j. Rubber & plastic products. k. Non-metallic mineral products. l. Iron & steel. m. Non-ferrous metals. n. Metal products. o. Non-electrical machinery. p. Office & computing machinery. q. Electrical apparatus, not elsewhere classified. r. Radio, TV & communication equipment. s. Professional goods. t. Motor vehicles. u. Shipbuilding & repairing. v. Aircraft. w. Other transport. x. Other manufacturing. y. Electricity, gas & water. z. Construction. aa. Wholesale & retail trade. bb. Restaurants & hotels. cc. Transport & storage. dd. Communication. ee. Finance & insurance. ff. Community, social & personal services. gg. Producers of government services

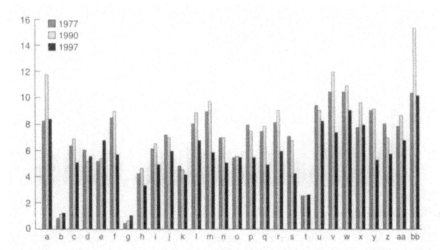

Fig. 4.1. Continued.

(e) The Netherlands. 1 Million (1997) NLG. a. Agriculture, forestry & fishing. b. Mining & quarrying. c. Food, beverages & tobacco. d. Textiles, apparel & leather. e. Wood products & furniture. f. Paper, paper products & printing. g. Petroleum & coal products. h. Industrial chemicals + drugs and medicines. i. Rubber & plastic products. j. Non-metallic mineral products. k. Iron & steel. l. Metal products. m. Non-electrical machinery. n. Office & computing machinery. o. Electrical apparatus, not elsewhere classified. p. Professional goods. q. Motor vehicles. r. Shipbuilding & repairing. s. Other transport. t. Other manufacturing. u. Electricity, gas & water. v. Construction. w. Wholesale & retail trade. x. Restaurants & hotels. y. Transport & storage. z. Communication. aa. Finance & insurance. bb. Real estate & business services. cc. Community, social & personal services. dd. Producers of government services

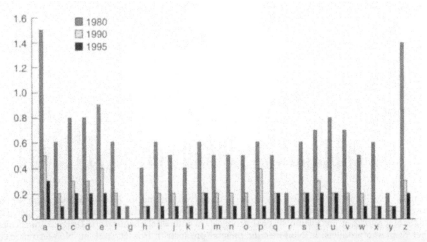

(f) Spain. 1 Million Pesetas. a. Agriculture, forestry & fishing. b. Mining & quarrying. c. Food, beverages & tobacco. d. Textiles, apparel & leather. e. Wood products & furniture. f. Paper, paper products & printing. g. Petroleum & coal products. h. Industrial chemicals. i. Drugs & medicines. j. Rubber & plastic products. k. Non-metallic mineral products. l. Basic Metals. m. Metal products. n. Machinery & Equipment. o. Electric & Optical Equipment. p. Motor vehicles. q. Other transport. r. Other manufacturing. s. Electricity, gas & water. t. Construction. u. Wholesale & retail trade. v. Restaurants & hotels. w. Transport & storage. x. Communication. y. Finance & insurance. z. Real estate & business services. aa. Community, social & personal services

The pattern of employment-intensities can be summarized through Spearman correlation coefficients for the sectoral rankings. In table 4.1 the upper panel shows the correlations within each country over time, and the lower panel the correlations across countries in the mid-1990s, the latest year available. The high value of the coefficients within each country, mostly between .7 and .9, indicates that within each country the employment-friendly sectors tend to remain the same over time. Across countries, also, considerable similarity can be seen. The correlation coefficients support the view that European economies tend to be quite similar to each other, with correlations all above .7, and less similar to the United States, with correlations mostly lower than .7. The European economy least similar to the United States in the mid-1990s was Germany, followed by France, and then the Netherlands and the

TABLE 4.1
Rank Correlation of Total Employment Created by Expenditure Stimuli to Each Sector

A. *Across time periods, by Country*

United States	1977	1990	1997	United Kingdom	1979	1990	1998
1977	1	0.815	0.705	1979	1	0.856	0.736
1990		1	0.871	1990		1	0.671
1997			1	1998			1

Germany	1978	1990	1995	France	1977	1990	1995
1978	1	0.816	0.720	1977	1	0.719	0.713
1990		1	0.766	1990		1	0.955
1995			1	1995			1

Netherlands	1977	1986	1997	Spain	1980	1990	1995
1977	1	0.891	0.826	1980	1	0.786	0.770
1986		1	0.947	1990		1	0.863
1997			1	1995			1

B. *Across countries, late 1990s*

	United States	United Kingdom	Germany	France	Netherlands	Spain
United States	1					
United Kingdom	0.630	1				
Germany	0.545	0.762	1			
France	0.570	0.724	0.836	1		
Netherlands	0.614	0.844	0.775	0.732	1	
Spain	0.740	0.751	0.863	0.824	0.794	1

United Kingdom, with Spain, perhaps surprisingly, the most similar to the United States in the relative employment-intensity of sectors.

EMPLOYMENT CREATION: MANUFACTURING VERSUS SERVICES

If services are income elastic, high-income economies will tend to consume more services. If the demand for services creates more jobs, then these economies will also tend to be high-employment economies. This line of argument is sometimes used as an explanation of the superior employment performance of the United States relative to most European economies. We now examine whether manufacturing and services products show systematic differences in employment intensity, measured on the product supply basis.

We divide the economy into the two broad groups, "manufacturing" and "services," allocating the available sectors appropriately.[4] The employment intensity of each group is calculated as the average number of jobs created on a product supply basis by the injection of one unit of final demand into each individual sector in the group. Comparison across the columns in table 4.2 shows clearly that there is no simple story of manufacturing generating more jobs than services, or vice versa. On average, the number of jobs generated economy-wide when final demand is allocated to manufacturing is of the same order of magnitude as when it is allocated to services. This result is robust both over time and across countries. Moreover, contrary to the received wisdom, in the United States and the United Kingdom demand for manufactures generates *more* jobs than an equal demand for services. In the continental European economies, on the other hand, demand for services generally generates more jobs than an equal amount of demand for manufactures.

The concept of the product supply chain stresses the important role played by the intermediate stages of production and the linkages between industries through them. As has recently been emphasized by Oulton (2001), industries with low productivity growth do not necessarily push the economy's productivity growth rate downwards towards zero. To the extent that stagnant industries produce for intermediate demand, any (positive) productivity growth there adds to the productivity growth

---

[4] Manufacturing comprises Agriculture (ISIC 1), Mining and Quarrying (ISIC 2), Manufacturing (ISIC3), Public Utilities (ISIC 4), and Construction (ISIC 5). Services comprise Wholesale Retail and Trade, Hotel and Restaurants (ISIC 6), Transport and Communications (ISIC 7), Finance, Insurance, Real Estate and Business Services (ISIC 8), and Community and Personal Services (ISIC 9).

TABLE 4.2
Total Job Creation from Expenditure Stimuli to Manufacturing
and Service Sectors

		Manufacturing	*Services*
United States	1977	38.6	36.5
	1990	19.0	16.6
	1997	13.3	12.2
United Kingdom	1979	132.3	112.8
	1990	48.9	43.2
	1998	24.5	20.6
Germany	1978	17.9	18.8
	1990	10.2	12.9
	1995	8.8	10.7
France	1977	9.5	13.5
	1990	2.9	3.9
	1995	1.9	2.7
Netherlands	1977	11.8	16.5
	1986	6.9	11.0
	1997	5.0	7.4
Spain	1980	0.6	0.7
	1990	0.2	0.2
	1995	0.1	0.1

Note: Manufacturing comprises Agriculture (ISIC 1), Mining and Quarrying (ISIC 2), Manufacturing (ISIC 3), Public Utilities (ISIC 4), and Construction (ISIC 5). Services comprise Wholesale Retail and Trade, Hotel and Restaurants (ISIC 6), Transport and Communications (ISIC 7), Finance and Insurance Real Estate and Business Services (ISIC 8), and Community and Personal Services (ISIC 9).

rate in the using sectors; comparing relative growth rates of productivity in final production only is liable to be misleading as a measure of the sector's contribution. We therefore now explore the nature and extent of this interdependence, as revealed through the location of the employment generated by an expenditure stimulus. In particular we distinguish between the share of new jobs generated that are located within the sector receiving the demand stimulus, the share arising in other sectors within the manufacturing or services group, and the share that spills over between these broad groups. Table 4.3 shows these shares for each year and country.

When demand is allocated to one of the sectors within manufacturing, on average between one-half and two-thirds of the jobs created occur

TABLE 4.3
Distribution of Jobs Created Following Expenditure Stimuli to Manufacturing
and Service Sectors

| | | Stimuli to Manufacturing Products | | | Stimuli to Service Products | | |
| | | | Spillovers to | | | Spillovers to | |
		Retained in Origin Sector (1)	Other Manu-facturing (2)	Services (3)	Retained in Origin Sector (4)	Manu-facturing (5)	Other Services (6)
United States	1977	0.52	0.24	0.24	0.73	0.12	0.15
	1990	0.51	0.21	0.28	0.72	0.09	0.18
	1997	0.50	0.19	0.31	0.71	0.10	0.20
United Kingdom	1979	0.56	0.20	0.24	0.76	0.10	0.14
	1990	0.54	0.15	0.31	0.72	0.07	0.21
	1998	0.57	0.16	0.27	0.72	0.07	0.21
Germany	1978	0.59	0.24	0.16	0.74	0.14	0.12
	1990	0.57	0.20	0.23	0.78	0.09	0.14
	1995	0.58	0.18	0.24	0.78	0.08	0.14
France	1977	0.58	0.21	0.22	0.81	0.08	0.11
	1990	0.53	0.16	0.31	0.81	0.05	0.14
	1995	0.57	0.18	0.25	0.84	0.06	0.10
Netherlands	1977	0.66	0.18	0.16	0.83	0.07	0.11
	1986	0.65	0.15	0.20	0.83	0.05	0.12
	1997	0.59	0.13	0.29	0.77	0.06	0.18
Spain	1980	0.62	0.24	0.14	0.69	0.20	0.11
	1990	0.62	0.21	0.17	0.75	0.13	0.12
	1995	0.55	0.21	0.24	0.76	0.11	0.13

Note: Manufacturing comprises Agriculture (ISIC 1), Mining and Quarrying (ISIC 2), Manufacturing (ISIC 3), Public Utilities (ISIC 4), and Construction (ISIC 5). Services comprises Wholesale Retail and Trade, Hotel and Restaurants (ISIC 6), Transport and Communications (ISIC 7), Finance and Insurance Real Estate and Business Services (ISIC 8), and Community and Personal Services (ISIC 9).

within the sector itself. This share has been very stable within each economy, with only the Netherlands and Spain and (marginally) the United States showing a declining trend. When the demand injection is to one of the services sectors, the proportion retained is significantly higher, at around three-quarters. This share has tended to fall over time in half of our countries (United States, United Kingdom, and the Netherlands), while increasing in the others (Germany, France, and Spain).

The new jobs not retained within the original sector spill over to the rest of the economy along the product supply chain. Here the trends are striking. From an original injection to one of the manufacturing sectors the share of jobs spilling over to other sectors within the manufacturing group has been tending to fall while the share located in services has increased sharply (columns 2 and 3). Manufacturing has been economizing on the use of manufactured inputs, and switching into expanded use of intermediate services. Similarly, when demand is injected into services the spillover of jobs to manufacturing has tended to decline, while the share of jobs generated within other parts of the services group has increased (columns 5 and 6). Services too have been economizing on the use of manufactured inputs and expanding their use of intermediate services. Rising spillovers to services both from manufacturing and from services themselves is clearly the dominant trend.

These developments can be interpreted as showing outsourcing in various forms. The reduced spillovers within and to manufactures are consistent with rising import penetration through the offshoring or outsourcing abroad of parts of the manufacturing supply chain. The rising spillovers to the service industries from both manufacturing and services are consistent with the outsourcing of functions, with firms increasingly restricting their activities to core competencies while buying in ancillary services previously provided in-house. They may, for example, no longer engage in their own recruitment, marketing, tax management, software development, cleaning, and catering, but purchase them from specialist (services) suppliers. It is sometimes argued that outsourcing along these functional lines generates no additional activities or jobs within the economy, only changing their sectoral location. But without anticipated efficiency gains the incentive to outsource would be lacking. A further possible source of the increasing spillovers of jobs from manufactures to services is that manufactured products not only increasingly include elements such as brand and marketing, but also explicit postsale service components such as maintenance contracts, help lines, and financing. Hardware may even become simply an adjunct to the service it supplies, as when a handset is provided as part of a mobile phone network subscription. The distinction between goods and services is becoming increasingly artificial in a modern economy.

THE EMPLOYMENT EFFECTS OF FINAL DEMAND AND
    CONSUMPTION MIXES WITHIN THE SIX ECONOMIES

The differing employment-intensities of individual sectors provide the channel through which demand patterns may affect a country's employment record. The European economies are characterized by a greater role for government expenditure in final demand and by higher export shares relative to the consumption orientation of the United States. If the sectors supplying government production and exports are less employment-intensive than those supplying household consumption, European employment rates will be lower. And similarly if the consumption mix chosen by American households is more employment-intensive, U.S. employment will be higher. As background to our analysis of the employment effects of demand and consumption mixes, table 4.4 summarizes the employment performance of the six economies.

Table 4.5 shows that the changing patterns of final demand in the European economies, mainly towards services, have been employment friendly; the demand mix of the late 1970s would give lower employment than its actual mix of the late 1990s. In most cases the effect has been significant, an implied employment increase of over 12 percent for Germany and 10 percent for the Netherlands. The United States stands in contrast, as the only economy where the pattern of demand changes has had an adverse effect on the level of employment, although this is small. Given the slow employment growth in the European economies, the shifting pattern of demand contributed one-third (36 percent) of the employment growth realized in Germany, 43 percent in the Netherlands, and 25 percent in Spain. In the United Kingdom employment would have fallen without the contribution from the changing demand mix, while in France the marginal fall in employment actually experienced would have been exacerbated. With the strong growth of employment in the United States, on the other hand, the "loss" of 1.6 percent over

TABLE 4.4
The Employment Record of the Six Economies

	Employment/ Population Ratio (%), Mid-1990s	Average Annual Growth Rate of FTE Employment, 1970s–90s
United States	72.5	2.0
United Kingdom	69.3	0.1
Germany[a]	64.7	1.2
France	59.0	−0.1
Netherlands	64.2	1.3
Spain	47.4	0.6

[a]Obtained by projecting West German employment in the period 1991–95 using the yearly compound employment growth rate computed on the period 1970–90. The gross employment growth rate including East Germany after 1991 is 2.5%.

TABLE 4.5
Employment Effect of Alternative Final Demand and Household Consumption
Mixes across Time Periods, by Country (%) (late 1970s mixes applied
to late 1990 final demand/household consumption)

	Final Demand on Total Employment	Household Consumption on Total Employment
United States (1977–97)	1.6	−1.2
United Kingdom (1979–98)	− 7.8	2.2
Germany (1978–95)	−12.5	−3.2
France (1977–95)	−6.1	3.8
Netherlands (1977–97)	−9.8	1.3
Spain (1980–95)	−2.1	−0.5

the 20 years due to the demand mix is less than the average growth in
a single year. For the European economies, therefore, the favorable shift
in the mix of final demand with its bias towards services has made an
important contribution to employment growth. For the United States
the effect was negative, but unimportant. This is clearly counter to the
hypothesis that the increasing service-orientation of the U.S. economy
has brought about its higher employment rate.

The growing role of services in consumption has received considerable
attention (Kalwij and Machin, this volume); we follow up on this literature by assessing the effects on employment. The household consumption columns in table 4.5 give the employment change associated with
alternative consumption mixes as a percentage of the employment generated by consumption activities and as a percentage of total employment.
The effects are small. In the European economies the changing mix of
household consumption fails to replicate the employment friendliness
found in final demand overall. Only in Germany (and very marginally
Spain) has the effect been positive at all. For France, the United Kingdom, and the Netherlands the change in the consumption mix has been
employment-reducing. In the United States the changing consumption
patterns have generated an increase in employment, but this is small in
absolute terms and particularly in the context of the U.S. record of
strong employment growth.

Given that the evolution of demand and consumption patterns within
the individual countries fails to explain the superior U.S. employment
performance over the period, is it the case that U.S. patterns of final
demand and consumption are more employment-friendly than in the Eu-

ropean economies? How far has the evolution of the United States into a service economy given rise to its higher employment rates? Because of the alleged importance of the service sectors in explaining the transatlantic employment gap, we will pay particular attention to the employment effects of the differing service mix and level of services overall in final demand and consumption across countries.

The estimated impact on employment of the differing national patterns of final demand and household consumption is shown in table 4.6. Each is calculated in three steps, changing consecutively the mix within services, the share of services in demand, and the mix within manufactures, which cumulate to give the total effect.[5] Taking first the mix of final demand (columns 1a–4a), far from being employment-unfriendly, the service mixes of the United Kingdom and the Netherlands in particular, but also Spain, would generate *higher* levels of employment in the United States. The patterns prevailing in Germany and France would generate lower employment, but by a negligible margin. This largely positive employment effect of the European mix of services in final demand is, however, counterbalanced by the negative employment effect of the lower share of services in each of the European economies. Overall, the final demand patterns of the United Kingdom, Netherlands, and Spain would generate higher levels of employment in the United States, while those of Germany and France would depress it. Conversely, the U.S. final demand pattern, applied in a European context, would result in a consistent, and significant, loss of employment, up to 9 percent in Germany and Spain (columns 1b–4b).

Turning to the final possibility, that the choices of the U.S. consumer, in terms of the mix within the consumption basket, may explain the higher U.S. level of employment, we find evidence in support of the superior job creation ability of the U.S. pattern (columns 5a–8a). Except for the United Kingdom, the European economies have a less employment-friendly pattern of consumption. This holds particularly for France and Germany. If the United States had the French pattern of household consumption, its employment would be 5.0 percent lower, and 3.6 percent on the German pattern; the U.S. employment rate would be reduced by 3.7 and 2.6 percentage points, narrowing the employment gap by the

[5] To estimate the employment effects for country A of the demand pattern of country B, the first step (service mix) computes the employment that would be generated in country A with unchanged demand for manufactures, and the demand for services unchanged in level but reallocated across individual services according to the pattern of country B. In the second step (service share) total expenditure on services country A is scaled to match the share in country B. In the third step (manufacturing mix) the demand for manufactures in country A is adjusted to mirror its pattern in country B. The sum of the three steps equals the overall effect.

TABLE 4.6
Employment Effect of Alternative Final Demand and Household Consumption Mixes across Countries (%)

	Final Demand				Household Consumption			
Panel A. European mixes applied to U.S. final demand/household consumption	Service Mix (1a)	Service Share (2a)	Manufacturing Mix (3a)	Final Demand Mix (4a)	Service Mix (5a)	Service Share (6a)	Manufacturing Mix (7a)	Consumption (8a)
United Kingdom	4.1	−0.8	−0.2	3.1	1.2	−1.1	0.4	0.5
Germany	−0.1	−2.3	0.8	−1.6	−3.4	−0.8	0.6	−3.6
France	−0.2	−1.6	0.7	−1.1	−4.7	−1.0	0.6	−5.0
Netherlands	4.2	−2.0	−0.2	2.0	−2.4	0.0	−0.1	−2.6
Spain	1.2	−1.4	2.8	2.6	−2.2	−0.8	1.7	−1.3

	Final Demand				Household Consumption			
Panel B. U.S. mixes applied to European final demand/ household consumption	Service Mix (1b)	Service Share (2b)	Manufacturing Mix (3b)	Final Demand Mix (4b)	Service Mix (5b)	Service Share (6b)	Manufacturing Mix (7b)	Consumption (8b)
United Kingdom	−6.1	0.6	1.5	−4.0	1.7	1.2	0.0	2.9
Germany	−10.5	1.5	0.0	−9.0	2.6	0.6	−0.3	2.9
France	−5.2	1.8	0.2	−3.2	2.9	1.9	−0.3	4.5
Netherlands	−6.8	2.0	1.4	−3.4	3.1	0.0	−0.1	3.0
Spain	−6.0	−0.1	−2.7	−8.7	−2.1	−0.2	−1.4	−3.7

Note: In panel A, Service mix is U.S. final demand/consumption, U.S. manufacturing mix, U.S. service share in final demand/consumption, country service mix. Service share is U.S. final demand/consumption, U.S. manufacturing mix, country service share in final demand/consumption, country service mix. Manufacturing mix is U.S. final demand/consumption, country manufacturing mix, country service share in final demand/consumption, country service mix. Final demand/consumption mix is service mix + service share + manufacturing mix. In panel B, Service mix is country final demand/consumption, country manufacturing mix, country service share in final demand/consumption, U.S. service mix. Service share is country final demand/consumption, country manufacturing mix, U.S. service share in final demand/consumption, U.S. service mix. Manufacturing mix is country final demand/consumption, manufacturing mix, U.S. service share in final demand/consumption, U.S. service mix. Final demand/consumption mix is service mix + service share + manufacturing mix.

same margin. For these two economies, therefore, one-quarter and one-third respectively of the employment gap can be attributed to the different private consumption mixes. The Spanish consumption pattern would lower U.S. employment only marginally, while the United Kingdom pattern would actually increase it.

A rather stronger picture of the greater employment-intensity of the U.S. consumption mix is given by the converse counterfactual, where the U.S. mix is applied to consumption in each European country (columns 5b–8b). Employment would increase by 4.5 percent in France and by around 3 percent in the United Kingdom, Germany, and the Netherlands; only in Spain would there be a fall. This would raise the employment-to-population ratio by about 2.1 percentage points in the United Kingdom, 1.8 in Germany, 2.6 in France, and 1.8 in Netherlands, but reduce it by 1.8 points in Spain. A U.S.-type consumption mix in the United Kingdom could halve its (small) employment gap with the United States; France and Germany could reduce theirs by one-fifth, and the Netherlands marginally; but the gap between the United States and Spain would widen.

We thus have contrasting messages about the implications for European as against U.S. employment from the analysis of the service mix in final demand, on the one hand, and the (service) consumption mix, on the other. The European final demand mix, in particular the service mix, is employment-enhancing, reducing the employment gap. The European consumption mix, on the other hand, depresses employment, widening the gap. We therefore turn to considering the issue of demand and employment in a wider context.

THE SOURCES OF EMPLOYMENT CHANGE IN PRODUCT SUPPLY

The estimates above have centered on the effects on employment of demand and consumption, taking as given the structure of the supply chain and employment requirements in each sector. We now broaden the focus to bring these in as well, decomposing the sources of employment change into the contributions from the growth final demand, changes in the supply chain, and labor productivity growth.

Returning to the formulation of the employment required for product supply given in equation (2) above, differencing gives

$$\Delta N = \hat{n}B(\Delta \hat{F}) + \hat{n}(\Delta B)\hat{F} + (\Delta \hat{n})B \ \hat{F}, \qquad (3)$$

where $B = (I - A)^{-1}$. The change in employment between two periods, ΔN, can be divided between ΔF, the growth of final demand, ΔB, structural change in input use along the supply chain, and $\Delta \hat{n}$, the growth of labor productivity.[6] It should be noted that ΔF subsumes the effects of both the changing level and the changing mix of final demand, which we will refer to simply as the change in final demand.[7]

The decompositions (table 4.7) reveal clearly that aggregate employment changes are the outcome of a two-way dynamic. In each of the economies the growth of final demand generates employment expansion, but this is offset by employment losses from the productivity gains throughout the supply chain. The contribution of structural change in input-output linkages (changing supply sources, outsourcing) is small everywhere. In terms of numbers of jobs, in the United States, where employment expanded by over 35 million FTEs over this period, the growth of final demand generated the equivalent of 60 million FTE jobs, with a further 4 million from the changing interindustry structure, while 28 million were eliminated by productivity growth. By contrast, in the United Kingdom, France, the Netherlands, and Spain labor productivity gains almost exactly offset the employment expansion generated by demand growth, leaving FTE employment almost unchanged.

The same dynamic is the norm when the decomposition is extended to selected major sectors (figure 4.2). For manufactures (i.e., nonservice products) only in the United States and Germany has growth in final demand generated more jobs than have been eliminated by the labor productivity gains in product supply. In the Netherlands and Spain the changing pattern of interindustry linkages in the supply of manufactures

TABLE 4.7

Decomposition of Employment Change across Productivity, Final Demand, and the Supply Chain (millions of FTE jobs)

| | | Changes in | | |
	Productivity	Final Demand	Supply Chain	Total
United States (1977–97)	−28.0	60.1	3.6	35.7
United Kingdom (1979–98)	−16.6	13.6	3.1	0.0
Germany (1978–95)	−8.4	16.1	0.6	8.3
France (1977–95)	−22.8	21.6	0.3	−0.9
Netherlands (1977–97)	−2.5	2.9	0.7	1.1
Spain (1980–95)	−26.6	26.4	1.2	1.0

[6] Labor productivity here is measured on a gross output basis; see Gordon 1996; Griliches 1992; Ten Raa and Schettkat 2001.

[7] For more formal development of the decomposition and discussion see Dietzenbacher and Los 1998.

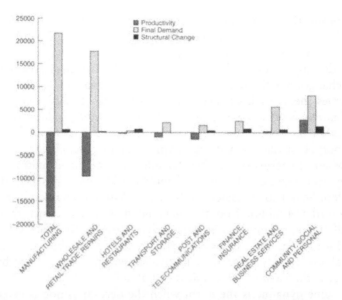

Fig. 4.2. Decomposition of Employment Change across Productivity, Final Demand, and the Supply Chain: Major Products (Thousands of Jobs).
(a) United States, 1977–97

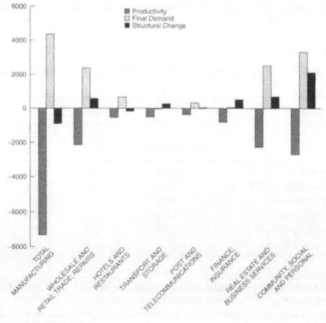

(b) United Kingdom, 1979–98

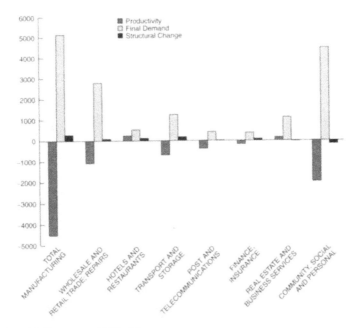

Fig. 4.2. (c) Germany, 1978–95

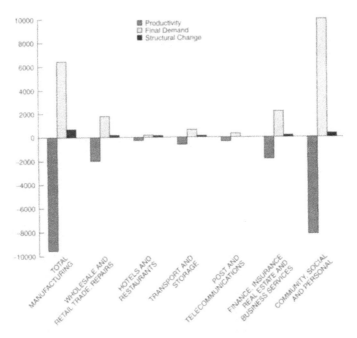

(d) France, 1977–95

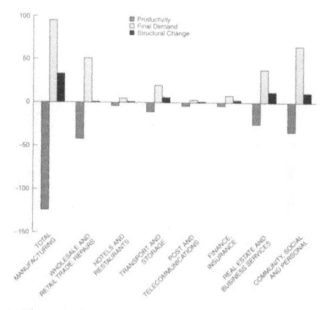

Fig. 4.2. (e) The Netherlands, 1986–97

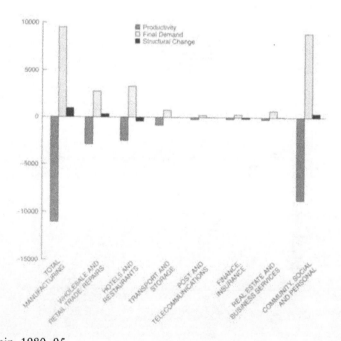

(ɪ) Spain, 1980–95
Total manufacturing comprises Agriculture (ISIC 1), Mining and Quarrying (ISIC 2), Manufacturing (ISIC3), Public Utilities (ISIC 4), and Construction (ISIC 5).

has been on balance job-creating, generating a significant number of additional jobs in conjunction with demand growth to balance the employment losses from rising labor productivity. The United Kingdom and France, on the other hand, have seen falls in the employment generated by manufactures as the expansion of demand has been weak relative to productivity growth, while changes in input use along the supply chain have been on balance job-destroying. Within services the big impetus to employment change has come from the three sectors Community, Social and Personal Services, Wholesale and Retail Trade, and Real Estate and Business Services. The same pattern of offsetting roles for demand and productivity changes is repeated, but with two significant differences. First, the job gains from demand growth typically outstrip the employment reductions from productivity gains. Second, in a significant minority of cases productivity gains over this period have been small, on occasion even negative. The most striking instance is in the provision of Community, Social and Personal Services in the United States, where on average labor productivity was falling; further instances can be noted in Germany, France, the Netherlands, and Spain.[8] Structural change, measured by changes in the interindustry linkages (Leontief inverse), plays at most a very small role in employment change. This contradicts the hypothesis that the observed growth in service employment is primarily due to outsourcing of intermediate services, as nonservice employers replace in-house provision by outside purchasing along the supply chain.[9]

These decompositions give a framework for interpreting the United States–Europe employment gap. In the United States the employment-creating effects of demand growth have been strong relative to the job-destroying effects of labor productivity gains. Both have been heavily concentrated by sector. The bulk of the employment growth has been driven by three sectors: Wholesale and Retail Trade, Community, Social and Personal Services, and Real Estate and Business Services. Demand growth in these three sectors has created 28.5 million new FTEs out of a total increase of 36 million over the period. The job-destroying effects of labor productivity growth have been concentrated in only two sec-

---

[8] Negative productivity growth in some U.S. service industries in the period 1973–87 has also been found in Appelbaum and Albin 1990.

[9] Similar findings have begun to emerge elsewhere. Ten Raa and Wolff 2001 find that growth in manufacturing TFP is due mainly to input saving in capital and labor, with a much smaller part due to outsourcing. in his analysis of a time series of Italian input-output tables for the period 1960–85 also finds that changes in the interindustry linkages (outsourcing) play only a minor role in the growth of service employment. in his survey reports that managers tend to overestimate the cost reduction aspects of outsourcing; moreover, he finds that outsourcing is often a consequence of output growth.

tors, Manufactures, and, again, Wholesale and Retail Services, eliminating 27.8 million FTE jobs. Productivity growth has been approximately employment-neutral (-0.2 million FTEs) across all the remaining sectors. The European economies, in contrast, show more muted employment gains from demand growth and markedly stronger employment losses from productivity growth. Both the gains and particularly the losses are more dispersed across sectors than in the United States. This differing balance between employment expansion and productivity gains is the key influence on the relative employment outcomes of the U.S. and the European economies.

Services and the United States–Europe Employment Gap

When employment is appropriately measured, as the jobs supported across the entire production chain in supplying individual final products, many of the casual generalizations about the role of services in employment creation fail to stand up. In particular, the employment intensity of services is no greater than that of manufactures. Nevertheless, there is a substantial amount of heterogeneity at the level of the individual product or service, which tends to persist over time, and which gives rise to the possibility that differing product mixes selected within individual countries could affect overall employment. In the European economies the growing orientation towards services within the structure of final demand since the 1970s has been to some extent employment-enhancing, but this has not been the case in the United States, casting doubt on the strength of any generalization. In the same vein, the evolution towards services within the structure of household consumption has been employment-depressing in all countries except the United States and Germany.

The European patterns of final demand, involving higher shares of government services and exports relative to the consumption orientation in the United States, are more favorable for employment except in Germany and France, where the negative employment effects generated by the share of services in final demand are not fully offset by the positive employment effects from the mix of services. On the other hand the consumption patterns of U.S. households generate more employment than their European counterparts. Overall, the product mix within final demand and consumption, and particularly the role of services within them, has at best mixed implications for relative employment between the United States and the European economies. Although they play some role in the cases of Germany and Spain, overall they make only a minor contribution to the employment gap between the United States and the European economies.

However, the *growth* of demand emerges as a major influence when we assess the sources of employment growth juxtaposed with labor productivity growth. Our analysis highlights the dynamic for each country between the job-creating effects of demand growth and the job-destroying effects of productivity growth. The systematic difference that emerges between the United States and the European economies is that, over the period on which we have focused, spanning the 1970s to the mid-1990s, the United States has shown massive employment creation at relatively low rates of productivity growth, while the European economies have been characterized by a bias towards more widespread productivity gains but accompanied by limited employment growth.

Times may now be changing. Since the second half of the 1990s the United States has moved into a period of substantial productivity growth, already sustained for close to a decade. This is beginning to again transform the perspective on the growth process. At the same time employment rates in the European economies have begun to rise, although they typically remain well short of the Lisbon targets or even the U.S. levels of the 1970s. Even if the quarter-century that we have analyzed turns out to have been an exceptional period for both the United States and the European economies in terms of the employment and productivity record, it was nonetheless a striking period, and the implications of the diverse growth patterns, in the emergence of the employment gap, have been profound.

APPENDIX A: DATA SOURCES

The principal data source used is the set of input-output tables prepared by the OECD. These are constructed from national sources, harmonized within the OECD. They are designed as far as possible to be on an industry-by-industry basis at basic prices. The Spanish tables prior to 1995, not available through the OECD, have been obtained from the Spanish Bureau of Statistics.

The analysis is based on the input-output tables alone because of the lack of harmonized supply-and-use (commodity by industry) tables. This limits us to analysis based on the product flows between industries as they are classified, and not on the primary activities (commodities) themselves. Against this, a significant advantage of industry-by-industry tables is that we can match the input-output sector directly with industry-level employment data.

For final demand and interindustry transactions we use the domestic use tables. Value added by industry, not available from the domestic use tables, is taken from the total use tables. All the tables used are at current prices.

Tables for 1970–90 are based on ISIC revision 2; those for 1995–98 are based on ISIC revision 3. The most important change introduced with the new classification involved the shift of the purchases of software from intermediate goods purchases to final demand (investment). As a consequence in all countries the ratio of intermediate goods to industry gross output in the business services drops slightly, and there is a contemporaneous increase in the share of investment in gross output. The changes are greatest for France, where the ratio of intermediate goods to gross output in business services dropped by eight percentage point between 1990 and 1995, while the share of (gross) private investment grew by six percentage points over the same period. The revised classification has also involved the shift of some minor manufacturing activities into the sector Other Manufacturing Industries.

Using data for Germany presents a specific problem because of unification. The 1997 German table includes East Germany, while the earlier tables do not. This is a problem affecting all longitudinal studies of the German economy. It should be noted that East Germany was rather a small economy in comparison to West Germany (26 percent in population and 10 percent in GDP), limiting the impact of the discontinuity. See Bibow 2003.

Employment data on a full-time equivalent (FTE) basis by industry have been obtained from the OECD data base STAN. Missing figures for the United Kingdom have been derived from the UK Labour Force Survey.

Detailed documentation on the OECD data, including the input-output tables, is available at www.oecd.org.

Minor issues arise in the industrial classification by country and year. These are described in the appendix to Gregory and Russo (2004).

APPENDIX B: THE ALLOCATION OF EMPLOYMENT ACROSS PRODUCT SUPPLY: A NUMERICAL EXAMPLE

The input-output flow table (table 4.B1) is shown for a three-industry economy producing outputs X1, X2, and X3. Each industry supplies its output as an intermediate good for further processing in all industries, including to other firms within its own industry, and to final demand. Gross output for each industry is obtained as the row sum of its sales to intermediate plus final demand. Equivalently, by the accounting balance, the value of the industry's gross output is obtained as the column

TABLE 4.B1
Input-Output Flow Table

	X1	X2	X3	Inter-mediate Sales	Final Demand	Gross Output	Employment
X1	70	30	15	115	110	225	10
X2	30	25	30	85	126	211	20
X3	50	20	25	95	55	150	80
Intermediate purchases	150	75	70				
Value added	75	136	80		291		
Gross output	225	211	150			586	

sum of its purchases of intermediate goods from all industries plus the value added (wages and profits) that it generates. The final column of the table shows employment in the industry.

The Leontief inverse matrix of input use coefficients is then derived as shown in table 4.B2.

The left-hand section in table 4.B3 shows the vector of industry employment coefficients n (labor input per unit of gross output) expressed as a diagonal matrix. The center section gives the matrix of gross output requirements from each industry to deliver the final demand vector. The right-hand section repeats the final demand vector, now expressed as a diagonal matrix.

By multiplication of these matrices we derive the employment required in each industry to deliver the vector of final demands, shown in table 4.B4.

Reading across the rows of the derived employment matrix n*B*FD, the elements give the employment generated in the industry, directly and indirectly, to supply the output of each column industry; the row total

TABLE 4.B2
Leontief Inverse Matrix

	$(I - A)$			$B = (I - A)^{-1}$	
0.69	−0.14	−0.10	1.59	0.28	0.26
−0.13	0.88	−0.20	0.35	1.23	0.34
−0.22	−0.09	0.83	0.46	0.22	1.31

TABLE 4.B3
Vector of Industry Employment Coefficients n, Matrix of Gross Output
Requirements, and Final Demand Vector

Employment Coefficients (n)			B*FD			Final Demand (FD)		
0.044	0	0	174.92	35.83	14.25	110	0	0
0	0.095	0	38.02	154.51	18.47	0	126	0
0	0	0.533	50.97	27.13	71.90	·0	0	55

TABLE 4.B4
Employment Required in Each Industry

	n*B*FD			Employment (row sum)
	7.77	1.59	0.63	10
	3.60	14.65	1.75	20
	27.18	14.47	38.35	80
Employment (column sum)	38.56	30.71	40.73	110

gives total employment in the industry, as in the original table. The column sum for each industry gives the total employment required from all industries to supply the final demand for its product, where each element within the column shows its location in the corresponding (row) industry.

Comparative Service Consumption in Six Countries

Adriaan S. Kalwij and Stephen Machin with
Laura Blow, Marijke van Deelen, François Gardes,
María-José Luengo-Prado, Javier Ruiz-Castillo, John Schmitt,
and Christophe Starzec

OVERVIEW

THIS STUDY presents cross-country comparative work on shifts in household expenditure patterns during the 1980s and 1990s in France, Germany, the Netherlands, Spain, the United Kingdom, and the United States. A key feature of this study is its emphasis on international comparability of the information available in consumer budget surveys. For this purpose, researchers from six countries have together worked out consistently defined commodity groupings over countries and time using household-level budget survey data. A uniform approach has then been taken for analyzing demand patterns and for assessing the importance of explanations put forward in the literature for changes in demand patterns. The explanations examined here are changes in household demo-

This study is part of the EU project Demand Patterns and Employment Growth in Europe and the United States, and its financial support is gratefully acknowledged. We thank all seminar participants at the Amsterdam and Seville Project meetings, and Rob Alessie for very useful comments and discussions.

Expert work on individual countries was developed with, and contributed by, the following: for the United States, John Schmitt (17th Street Economics, Washington); for the United Kingdom, Laura Blow (Institute for Fiscal Studies, London); for Germany, Marijke Deelen (University of Utrecht); for France, François Gardes (Université de Paris–I, Panthéon-Sorbonne, INSEE) and Christophe Starzec (Université de Paris–I, Panthéon-Sorbonne, INSEE); for Spain, Javier Ruiz-Castillo (Universidad Carlos III) and María-José Luengo-Prado (Northeastern University).

The country papers are available at http://www.uva-aias.net/lower.asp?id=30&lang =en).

graphic composition and employment, changes in the budget, and relative price changes. In particular this study is aimed in explaining the change in the demand for service-sector-related commodities. The empirical findings are summarized as follows:

1. The overall trend in all countries is that the traditional household, consisting of a one-earner household with two children, is losing ground, with couples having fewer children and a marked increase in employed single-person households.

2. Spain and the United Kingdom report strong increases in real expenditures at around 2 percent per year, while the Netherlands, France, the United States, and Germany experienced much lower growth, at around 0.3–1 percent per year.

3. The most dominant changes in demand patterns on an aggregate level are caused by a strong increase in expenditures on housing.

4. Within nondurable goods and services the decrease in the budget share of "food and nonalcoholic beverages" is strongest for all countries and the expenditure shares on services increase markedly over time for all countries. This increase is mainly due to an increase in "food and beverages away from home," "private transport services," "communication services," and to some extent "entertainment services" in some of the countries.

5. Concerning relative prices, it seems that for all countries services became more expensive over time, and, consequently, goods became relatively cheaper. This is in line with Baumol's cost disease applied to the labor-intensive service sector, which experiences lower productivity gains than goods-related sectors.

6. In terms of the overall share of services, demographic changes explain about 10–20 percent of the change over time. Changes in household employment explain little of the changes in the services share once controlled for budget effects.

7. The impact of increases in expenditures on the budget share of services depends on the budget elasticity. The estimated budget elasticities show services to be a luxury commodity. Increases in household total expenditures explain over 40 percent of the increase in the services share in Spain, over 30 percent in France and the United Kingdom, and 17 percent in Germany. In the Netherlands the overall expenditure effects are relatively small (7 percent), and in the United States we even find a small negative impact, which is due to a decrease in the real expenditures on nondurable goods and services.

8. Price effects are relatively large. Under the assumption of price inelastic demand, price changes yield an increase in the services share between 21 percent for the Netherlands and 68 percent for the United Kingdom.

The importance of the different explanations examined in this study differs by country. Nevertheless, overall we may conclude that across countries rising household expenditures explain about 21 percent of the increase over time in the budget share of consistently defined service-related expenditures, and the changing household demographic composition explains about 16 percent of the increase. Under the assumption of inelastic demand, the shifts in relative prices would account for about 45 percent of the increase in services. Furthermore, we find no evidence of a closing gap between Europe and the United States in the share of services in consumer expenditures.

1. Introduction

Recent changes over the last few decades in consumer demand are commonly believed to be most apparent in service-sector-related expenditures. For instance, nowadays households spend relatively more on holidays or food in restaurants than they did a couple of decades ago. This study is concerned with examining household expenditures and household demand patterns over the last two decades. In particular it provides a detailed examination of changes in the demand for service-sector-related commodities (services) and relates these changes to possible explanations for the observed changes put forward in the literature (and which are discussed in the overview chapter of this book by Salverda and Schettkat). The countries under investigation are France, (West) Germany, the Netherlands, Spain, the United Kingdom, and the United States.

There is an enormous literature on consumption and demand patterns that dates back a long time. There are huge numbers of within-country studies that use household-level data to examine a multitude of issues relating to consumer demand. However, largely due to substantial issues of survey and data comparability, much less cross-country comparative work based on microdata exists. This study attempts to fill this lacuna, using the data drawn from six country studies that have jointly tackled the issue of cross-country data comparability head-on. The individual country studies are Gardes and Starzec (2003) for France, Deelen and Schettkat (2004) for Germany, Kalwij and Salverda (2004) for the Netherlands, Luengo-Prado and Ruiz-Castillo (2004) for Spain, Blow (2004) for the United Kingdom, and Schmitt (2004) for the United States. The innovative feature of these six country studies is that the key target of the participating researchers was cross-country comparability of the analysis of consumer demand patterns for each country based on household-level budget surveys.

Using the data drawn from these six country studies, we examine cross-country changes in households' demand patterns over the last two decades. As we have already noted, serious measurement and survey definition issues arise if one wishes to compare household-level survey data across countries. The next part of this chapter therefore devotes some time to explaining these issues. A first objective is to obtain statistics that are comparable across countries, and a lot of work has been done in the country studies to facilitate this comparability. Based on budget household data, the six country studies have created comparable expenditure categories and variables for the household demographic and employment composition from the microdata from each of the countries. There are, of course, a number of difficulties in doing so, and these are also addressed in this study.

Following the discussion of issues of comparability, the next part of the chapter presents empirical evidence on changes in consumption patterns that have been seen in the countries we study. To get some insights in the data, we use the consistently defined budget shares to look for cross-country commonalities in temporal changes in consumption patterns. Next we examine several explanations for the observed changes in demand that have been suggested in the literature. A common empirical framework is adopted based on estimating identically specified Engel curves across countries. The estimates that emerge are then used to examine the following two explanations put forward in the literature for the change in services expenditures: (1) household compositional effects, such as changes in households' demographic composition and employment structure; (2) budget effects arising from the way in which households' total expenditures affect the demand for particular commodities. This budget effect depends on whether a commodity is a luxury, a necessity, or an inferior commodity. A further explanation put forward in the literature for a change in demand patterns is changes in relative prices. This we refer to as *price effects*; it may relate in part to Baumol's cost disease. Baumol asserts that certain sectors, such as the service sector, experience relatively lower productivity growth and, consequently, face relatively higher increasing costs (Baumol 1967).[1] This would translate into relatively higher prices of the commodities produced in these sectors. Consequently, in the case where demand is price inelastic, the budget shares of these commodities increase. Of course, consumer demand will most likely respond to relative price changes, and also other factors may have affected demand patterns. Data limitations prevent the estimation of price responses, which will be considered as part of the unexplained or residual effects.

The structure of the rest of this study is as follows. Section 2 describes the household budget data for each country and the commodity classifi-

---

[1] We cannot directly test the cost-disease hypothesis since this requires testing in terms of industries or vertically integrated sectors.

cation that is defined on a consistent basis across countries. Section 3 provides descriptive background statistics on changes in household composition, employment and household expenditures, and household demand patterns over time. Section 4 contains the main empirical analysis, beginning with the descriptive cross-country analysis of temporal changes in consumption patterns, and then moving on to the statistical estimates and the examination of the explanations for the observed changes in household expenditure patterns. Section 5 concludes.

2. Data Sources and Commodity Classifications

This section describes briefly the data sources for each country on which all tables and analyses in this study are based. More detailed descriptions and statistics are available in the six country studies. In these studies, also, details are found on each country's household-level expenditure survey and on comparisons with expenditures statistics from the National Accounts. A very brief and cursory description of the data we use now follows.

The Data

The years under investigation for this study are 1979, 1990, and 1995 for France, 1978 and 1993 for Germany, 1979, 1989, and 1998 for the Netherlands, 1980 and 1990 for Spain, 1980, 1990, and 1998 for the United Kingdom, and 1980, 1990, and 1997 for the United States.

FRANCE

The main source of statistical information used in this study for France is based on the Budget des Familles (FBS, Family Budget Surveys). The FBS project has a very long history and has been modified continuously during its period of its existence. Some methodological changes were minor from the comparative point of view, but others could influence consistency over time. The present study is based on surveys that belong to the same generation (1979–95) with almost identical methodological choices, guaranteeing comparability across time. In 1980 and 1995 the sample sizes of the FBS are, respectively, 10,645 and 12,102 households.

GERMANY

Information on income and expenditures of households in (West) Germany is collected every 5 years in the so-called EVS (Einkommens- und Verbrauchs-Stichprobe). This has fairly large sample sizes (about 35,000 households in West Germany), with some variations between survey years. The major purpose of the EVS is to record all income sources and expenditures as well as the stock of household durables, the housing situation, and the financial situation of households (savings, financial assets, insurances). At the beginning of the survey period the household's socio-demographic characteristics are recorded, and in the following four months households report their expenditures. To capture smaller and frequent expenditures (such as expenditures on food, beverages, etc.) about a fifth of the households over one month report these detailed expenditures in a diary. The figures reported in this detailed diary are multiplied by twelve to obtain an annual amount. Households of foreigners have been included in the EVS only since 1993. The institutional population is never included. The final sample of the EVS in this study uses the 1978 and 1993 years that have information on, respectively, 22,468 and 31,774 households in West Germany (referred to as Germany from here onwards).

THE NETHERLANDS

The data for the Netherlands are taken from the Dutch budget survey, which has been held by Statistics Netherlands on a yearly basis since 1978. For this study the 1979, 1989, and 1998 waves are available. Each wave consists of about two thousand households. All households keep a daily record of all expenses per item, over and above a threshold amount, during one year except when being on holidays. The latter expenditures are recorded in a separate holidays-diary. The threshold amount for the daily records was 25 guilders (Ç11) in 1979 and increased to 35 guilders (Ç16) in 1998. For a limited time period all expenses are recorded, from which yearly expenses are deduced on goods with a price below this threshold amount. This period equaled one month in 1979 but was reduced to seven or eight days in 1998. The survey contains information on income and family composition, and background information on all members of the household such as age, education, and labor market status. All expenditures are directly observed except the rental value of the house for homeowners, and this is imputed by Statistics Netherlands. The final sample consists of 1,884 households in 1979 and 1,904 households in 1998.

SPAIN

The data from Spain are taken from the Encuestas de Presupuestos Familiares (EPF) collected by the Instituto Nacional de Estadística (INE) in 1980–81 and 1990–91. The observation periods are from the third quarter up to and including the second quarter in the next year. These periods are referred to as 1980 and 1990. These surveys consist of 23,707, and 21,155 household observations representative of a population of approximately 10 and 11 million households in, respectively, 1980 and 1990, occupying private residential housing in all of Spain.

THE UNITED KINGDOM

The UK Family Expenditure Survey (FES) is a continuous household survey that began in 1957 and is carried out by the Office for National Statistics. The FES provides detailed information about household expenditure on goods and services (including housing costs, food, fuel, travel, clothing, and leisure), with considerable detail in the categories used. It provides information about the ownership of consumer durables and cars; plus basic information on housing and a range of demographic and socioeconomic variables. For each sampled household, information is collected about the household (housing tenure, number of rooms, amenities) and about each usually resident member (such as age, sex, marital status, and relationship to the head of household). The final sample of the FES in this study uses the 1980, 1990, and 1998 years that have information on over 6,000 households per year.

THE UNITED STATES

The Consumer Expenditure Survey (CEX) is a relatively small, but detailed, survey of the expenditure patterns of U.S. households. The principal purpose of the survey is to gather household-expenditure information for use in connection with the maintenance of the official Consumer Price Index. The Bureau of Labor Statistics (BLS) estimates that the expenditures collected in the interview portion typically cover 80–95 percent of total household expenditures. The interview questionnaire collects fairly detailed information on 60–70 percent of total expenditures and less-detailed information on an additional 20–25 percent of total expenditures, including food (again, all percentages are BLS estimates). The diary portion collects expenditure data on small, frequently purchased items that are not collected in the interview portion. The dairy portion covers about 5–15 percent of the remaining household expenditures, including food away from home, housekeeping supplies, personal care products, or nonprescription drugs. The final sample of the BLS/CEX in this study uses the 1980, 1990, and 1997 years that have information on around 6,000 households.

Definitions and the Commodity Classification

The unit of observation in all budget surveys used in this study is the household. The respondent is normally the head of household. A household is defined as a single-person household in case where the head of household is the only adult in the home. Where the head of household is married or cohabiting and there are two adults in this household, then a household is defined as a couple, and otherwise the household is defined as "other." If the couple has children, they are registered as such. The exception is France, where a child is defined as a household member younger than 15 years of age. In most countries the "other" group is small, but in countries such as Spain it is common to have parents or parents-in-law of the head of household living in the household, and such a household is defined as "other." A household in which the head of household is over 64 years of age is defined as retired. The employment status is defined based on having a job with positive earnings, irrespective of the number of hours of work. For example, a person on welfare is classified as jobless.

Gross household income—if available in the survey—includes gross labor income of all household members, gross income of other activities, asset income, rent subsidies, child allowances, social security benefits, pension income, and other monetary transfers such as inheritance, scholarships, and alimony. To arrive at net household income, social security contributions and labor and income tax are deducted from gross household income. In addition mandatory health insurance contributions are deducted from net income, and the rental value of the house is added to net income. In the case of a public health plan the premiums are known and, depending on the scheme, may be income dependent. In the case of a private health plan only the premium for the mandatory basic private health insurance is deducted. Additional insurances, which are optional, are registered as expenditures on health services. The definition of household income used in this study deviates from net household income by taking into account mandatory health insurance premiums, interest payments, and the rental value of the house for homeowners. This income concept is closely linked to household expenditures. The difference between household income as defined in this study and disposable income is the interest payments that are not reported on in most of the surveys in every year. Income is poorly measured in several countries and is not a key variable for this study. Given this discussion, savings can clearly not be deduced from the difference between income and expenditures.

A significant methodological advance made in the six country studies has been to establish a set of consistently defined aggregated commodity groupings. After a long and painstaking process of seeing what exists in each country's budget surveys, assessing how well measured the items were, these studies came up with a consistently defined set of 20 categories. These categories are reproduced in the appendix, which provides a description of the expenditure categories. This commodity classification is more detailed than that in other studies, in particular for the service-related commodities. Some of the service categories are too small to make robust inferences, and for this reason we often only make inferences on the aggregate of all services-related commodities later on. The results on the most detailed level are, of course, always reported on.

The statistics reported in this study are weighted sample statistics; hence for each country we provide a representative picture of the population. Furthermore, all budget shares are expressed in current prices. Data cleaning is done in a similar way across countries. Trimming is used to deal with outliers that may influence the empirical results and is carried out on the expenditure shares, that is, expenditures on a certain commodities over total expenditures. Households who report a budget share over the average share plus six times the standard deviation are removed from the sample. This yields a removal of only a small proportion of the samples; details are provided in the six country studies.

3. Changes in Household Composition, Employment, and Expenditures

This section sets the scene for the statistical analysis by providing descriptive statistics on the nature of shifts in household composition (by demographics and employment structure) and on expenditure patterns over time for each country. As discussed above, for several countries more than two years of budget survey are available, but for expositional reasons we mostly present results based on the data from the first and last years of the available survey. We refer to the six country studies for more detailed descriptions using more than two years and on country-specific features.

Household Composition and Employment

Table 5.1 shows the major demographic changes in the six countries. Panel A shows that average household size has decreased in all countries, mainly due to a decrease in the number of children in the household and to a lesser extent due to a decrease in the number of adults. Spain even experienced a slight increase in the number of adults in the household. However, as panel B shows, all countries experienced an increase in the number of single-person households. The most notable demographic change is the decrease in the percentage of households with children. Furthermore, an increase in lone parents is observed in all countries. Finally, the data show the aging of the population by increasing percentages of retired household (age 65 or over).

Panel C of table 5.1 shows the major trends in household employment that have occurred over time, and panel D focuses on particular groups

TABLE 5.1
Household Composition and Employment over Time and Across Countries

	SP 1980	SP 1990	NL 1979	NL 1998	US 1980	US 1997	FR 1979	FR 1995	UK 1980	UK 1998	GER 1984	GER 1998
Panel A. Absolute												
Average household size (in persons)	3.70	3.41	2.87	2.30	2.73	2.54	3.05	2.58	2.71	2.42	2.34	2.06
Average number of children	1.20	0.86	1.05	0.68	0.80	0.70	0.70	0.51	0.74	0.62	0.68	0.53
Average number of adults	2.50	2.55	1.82	1.62	1.93	1.83	2.35	2.07	1.97	1.80	1.66	1.54
Panel B. Demographics (%)												
Single	3.1	3.6	11.0	21.4	16.1	18.3	8.7	14.4	8.7	15.1	19.2	25.1
Single parents	3.9	5.2	3.6	6.2	5.4	6.3	3.4	4.6	5.5	8.8	2.5	4.1
Couple, childless	8.4	7.5	17.2	22.6	20.9	18.6	15.6	15.6	17.1	18.9	23.3	22.5
Couple with children	52.4	51.1	46.2	29.4	31.0	24.8	34.9	25.7	38.3	28.9	24.2	18.2
Retired	12.4	15.9	16.8	19.2	17.8	19.5	13.7	21.2	22.0	22.6	24.4	25.2
Other	19.8	16.8	5.2	1.3	8.7	12.5	23.7	18.5	8.4	5.8	6.4	5.0
	100.0	100.0	100.0	100.0	100.0	100.0	100.0	100.0	100.0	100.0	100.0	100.0
Panel C. Employment (%)												
Single, no job	2.6	3.6	8.3	10.7	3.0	3.0	3.7	7.7	4.4	9.5	7.6	7.7
Single, one job	4.4	5.2	6.3	16.8	18.5	21.6	8.4	11.3	9.8	14.5	14.1	21.5
Couple, no job	6.3	7.2	9.5	7.1	1.6	1.5	2.3	5.3	2.9	4.5	4.0	3.2
Couple, one job	37.9	31.3	42.1	22.0	13.4	9.6	21.5	13.8	17.8	11.1	21.1	16.2
Couple, two jobs	16.6	20.2	11.8	22.9	36.9	32.4	26.7	22.2	34.6	32.1	22.5	21.3
Retired	12.4	15.9	16.8	19.2	17.8	19.5	13.7	21.2	22.0	22.6	24.4	25.2
Other	19.8	16.8	5.2	1.3	8.7	12.5	23.7	18.5	8.4	5.8	6.4	5.0
	100.0	100.0	100.0	100.0	100.0	100.0	100.0	100.0	100.0	100.0	100.0	100.0
Panel D. Specific types (%)												
A couple with children and one job	32.9	27.7	33.0	15.8	8.5	5.5	15.7	9.1	12.8	6.8	12.9	9.3
Workless households	8.9	10.7	17.8	17.8	4.6	4.4	6.0	13.0	7.4	14.0	11.6	10.9
Two earners with children	15.1	18.5	7.2	11.9	22.1	19.0	18.6	15.5	23.8	20.2	10.3	8.4

of interest. Panel D reports a decrease in all countries of the percentage of "traditional" households of a couple with children in which only one adult works (the "male breadwinner" household structure). This decrease has been largest in the Netherlands, which experienced a fast increase in part-time employed women during the 1990s. This latter aspect is clear in panel C, with a doubling in the Netherlands of two-job couples. Interestingly, there are very sharp rises in the number of employed people living alone, as the "single, one job" category shows.

Panel D of table 5.1 shows that, in contrast to some common beliefs, the percentage of two-job couples with children has decreased somewhat in the United States, France, the United Kingdom, and Germany. The percentage of jobless households has in particular risen (doubled) in France and the United Kingdom and remained stable in the other countries (panel D, table 5.1). In this respect France and the United Kingdom have passed the level of Spain and became closer to the infamous high Dutch level of jobless households. The United States remains with a low percentage of jobless households. These findings are in particular noteworthy given the reported relatively low unemployment rates reported by the OECD in the late 1990s, especially in counties like the United Kingdom and the Netherlands, that match U.S. levels. On a household level there is no sign that the percentages of jobless households got any closer to the low U.S. levels.

In short, the overall trend in all countries is that the traditional household is losing ground, with a marked increase in employed single-person households and couples having fewer children.

Household Expenditures

Table 5.2 reports on real household total expenditures. Spain and the United Kingdom report strong increases in real expenditures at around 2 percent per year, while the Netherlands, France, the United States, and Germany experienced much lower growth, at around 0.3–1 percent per year. Expenditure inequality—based on the ratio of the 90th to the 10th percentile of the expenditure distribution (P90/P10)—remained relatively stable in the Netherlands, the United States, and the United Kingdom and decreased in Spain and France.

Clearly, these are raw statistics in the sense that they are not based on adult-equivalent expenditures, as they do not take household composition into account. At the bottom of table 5.2 average household total expenditures are broken down into several major categories. Most notable is the steep increase in expenditures on housing. We return to this breakdown below.

Table 5.3 reports on the distribution of total expenditures over the

TABLE 5.2
Household Real Total Expenditures per Year and across Countries (in real local currency)

	SP 1980	SP 1990	NL 1979	NL 1998	US 1980	US 1997	FR 1979	FR 1995	UK 1980	UK 1998	GER 1978	GER 1993
	(pesetas, 1000s)		(guilders)		(dollars)		(francs)		(pounds)		(DM)	
Mean	2,040	2,451	42,286	48,559	30,331	32,709	178,165	187,644	13,782	19,221	45,646	49,582
Percentiles												
10th	642	830	19,571	22,240	10,840	12,343	69,800	82,311	4,622	6,966		20,696
50th	1,777	2,138	39,113	44,913	26,781	27,975	157,127	164,220	11,910	15,756		44,158
90th	3,860	4,538	69,889	78,508	53,980	58,743	306,059	318,585	24,814	35,073		85,787
Inequality measures												
P90/P10	6.01	5.46	3.57	3.53	4.98	4.76	4.38	3.87	5.37	5.03		4.15
Theil Index	0.23	0.21	0.11	0.12	0.18	0.18	0.20	0.20	0.20	0.20		
Disaggregated Total Expenditures												
Durables	158	200	6,073	5,775	3,894	4,575	16,805	15,706	1,560	2,539	8,707	7,034
Health	52	38	570	609	1,343	1,749	8,144	8,557	109	267	2,166	3,420
Education	44	65	291	488	346	486	1,179	807	85	217	0	0
Housing	235	491	8,341	13,055	6,127	8,378	32,163	45,935	2,207	4,568	7,440	9,424
Nondurables and services	1,458	1,765	27,010	28,631	18,621	17,521	122,064	132,359	9,820	11,630	27,334	29,705
Total expenditures	1,946	2,560	42,286	48,559	30,331	32,709	178,586	187,644	13,782	19,221	45,646	49,582

TABLE 5.3
The Distribution of Expenditures on the 20 Commodities over Time and across Countries (%)

	SP 1980	SP 1990	NL 1979	NL 1998	US 1980	US 1997	FR 1979	FR 1995	UK 1980	UK 1998	GER 1978	GER 1993
Gross household income	87.7	84.0	167.1	153.3	110.5	121.1	89.1	80.0	144.2	121.3	141.2	146.0
Disposable net Income			127.9	131.6	96.5	110.9	97.0	88.6	116.4	106.3	118.6	121.4
All goods and services	100.0	100.0	100.0	100.0	100.0	100.0	100.0	100.0	100.0	100.0	100.0	100.0
1. Food and nonalcoholic beverages	35.5	27.5	19.9	12.5	16.3	12.4	19.8	14.4	21.9	12.8	14.7	11.6
2. Alcoholic beverages and tobacco	2.8	2.5	3.7	2.4	2.9	1.8	2.6	2.4	7.9	5.4	4.0	2.8
3. Clothing and footwear	8.2	8.8	9.6	6.4	4.6	3.8	7.7	5.0	7.0	5.2	8.1	6.8
4. Private transport goods	5.5	5.7	6.6	6.2	11.8	9.2	10.4	9.5	7.2	7.9	10.0	8.5
5. Furnishing and appliances	6.0	4.5	7.2	5.5	3.3	2.6	6.3	4.7	4.1	4.9	8.3	5.7
6. Entertainment goods	2.5	2.7	5.9	6.0	2.9	3.2	5.7	6.4	4.5	4.6	5.9	5.5
7. Personal goods	0.8	1.0	0.9	1.3	2.8	2.7	1.4	1.4	1.3	1.3	2.1	2.0
8. Home energy	4.0	4.0	7.5	5.4	5.3	4.7	4.1	3.9	7.3	5.7	5.3	5.0
9. Food and beverages away from home	5.0	7.7	2.4	3.6	3.6	3.3	4.2	4.4	3.8	4.2	2.6	2.1
10. Holiday services	0.3	0.6	4.8	4.8	2.2	2.0	1.9	1.9	1.3	2.0	5.3	7.0
11. Housing	15.8	20.2	20.8	29.5	22.6	28.4	18.0	24.5	19.1	29.2	14.7	19.0
12. Household services	1.6	1.3	0.9	1.4	1.6	1.6	1.4	1.3	1.0	0.9	0.6	0.3
13. Health goods and services	2.2	2.4	1.2	1.4	4.6	5.7	4.6	4.6	0.8	1.2	4.7	6.9
14. Personal services	0.6	0.6	0.7	0.7	0.9	0.9	1.3	1.2	0.7	0.6	0.7	1.0
15. Public transport services	1.4	1.0	0.8	1.1	1.1	1.0	1.2	2.0	2.0	1.5	0.9	0.9
16. Private transport services	2.9	3.1	2.6	3.9	4.1	4.8	5.4	7.7	2.5	3.5	3.0	4.6
17. Communication services	0.9	1.3	2.0	2.5	2.3	3.4	1.2	1.6	1.8	2.3	1.8	2.0
18. Education and training services	1.2	1.1	0.6	1.0	1.0	1.4	0.7	0.4	0.4	0.7	0.0	0.0
19. Entertainment services	1.8	1.8	1.2	2.5	1.2	2.2	1.6	2.4	3.4	3.7	1.8	2.9
20. Miscellaneous services	1.0	2.2	0.7	1.9	4.9	4.7	0.6	0.4	1.9	2.3	5.5	5.6
Goods (1–8)	65.3	56.7	61.3	45.7	50.0	40.6	58.0	47.6	61.3	47.9	58.4	47.7
Services (9–20)	34.7	43.3	38.7	54.3	50.0	59.4	42.0	52.4	38.7	52.1	41.6	52.3

20 commodity groups. Descriptions of these 20 commodity groups are provided in the appendix. At the bottom of table 5.3 we summarize the results in two main aggregated groups, goods and services. The share of goods decreases in all countries, and this is mainly due to a decrease in the budget share of food and nonalcoholic beverages and clothing and footwear. Correspondingly, the budget share of services has gone up in all countries. To some extent the increase in services is due to increases in services-related commodities such as food and beverages away from home and private transport services. However, the biggest increase is in housing, with tincreases of about 5 percentage points for Spain, France Germany, the United States, and up to almost 10 percentage points in the Netherlands and the United Kingdom.

Table 5.4 provides a clearer picture of what is going on across countries and over time. It distinguishes between expenditures on durable goods, health, education, housing, and nondurable goods and services. This latter category, the restricted grouping, is broken down over the 17 commodity groupings. Note that we keep the numbering consistent with the numbering in table 5.3.

Durable goods (included in table 5.3 among the 20 categories) such as cars are considered investment goods and not consumption goods. For this reason we examine them separately from nondurable goods and services; they are excluded from the detailed empirical analysis of household expenditure patterns in the next section. The durable goods are lumped into one durable goods category (see the appendix for details). Table 5.4 shows that the expenditure share on durables increases somewhat in the United States, and decreases somewhat in the Netherlands and France.

The differences across countries in the budget shares on education and health are largely determined by institutional differences and the extent to which these services are provided directly by the government. For instance, tables 5.5 and 5.6 make clear that the health and education sectors are largely publicly financed, with the exception of the U.S. health system. For this reason we report on health and education expenditures separately; as can be seen in table 5.5, private expenditures on health care are relatively small except in the United States.

Because of these differences some of the analysis in section 4, particularly that looking for cross-country commonalities in temporal shifts in consumption behavior, will focus not on the broad 20-commodity definition, but on the narrower 17-commodity definition. This is to ensure close comparability across country definitions.

As discussed above, the expenditures on housing and the trend over time vary considerably across countries. These differences may be associated with differences in the housing market, but there are fundamental

TABLE 5.4
Durables, Health, Education, and Nondurable Goods and Services over Time and across Countries (%)

	SP 1980	SP 1990	NL 1979	NL 1998	US 1980	US 1997	FR 1979	FR 1995	UK 1980	UK 1998	GER 1978	GER 1993
Share of total expenditures												
Durables	7.0	6.1	12.2	10.0	9.4	9.5	9.4	8.4	7.9	9.2	18.3	14.2
13. Health services	2.2	2.4	1.2	1.4	4.6	5.7	4.6	4.6	0.8	1.2	4.7	6.9
18. Education services	1.2	1.1	0.6	1.0	1.0	1.4	0.7	0.4	0.4	0.7	0	0
11. Housing	15.8	20.2	20.8	29.5	22.6	28.4	18.0	24.5	19.1	29.2	14.7	19.0
Nondurable goods and services	73.7	70.2	65.2	58.2	62.4	55.0	67.4	62.2	71.8	59.7	62.3	59.9
As a share of nondurable goods and services												
1. Food and nonalcoholic beverages	47.9	39.5	30.5	21.5	26.3	22.8	25.9	20.4	30.9	22.2	23.6	19.3
2. Alcoholic beverages and tobacco	3.7	3.4	5.6	4.0	4.5	3.2	3.4	3.4	10.6	8.8	6.4	4.7
3. Clothing and footwear	11.2	12.2	14.6	10.9	6.4	5.9	10.0	7.1	9.5	8.2	13.1	11.3
4. Private transport goods	4.5	4.2	3.3	5.1	11.0	7.0	13.5	13.4	4.5	5.5		
5. Furnishing and appliances	3.3	3.1	2.3	1.8	1.0	1.1	8.2	6.7	1.4	2.5		
6. Entertainment goods	1.8	2.4	6.0	6.5	2.7	2.9	7.4	9.0	5.1	5.7	9.5	9.1
7. Personal goods	1.0	1.3	1.4	2.1	4.5	5.0	1.8	2.0	1.9	2.1	3.4	3.3
8. Home energy	5.7	5.9	11.7	9.8	8.7	8.9	5.4	5.5	10.5	10.3	8.5	8.3
9. Food and beverages away from home	6.7	10.7	3.6	6.1	5.7	5.9	7.9	9.0	5.2	7.0	4.2	3.4
10. Holiday services	0.4	0.9	7.1	7.8	3.4	3.5	0.0	0.0	1.6	2.8	8.6	11.7
12. Household services	2.3	1.9	1.5	2.4	2.6	2.9	1.9	1.8	1.5	1.5	1.0	0.5
14. Personal services	0.8	0.9	1.0	1.2	1.4	1.7	1.7	1.7	1.1	1.1	1.1	1.7
15. Public transport services	1.9	1.5	1.2	1.9	1.7	1.8	1.6	2.8	2.7	2.4	1.4	1.5
16. Private transport services	3.9	4.4	4.2	6.8	6.5	8.7	7.0	10.9	3.5	6.0	4.7	7.7
17. Communication services	1.3	2.0	3.2	4.4	3.8	6.1	1.6	2.3	2.6	4.1	2.9	3.3
19. Entertainment services	2.4	2.5	1.9	4.4	1.9	4.1	2.1	3.4	4.7	6.1	2.9	4.8
20. Miscellaneous services	1.4	3.1	1.0	3.3	8.0	8.6	0.8	0.6	2.6	3.6	8.8	9.3
Nondurable goods (1–8)	79.1	72.1	75.3	61.7	65.0	56.7	75.5	67.5	74.5	65.4	64.4	56.0
Services (9, 10, 12, 14–17, 19, 20)	20.9	27.9	24.7	38.3	35.0	43.3	24.5	32.5	25.5	34.6	35.6	44.0

TABLE 5.5
Health Expenditures as a Percentage of GDP for Each Country in 1998

	Total	Public	Private
France	9.5	7.2	2.3
Germany	10.6	7.9	2.7
Netherlands	8.6	6.0	2.6
Spain	7.1	5.4	1.7
United Kingdom	6.7	5.6	1.1
United States	13.6	6.1	7.5

Source: Schmitt 2004.

differences across countries in the way imputed rent is calculated (see the six country studies). For this reason we conclude that housing expenditures are not comparable across countries, and they are analyzed separately from the commodities we analyze in detail in the next section (nondurable goods and services). A final note is that housing allowances (rent subsidies) are considered to be disposable income; hence we report on "gross" rents.

To summarize the top of table 5.4: the main increase is observed in the expenditure share on housing (as in table 5.3) and the main decrease is in the expenditure shares on nondurable goods and services.

Next we turn to the categories within nondurable goods and services, which are considered comparable across countries. The summary at the bottom of table 5.4 shows that expenditure shares on services increase over time for all countries. This increase is mainly due to an increase in food and beverages away from home, private transport services, communication and to some extent due to an increase in entertainment services in some of the countries. Explanations for these observed changes are examined in section 4.

TABLE 5.6
Education Expenditures as a Percentage of GDP for Each Country in 1998

	Total	Public	Private
France	6.2	5.9	0.4
Germany	5.5	4.4	1.2
Netherlands	4.6	4.5	0.1
Spain	5.3	4.4	0.9
United Kingdom	4.9	4.6	0.3
United States	6.4	4.8	1.6

Source: Schmitt 2004.

Table 5.7 reports on the average price changes per year. Durable goods have become relatively cheaper in all countries except Germany. Prices of health services and education services have in particular increased in the United States and United Kingdom. The price of housing has sharply increased in the Netherlands, France, and the United Kingdom and has decreased somewhat in the United States. Except for Spain, nondurable goods and services have become relatively cheaper. Services became more expensive over time for all countries, and, consequently, nondurable goods became relatively cheaper. This observation is in line with Baumol's cost disease applied to the labor-intensive service sectors that experience lower productivity gains than goods-related sectors of industries.

4. Analyzing Trends in Expenditure Patterns across Countries and Time

In this section we consider a more formal statistical set of analyses looking at cross-country comparisons of consumption changes over time and what might best explain them. We begin with the descriptive cross-country analysis of temporal changes in consumption patterns, then move on to the statistical estimates and the examination of the explanations for the observed changes in household expenditure patterns.

Looking for Cross-Country Commonalities in Changes in Private Consumption

The purpose of this subsection is to exploit the fact that we have data on consistently defined commodity groups across countries over time. These groupings enable us to study how consumption has altered and the extent to which one can pin down common changes across countries. Of course, at a broad level the service versus goods share of consumption has been rising for all our countries over time, as the discussion in the previous section showed. But we would like to study this pattern in more detail, and that is what we do here. Germany does not feature in this analysis because of definitional problems, especially in the 1990s.

We focus upon the 17 restricted commodity groupings (i.e., leaving out durables, housing, and health and education services). One can begin by looking at cross-country pairwise correlations in changes in budget shares for these commodity groups. This can be done by defining annualized changes in budget shares between period $t - 1$ and t as $\Delta S_j = (S_j^t - S_j^{t-1})$ for consumption category j and where $\Sigma_{j=1}^J S_j = 1$, with $S_j = EXP_j / \Sigma_{j=1}^J EXP_j$, EXP_j denotes expenditure on commodity j, and J is the

TABLE 5.7
Price Changes, in Average %-change per Year, across Countries

	SP 1980–90	NL 1979–98	US 1980–97	FR 1980–95	UK 1980–98	GER 1978–93
All goods and services	14.1	2.8	5.7	8.5	7.4	4.0
Within all goods and services						
Durable goods	−2.1	−0.6	−1.2	−1.6	−1.6	0.0
Health services	−1.2	0.1	3.6	−1.4	2.3	1.1
Education services	0.0	0.7	5.7	2.0	4.3	—
Housing	0.7	2.0	−0.1	1.3	2.5	1.0
Nondurable goods and services	0.1	−0.6	−0.2	−0.2	−0.2	−0.3
Within nondurable goods and services						
1. Food and nonalcoholic beverages	−0.1	−0.3	−0.4	−1.0	−0.8	−0.9
2. Alcoholic beverages and tobacco	0.2	1.5	0.2	1.3	2.8	−0.9
3. Clothing and footwear	0.3	−1.1	−1.7	−0.2	−2.4	−0.2
4. Private transport goods	−0.2	0.7	−0.6	−0.8	−1.4	
5. Furnishing and appliances	−0.8	−0.4	−2.0	−0.4	−0.3	
6. Entertainment goods	0.2	−0.5	−0.6	−1.3	−0.7	−1.0
7. Personal goods	−1.7	−0.1	−0.3	−0.7	1.8	1.3
8. Home energy	−0.5	0.4	−0.5	−0.6	−0.8	0.5
9. Food and beverages away from home	1.4	1.4	−0.1	1.6	1.6	−3.3
10. Holiday services	3.3	0.3	2.3	1.3	4.0	1.9
12. Household services	0.6	1.5	0.2	1.5	1.7	−0.3
14. Personal services	1.2	−0.1	0.1	1.1	4.0	0.2
15. Public transport services	0.5	2.2	2.4	0.2	0.8	0.9
16. Private transport services	2.1	0.9	1.1	−6.7	2.4	1.2
17. Communication services	−2.1	−0.1	−0.9	−2.8	−1.5	0.9
19. Entertainment services	−0.1	0.0	1.0	−1.3	1.3	−1.0
20. Miscellaneous services	−0.9	0.0	2.3	1.3	1.4	2.5
Nondurable goods (1–8)	−0.1	−0.2	−0.6	−0.7	−0.4	−0.5
Services (9–20)	0.8	0.6	1.0	0.8	1.3	0.9

TABLE 5.8
Sample Periods Used to Define 1980s and 1990s Changes

Country	Years	'1980s' Change	'1990s' Change
United States	1980, 1990, 1997	$(S_j^{1990} - S_j^{1980})/10$	$(S_j^{1997} - S_j^{1990})/7$
United Kingdom	1980, 1990, 1998	$(S_j^{1990} - S_j^{1980})/10$	$(S_j^{1998} - S_j^{1990})/8$
Netherlands	1979, 1989, 1998	$(S_j^{1989} - S_j^{1979})/10$	$(S_j^{1998} - S_j^{1989})/9$
Spain	1980/81, 1990/91	$(S_j^{1991} - S_j^{1981})/10$	—
France	1980, 1990, 1995	$(S_j^{1990} - S_j^{1980})/10$	$(S_j^{1995} - S_j^{1990})/5$

number of commodity groupings. We are interested in the pairwise correlation between ΔS_{jc} and $\Delta S_{jc'}$ for countries c and c' and commodity groups j.

This can be done for the data periods shown in table 5.8 for each country to get as close to decade differences as the data available permits. Table 5.9 reports the pairwise correlations, for the 1990s change

TABLE 5.9
Cross-Country Correlations of Changes in Budget Shares in the 1980s and 1990s

Panel A
1990s Changes in Budget Shares

	US	UK	Netherlands
United Kingdom	.85		
	(.00)		
Netherlands	.87	.88	
	(.00)	(.00)	
France	.50	.35	.70
	(.04)	(.17)	(.00)

Panel B
1980s Changes in Budget Shares

	US	UK	Netherlands	France
United Kingdom	.53			
	(.02)			
Netherlands	.40	.83		
	(.11)	(.00)		
France	.24	.77	.87	(.00)
	(.35)	(.00)		
Spain	.63	.91	.89	.87
	(.01)	(.00)	(.00)	(.00)

Note: Figures are correlation coefficients; *p*-values are given in parentheses.

in panel A and for the 1980s change in panel B. The existence of common changes in consumption shares over the 1990s is evident from panel A. All six pairwise correlations are positive, and five are significant at the 5 percent level or better. Certainly for the 17-category grouping we consider here, there is evidence that the same commodities either increased or decreased their budget shares in the 1990s in a similar way across countries.

What of the 1980s? Here the pattern is less clear, although again all correlation coefficients are positive. Fewer are statistically significant, however, and perhaps even more interesting, there is something of a clustering where the correlations with the United States are mostly weaker (especially for France and for the Netherlands).

We can place more structure upon these patterns of change by considering how successfully one can identify common consumption commodity effects operating in a similar way in shaping consumption changes across countries. Consider the following simple empirical model of changes in budget shares for commodity j in country i in year t:

$$\Delta S_{ji}^t = \alpha_j + \varepsilon_{ji}^t. \tag{1}$$

This equation breaks down the change in budget shares into a common commodity effect (α_j) and ε_{ji}^t, a time- and country-specific random error term.

Looking for the commodities that matter most for explaining common consumption changes over time involves obtaining estimates of α_j. Table 5.10 reports estimates of significant terms in the above regression, for the 1980s and 1990s pooled together and for them separately. The α_j estimates are, by definition, scaled to have a mean of zero so that one can ascertain significant positive and negative commodity effects relative to zero.

The results are helpful in discerning the structure of the common nature of shifts in consumption. The specification in column 1 of table 5.10, for the pooled sample, shows there to be six statistically significant commodity effects, four of which are positive, two of which are negative. All of the four positive effects are in services (private transport services, food and beverages away from home, entertainment services, and communication services), while the two significant negative effects are in goods (food and nonalcoholic beverages and clothing and footwear). The decade differences show the same kind of pattern, though it is interesting that there is no consistent ranking across decades.

Empirical Analysis: Decomposition

This section follows on to examine possible explanations for the changes in the expenditure patterns over time, as discussed in the introduction.

TABLE 5.10
Statistically Significant Consumption Commodity Effects (significant common group effects, α_i)

Pooled		1990s		1980s	
1. Private transport services (group 16)	.144 (4.22)	1. Private transport services (group 16)	.163 (3.81)	1. Food and beverages away from home (group 9)	.227 (2.38)
2. Food and beverages away from home (group 9)	.135 (2.13)	2. Entertainment services (group 19)	.155 (4.19)	2. Private transport services (group 16)	.127 (2.49)
3. Entertainment services (group 19)	.099 (3.03)	3. Communication services (group 17)	.056 (2.16)	3. Miscellaneous services (group 20)	.081 (2.05)
4. Communication services (group 17)	.070 (2.48)				
16. Clothing and footwear (group 3)	-.086 (2.03)	16. Clothing and footwear (group 3)	-.132 (2.95)		
17. Food and nonalcoholic beverages (group 1)	-.403 (5.92)	17. Food and nonalcoholic beverages (group 1)	-.439 (4.14)	17. Food and nonalcoholic beverages (group 1)	-.359 (4.08)
Sample size	153		68		85
R-squared	.56		.61		.61

Note: The dependent variable is defined in annualized percentage point changes; t-ratios are given in parentheses. In each column groups are listed in order of decreasing magnitude of α_i; the group's rank among the 17 groups is listed. "Significant" is defined as $p < .05$.

In particular we are interested in explaining why the services share, particularly for some services as highlighted in the previous subsection, has increased over time. For this purpose a system of Engel curves is estimated; based on these estimates the change is decomposed with respect to demographic, employment, and household total expenditures changes. Important here to note is that the same analysis is carried out for each country; hence the empirical results are fully comparable across countries.

A brief description of the procedure implemented is as follows. For each country a system of reduced form Engel curves is estimated where the expenditure shares of the 17 restricted commodity groups are related to the logarithm of household total expenditures and demographic and employment variables. A popular empirical specification relates each budget share to the logarithm of household total expenditures and other household characteristics (see Deaton and Muellbauer 1980):

$$S_{j,h}^t = \alpha_j^t + \gamma_j^{d,t} z_h^{d,t} + \gamma_j^{e,t} z_h^{e,t} + \beta_j^t \ln(x_h^t) + \varepsilon_{j,h}^t, \tag{2}$$
$$h \in \{1, \ldots, H_t\}, t \in \{1, \ldots, T\}, j \in \{1, \ldots, J\},$$

where $S_{j,h}^t$ is the budget share of commodity j of household h in time period t, $z_h^{d,t}$ and $z_h^{e,t}$ are vectors containing demographic and employment variables, respectively, x_h^t is household total expenditures, α_j^t, γ_j^t, and β_j^t are the parameters of interest of the budget share equation for commodity k in year t, and $\varepsilon_{j,h}^t$ is an idiosyncratic error term. Prices are not explicitly included as explanatory variables in equation (2) since within a period all households are assumed to face the same prices. Equation (2) is estimated using instrumental variables to take into account possible measurement errors in total expenditures. Household income is used as an instrument.

For the purpose of this study, equation (2) needs to be estimated for only one base-period. The explanatory variables used in the empirical analysis are defined the same for all countries as follows:

A. Household expenditures on nondurable goods and services:
   - Logarithm of expenditures
B. Household demographic variables:
   - Logarithm of household size
   - Number of persons under 6 years of age divided by household size
   - Number of persons over 5 and under 18 years of age divided by household size
   - Number of persons over 17 and under 31 years of age divided by household size
   - Number of persons over 30 and under 65 years of age divided by household size

- Number of persons over 64 years of age divided by household size
- Age and age squared of the head of household

C. Household employment variables:
- Number of employed persons in the household
- A dummy variable equal to 1 if all adults are employed, 0 otherwise
- A dummy variable equal to 1 if all adults are employed and a person under 6 years of age is present in the household, 0 otherwise

Using the estimation results of equation (2) for a base year of each country, we decompose the observed average changes (table 5.4) with respect to demographic, employment, and household total expenditures changes. We refer to Blow, Kalwij, and Ruiz-Castillo (2004) for more details on the decomposition and to the six country studies for the details on the estimation results. Underneath we link the decomposition to the possible explanations put forward in the introduction:

Changes in household composition. Here we distinguish demographic changes and changes in household employment (variable sets B and C, above).

A change in household expenditures on nondurables and services (variable set A, above). Here we distinguish between changes in the average budget and changes in expenditures inequality. For this the following decomposition is exploited:

$$\overline{\ln(x_h^t)} = \ln(x^t) - \Gamma^t, \; with \; \ln(x^t) = \ln\left(\frac{1}{H_t}\sum_h x_h^t\right) \; and \; \Gamma^t = \frac{1}{H_t}\sum_h \ln\left(\frac{x^t}{x_h^t}\right)$$

The first term is the log-average expenditures, and the second term is the well-known (negative of the) Theil inequality index, denoted by Γ^t (Theil 1967). In the case that the estimated budget effect implies the commodity is a luxury, an increase in the average budget increases the share for this particular commodity. An increase in budget inequality, as measured by the Theil index, yields a decrease in the expenditure share for this commodity.

Price effects. This is the increase in the budget share due to an increase in the relative price of this commodity, under the assumption that there are no price-substitution effects (i.e., inelastic demand). The price indices of table 5.7 are used. As Blow et al. show (2004, appendix D), the price effect on the budget shares in the years 1 and 2, using year 1 as base period, can be calculated as $S_j^1 \Delta p_j$, where S_j^1 is the average budget share of commodity j in base year 1, and Δp_j denotes the change in the relative price of commodity j between years 1 and 2.

Table 5.11 summarizes the decomposition. Table 5.12 reports on the contributions of these explanations to the observed change in the budget

TABLE 5.11
Decomposition, Based on Equation (2)

	$P(S_j^2 - S_j^1)$, Predicted Change
Explanation (1), compositional effects	
Demographics	$\hat{\gamma}_j^{d,1}(z^{d,2} - z^{d,1})$
Household employment	$\hat{\gamma}_j^{e,1}(z^{e,2} - z^{e,1})$
Explanation (2), budget effects	
Average budget	$\hat{\beta}_j^1(\ln(x^2) - \ln(x^1))$
Distributional aspect (inequality)	$\hat{\beta}_j^1(-\Gamma^2 + \Gamma^1)$
Explanation (3), price effect	$S_j^1 \Delta p_i$
Unexplained	Residual (difference between observed and predicted)

shares of the two aggregate commodities nondurable goods and services, in percentage points. In terms of the overall services or, equivalently, nondurable goods share, demographic changes explain about 10–20 percent of the change. Household employment effects are observed to be small (as described in the first part of section 3) and explain little of the changes in the services share, once controlled for budget effects.

The way increases in expenditures affect the budget share of services depends on the budget elasticity. Table 5.13 reports estimated elasticities, showing services to be a luxury. Hence we expect an increase in the share of services as expenditure rises. Increases in household total expenditures explain over 40 percent of the increase in the services share in Spain, over 30 percent in France and the United Kingdom, and 17 percent in Germany. In the Netherlands the overall expenditure effects are relatively small (7 percent) and in the United States we even find a small negative impact, which is due to a decrease in the real expenditures on nondurable goods and services. Price effects are relatively large. Under the assumption of price inelastic demand, price changes yield an increase in the services share of between 21 percent for the Netherlands and 68 percent for the United Kingdom. As a result of the small changes in expenditures inequality (see table 5.2), inequality effects are close to zero for most countries.

The final set of results is given in table 5.14, which reports the decomposition on the 17 commodities averaged across countries (country-specific estimates are given in table 5.A1). This provides important insights in the trends over time. In all countries the decrease in the budget share of "food and nonalcoholic beverages" is strongest and relatively large, and there is an important impact on expenditure increases at –.15 of the

TABLE 5.12
Empirical Results on Explanations for the Change between circa 1980 and the 1990s in the Expenditure Shares on Nondurable Goods and Services

	Total Change	Demographics	Employment	Budget Level	Budget Inequality	Price Effects	Unexplained
Spain, 1980–90							
Nondurable goods (1–8)	−7.0	−1.0	0.1	−3.0	0.0	−1.9	−1.2
Services (9–20)	7.0	1.0	−0.1	3.0	0.0	1.9	1.2
Netherlands, 1979–98							
Nondurable goods (1–8)	−13.6	−2.6	−0.1	−0.9	0.6	−2.9	−7.7
Services (9–20)	13.6	2.6	0.1	0.9	−0.6	2.9	7.7
United States, 1980–1997							
Nondurable goods (1–8)	−8.3	−0.8	0.1	0.9	0.0	−3.2	−5.1
Services (9–20)	8.3	0.8	−0.1	−0.9	0.0	3.2	5.1
France, 1980–95							
Nondurable goods (1–8)	−8.0	−1.1	0.2	−2.6	0.0	−5.2	0.7
Services (9–20)	8.0	1.1	−0.2	2.6	0.0	5.2	−0.7
United Kingdom, 1980–98							
Nondurable goods (1–8)	−9.2	−1.6	−0.1	−2.8	0.5	−6.3	1.1
Services (9–20)	9.2	1.6	0.1	2.8	−0.5	6.3	−1.1
Germany, 1978–93							
Nondurable goods (1–8)	−8.4	−1.5	0.0	−1.4	0.0	−4.6	−0.8
Services (9–20)	8.4	1.5	0.0	1.4	0.0	4.6	0.8

Note: Figures are percentage points.

TABLE 5.13
Estimated Budget Elasticities for Each Country around 1980

	ES 1980	NL 1979	US 1980	FR 1980	UK 1980	GER 1978
1. Food and nonalcoholic beverages	0.58	0.42	0.51	0.55	0.39	0.33
2. Alcoholic beverages and tobacco	0.56	0.72	0.91	0.59	0.87	0.62
3. Clothing and footwear	1.25	1.15	1.04	1.17	1.43	1.24
4. Private transport goods	1.71	2.28	1.15	1.68	1.90	
5. Furnishing and appliances	0.88	1.39	1.51	0.86	1.08	
6. Entertainment goods	2.16	1.09	1.20	1.37	0.99	1.30
7. Personal goods	1.29	1.07	0.67	1.34	0.86	1.40
8. Home energy	0.84	0.68	0.84	0.14	0.56	0.39
9. Food and beverages away from home	1.42	1.73	1.14	1.16	1.63	1.21
10. Holiday services	3.26	2.10	1.57		2.63	1.74
12. Household services	2.63	2.13	1.33	1.71	3.00	0.90
14. Personal services	1.93	1.56	1.36	1.15	1.28	1.24
15. Public transport services	1.12	0.09	1.23	1.22	1.07	0.86
16. Private transport services	1.75	2.01	1.52	1.26	2.15	1.48
17. Communication services	1.96	0.85	0.65	0.02	1.27	1.03
19. Entertainment services	1.52	0.95	1.49	1.26	0.85	1.05
20. Miscellaneous services	1.62	0.79	1.72	−2.59	2.33	1.72
Nondurable goods (1–8)	0.82	0.80	0.80	0.97	0.77	0.75
Services (9–20)	1.70	1.61	1.38	1.09	1.66	1.45

−.44 fall. Price effects seem important for almost all goods and service commodities, lending some weight to notions of the cost disease type. Interestingly, compositional changes reflected by changing demographic or household employment structure are only of secondary importance in the decomposition.

5. CONCLUSIONS

This study presents cross-country comparative work on shifts in consumption patterns over time for six countries. A key feature is a strong emphasis on international comparability, facilitated by researchers from the six countries getting together to work out what is and what is not consistently defined in the household surveys from their respective countries. This results in the analysis being based upon consistently defined commodity groupings for each country over time. Therefore, the main advance made in this study is in terms of making the micro-level expen-

TABLE 5.14
Averages over Countries of the Changes in Budget Shares and the Extent to Which Changes in Demographics, Employment, the Budget, and Prices Attributed to These Changes in Budget Shares

	Total Change	Demo-graphics	Employ-ment	Budget Level	Budget Inequality	Price Effects	Unexplained
1. Food and nonalcoholic beverages	-0.44	-0.09	0.01	-0.15	0.01	-0.13	-0.09
2. Alcoholic beverages and tobacco	-0.07	-0.01	0.00	-0.02	0.00	0.03	-0.07
3. Clothing and footwear	-0.08	0.00	0.00	0.02	0.00	-0.05	-0.05
4. Private transport goods	-0.02	0.00	0.00	0.02	0.00	-0.09	0.05
5. Furnishing and appliances	-0.01	0.00	0.00	0.01	0.00	0.00	-0.02
6. Entertainment goods	0.04	0.00	0.00	0.02	0.00	-0.03	0.05
7. Personal goods	0.02	0.00	0.00	0.00	0.00	0.02	0.00
8. Home energy	-0.02	0.01	0.00	-0.03	0.00	0.01	0.00
9. Food and beverages away from home	0.11	0.02	0.00	0.03	0.00	0.04	0.03
10. Holiday services	0.06	0.02	0.00	0.02	0.00	0.03	-0.01
12. Household services	0.00	0.01	0.00	0.02	0.00	0.02	-0.05
14. Personal services	0.01	0.01	0.00	0.01	0.00	0.01	-0.01
15. Public transport services	0.01	0.00	0.00	0.00	0.00	0.01	0.00
16. Private transport services	0.15	0.01	0.00	0.02	0.00	0.08	0.05
17. Communication services	0.07	0.01	0.00	0.00	0.00	0.01	0.05
19. Entertainment services	0.09	0.00	0.00	0.01	0.00	0.02	0.07
20. Miscellaneous services	0.07	0.02	0.00	0.02	0.00	0.03	0.01
Nondurable goods (1–8)	-0.58	-0.09	0.00	-0.12	0.01	-0.26	-0.13
Services (9–20)	0.58	0.09	0.00	0.12	-0.01	0.26	0.13

Note: Figures are yearly changes in percentage points.

ditures data and empirical analysis comparable across countries, yielding interesting and new findings on consumer behavior across countries.

Out of these consistently defined cross-country classifications, several key findings on the changing nature of consumption patterns emerge. First, there are clear commonalities in trends in cross-country consumption patterns over the last two decades. The most dominant changes in demand patterns on an aggregate level are caused by the strong increase in expenditures on housing, absorbing most if the observed increase in households' total expenditures, a strong decrease in the budget share of food and nonalcoholic beverages, and an increase in the share of services in all countries. This latter increase is mainly due to an increase in food and beverages away from home, private transport services, communication services, and to some extent due to an increase in entertainment services in some of the countries. Second, when one looks for explanations of these shifts from estimating Engel curves, one uncovers evidence that relative price and budget effects are important, but with less contribution from changes in the demographic and employment structure of households. The importance of the different explanations examined in this study differs by country. Nevertheless, overall we may conclude that across countries, rising household expenditures explain about 21 percent of the increase over time in the budget share of consistently defined service-related expenditures, and the changing household demographic composition explains about 16 percent of the increase. Under the assumption of inelastic demand, the shifts in relative prices would account for about 45 percent of the increase in services. Furthermore, we find no evidence of a closing gap between Europe and the United States in the share of services in consumer expenditures.

APPENDIX: COMMODITY CLASSIFICATION, DESCRIPTION

Expenditures do not include savings-related insurances such as a life insurance. The categories of durable goods that are lumped together are purchase of cars and bikes; furnishings; appliances; books, newspapers, and computer; audio and video equipment; toys and hobbies; and holiday goods.

COMMODITY GROUPS

For full listings see the individual country studies listed in the DEMPATEM working papers. Typical items covered are:

1. Food and nonalcoholic beverages at home
   Includes among other items bakery products, potatoes, fruit, vegetables, oil and butter, meat, fish, milk products, and spices.
2. Alcoholic beverages and tobacco
   Excludes beverages away from home (see group 9).
3. Clothing and footwear
   Includes sport-wear and accessories such as belt, watch, jewelry, and handbag.
4. Private transport goods
   Includes bikes, car purchase, and fuel; excludes repairs.
5. Furnishings and appliances
   Includes furnishings, insurance, cutlery, refrigerator (excludes detergents; see group 11).
6. Entertainment goods
   Computer, audio and video equipment, musical instruments, pets, camping, photography, camcorder.
7. Personal goods
   Hairdryer, electric shaver, toiletries
8. Home energy
   Includes gas, electricity, and water.
9. Food and beverages away from home
   Excludes expenditures made during holidays.
10. Holidays services
    Includes all expenditures made during holidays or weekend outings both domestic and abroad; tours; insurances.
11. Housing
    Rent or rental value, service and maintenance costs (also of the heating system or other sunk equipment)
12. Household services
    Servants' wages, including the cleaning maid and window cleaner; child care, launderette; repairs of footwear, clothing, and household equipment
13. Health goods and services
    Includes reimbursements as negative expenditures, in particular basic health insurance and medicines; health care, mainly payments to optician; includes health insurance premium; self-medication; eyeglasses or contacts; hearing aid; medicines.
14. Personal services
    Hairdresser and beauty parlor
15. Public transport services
    Includes taxi, bus, train, metro (plane in the United States).
16. Private transport services
    Repairs to vehicles, parking fees, insurance, road tax, driving lessons.

Table 5.A1
Empirical Results on the Explanations for the Change in the Expenditure Shares
on Nondurable Goods and Services

	Spain, 1980–90						
	T	D	E	B	I	P	S
1. Food and nonalcoholic beverages	−8.4	−0.7	0.1	−3.5	0.1	−0.1	−4.2
2. Alcoholic beverages and tobacco	−0.3	−0.2	0.0	−0.4	0.0	0.0	0.3
3. Clothing and footwear	1.0	−0.1	0.0	0.6	0.0	0.5	0.0
4. Private transport goods	−0.3	−0.1	0.0	0.2	0.0	−1.8	1.5
5. Furnishing and appliances	−0.2	0.0	0.0	−0.2	0.0	−0.2	0.2
6. Entertainment goods	0.6	0.0	0.0	0.4	0.0	0.1	0.2
7. Personal goods	0.3	0.0	0.0	0.0	0.0	−0.2	0.4
8. Home energy	0.2	0.1	0.0	−0.2	0.0	−0.2	0.4
9. Food and beverages away from home	4.1	0.2	−0.1	0.6	0.0	0.9	2.5
10. Holiday services	0.5	0.1	0.0	0.3	0.0	0.1	0.0
12. Household services	−0.4	0.1	0.0	0.7	0.0	0.1	−1.3
14. Personal services	0.2	0.1	0.0	0.1	0.0	0.1	−0.1
15. Public transport services	−0.4	0.0	0.0	0.0	0.0	0.1	−0.5
16. Private transport services	0.5	0.0	0.0	0.6	0.0	0.8	−0.8
17. Communication services	0.7	0.1	0.0	0.2	0.0	−0.2	0.6
19. Entertainment services	0.1	0.0	0.0	0.2	0.0	0.0	−0.1
20. Miscellaneous services	1.7	0.2	0.0	0.4	0.0	0.1	1.0

	France, 1980–95						
	T	D	E	B	I	P	S
1. Food and nonalcoholic beverages	−5.5	−0.7	0.1	−4.0	0.0	−3.1	2.2
2. Alcoholic beverages and tobacco	0.0	−0.2	0.0	−0.6	0.0	0.8	−0.1
3. Clothing and footwear	−2.9	−0.1	0.0	0.3	0.0	0.1	−3.2
4. Private transport goods	−0.1	−0.4	−0.2	0.8	0.0	−1.2	0.9
5. Furnishing and appliances	−1.5	−0.1	0.1	0.8	0.0	−0.2	−2.2
6. Entertainment goods	1.6	0.1	0.0	0.9	0.0	−1.2	1.7
7. Personal goods	0.2	0.0	0.0	0.2	0.0	−0.1	0.1
8. Home energy	0.0	0.3	−0.1	−1.1	0.0	−0.3	1.2
9. Food and beverages away from home	1.1	0.2	0.0	1.5	0.0	2.2	−2.9
10. Holiday services	0.0	0.0	0.0	0.0	0.0	0.0	0.0
12. Household services	−0.1	0.2	0.0	0.7	0.0	0.5	−1.5
14. Personal services	0.0	0.2	0.0	0.2	0.0	0.4	−0.8
15. Public transport services	1.3	0.0	0.1	0.1	0.0	0.1	1.0
16. Private transport services	3.9	0.2	−0.3	−0.1	0.0	2.8	1.4
17. Communication services	0.7	0.1	0.0	−0.2	0.0	−0.6	1.3
19. Entertainment services	1.4	0.0	0.0	0.4	0.0	−0.3	1.4
20. Miscellaneous services	−0.2	0.1	0.0	0.1	0.0	0.2	−0.6

T = total change, D = demographics, E = employment, B = budget level, I = budget inequality, P = price effects, S = unexplained.

Netherlands, 1979–98							United States, 1980–97						
T	D	E	B	I	P	S	T	D	E	B	I	P	S
−9.0	−3.5	0.0	−1.0	0.7	−1.9	−3.3	−3.5	−0.6	0.1	0.8	0.0	−2.6	−1.2
−1.5	−0.2	0.1	−0.1	0.1	1.6	−3.0	−1.3	0.0	0.0	0.1	0.0	−1.5	0.1
−3.7	0.1	0.0	0.1	−0.1	−3.2	−0.6	−0.5	−0.1	0.0	0.0	0.0	1.6	−1.9
1.8	0.5	0.0	0.2	−0.2	0.4	0.7	−4.0	−0.2	0.0	0.0	0.0	−3.3	−0.4
−0.5	0.2	0.0	0.1	0.0	−0.2	−0.4	0.1	0.0	0.0	0.0	0.0	0.6	−0.5
0.5	0.1	0.1	0.0	0.0	−0.6	0.9	0.2	0.0	0.0	−0.1	0.0	0.5	−0.2
0.8	0.0	0.0	0.0	0.0	0.0	0.8	0.5	−0.1	0.0	0.1	0.0	0.6	−0.2
−1.9	0.2	−0.2	−0.2	0.1	0.9	−2.7	0.2	0.1	0.0	0.1	0.0	0.8	−0.8
2.5	0.4	0.1	0.2	−0.1	1.0	1.0	0.2	0.1	0.0	−0.1	0.0	0.2	0.0
0.7	1.2	0.1	0.5	−0.3	0.4	−1.2	0.1	0.1	0.0	−0.2	0.0	−0.8	1.0
0.9	0.4	0.0	0.1	−0.1	0.4	0.1	0.3	0.2	0.0	−0.1	0.0	0.1	0.1
0.2	0.1	0.0	0.0	0.0	0.0	0.1	0.3	0.0	0.0	0.0	0.0	0.3	0.0
0.7	−0.1	0.0	−0.1	0.0	0.5	0.3	0.1	0.1	0.0	0.0	0.0	−0.4	0.5
2.6	0.4	−0.1	0.2	−0.2	0.7	1.5	2.2	0.0	0.0	−0.2	0.0	0.8	1.6
1.2	0.3	0.0	0.0	0.0	0.0	1.0	2.3	0.0	0.0	0.1	0.0	3.3	−1.0
2.5	0.0	0.0	0.0	0.0	0.0	2.4	2.2	0.0	0.0	−0.1	0.0	1.6	0.7
2.3	−0.2	0.0	0.0	0.0	0.0	2.5	0.6	0.3	0.0	−0.3	0.0	−1.8	2.3

United Kingdom, 1980–98							Germany, 1978–93						
T	D	E	B	I	P	S	T	D	E	B	I	P	S
−8.7	−1.8	0.2	−3.2	0.6	−2.3	−2.1	−4.3	−1.1	0.0	−1.4	0.0	−3.2	1.4
−1.8	−0.2	−0.1	−0.2	0.0	2.9	−4.3	−1.7	0.0	0.1	−0.2	0.0	−0.9	−0.6
−1.3	0.2	−0.1	0.7	−0.1	−4.5	2.6	−1.8	−0.2	−0.1	0.3	0.0	−0.4	−1.3
1.0	0.2	0.1	0.7	−0.1	−1.5	1.6	0.0	0.0	0.0	0.0	0.0	0.0	0.0
1.1	0.0	0.0	0.0	0.0	0.0	1.0	0.0	0.0	0.0	0.0	0.0	0.0	0.0
0.6	0.0	0.0	0.0	0.0	−0.4	1.0	−0.3	0.1	0.0	0.2	0.0	−1.5	0.7
0.3	0.0	0.0	0.0	0.0	0.6	−0.3	−0.1	0.0	0.0	0.1	0.0	0.7	−0.8
−0.2	0.1	−0.1	−0.8	0.1	−1.1	1.4	−0.2	−0.2	0.0	−0.4	0.0	0.6	−0.2
1.8	0.3	−0.1	0.6	−0.1	1.6	−0.5	−0.8	0.3	−0.2	0.1	0.0	−2.1	1.2
1.2	0.2	0.0	0.4	−0.1	0.8	−0.2	3.1	0.4	0.1	0.5	0.0	2.5	−0.5
0.0	0.3	0.1	0.5	−0.1	0.4	−1.1	−0.5	0.0	0.0	0.0	0.0	0.0	−0.5
0.0	0.1	0.0	0.1	0.0	0.5	−0.6	0.6	0.0	0.0	0.0	0.0	0.0	0.6
−0.3	0.1	−0.1	0.0	0.0	0.3	−0.6	0.1	0.0	0.1	0.0	0.0	0.2	−0.2
2.5	0.2	0.1	0.7	−0.1	1.9	−0.3	3.0	0.0	0.1	0.2	0.0	0.9	1.8
1.4	0.1	0.1	0.1	0.0	−1.3	2.4	0.4	0.0	0.0	0.0	0.0	0.4	0.0
1.4	0.0	−0.1	−0.1	0.0	1.3	0.3	1.8	0.0	0.0	0.0	0.0	−0.5	2.3
1.0	0.3	0.1	0.6	−0.1	0.7	−0.6	0.5	0.7	−0.1	0.5	0.0	3.3	−3.9

17. Communications services
    Telephone and mail
18. Education and training services
    Tuition fees
19. Entertainment services
    Music and dance lessons, sport rental, contributions to societies, entrance fees to, e.g., cinema.
20. Miscellaneous services
    Insurances, donations

CHAPTER 6

Employment Differences in Distribution: Wages, Productivity, and Demand

Andrew Glyn, Joachim Möller, Wiemer Salverda,
John Schmitt, and Michel Sollogoub

CHAPTER 1 describes how the employment gap between the United States and Europe opened up over the last three decades. The decline in employment in European agriculture and industry exposed a long-run shortfall in service jobs. Within the service sector, the gap, as compared to the United States, is concentrated in community and personal services and in trade, hotels, and catering. The former are publicly financed to varying degrees in different countries—but are still strongly consumer-oriented, as shown in chapter 1. Inevitably, the former activities are also affected by developments in the labor market (wage costs), technology (productivity), and product demand, as discussed in the chapters by Fuchs and by Baumol. However, these services are more dependent on political decision-making and less directly subject to market forces. Thus we focus this chapter on retailing, hotels, and catering[1] as the quintessential private service industry, heavily dependent on the bottom end of the labor market, where the evidence for the contending explanations for the employment gap should be most apparent.

First we discuss some frequently suggested explanations of the employment gap, including lack of wage flexibility in Europe reflected in lack of low-productivity jobs, regulations in the product market, and the overall level of demand. In section 2, we will analyze the distribution sector in detail, examining in particular whether the employment, wage, and productivity patterns we uncover, especially in retail trade, support

The authors wish to thank Maxim Bouev (Oxford), David Hollanders (Amsterdam), Alisher Aldashev (Regensburg), and Sarah Voitchovsky (Oxford) for their excellent research assistance. A detailed previous version of the chapter is available as DEMPATEM Working Paper No. 12 at www.uva.nl/aias/lower.
[1] The distribution sector comprises wholesale trade, retailing, and hotels and catering (eating and drinking places). The three are often lumped together in statistics of production, employment, and earnings.

the labor-market flexibility argument. Finally, in section 3, we analyze the role of aggregate consumer spending and productivity levels in distribution in generating the employment differences in distribution between the United States and Europe.

1. EXPLAINING THE EMPLOYMENT GAP

The first and probably most influential explanation for the service-sector employment gap is that common features of European labor markets—including strong unions and wide-ranging collective agreements, generous unemployment benefits, strict employment protection legislation, and high minimum wages—keep wages in European services "too high," thereby pricing less-skilled workers out of employment. According to this view, lowering the effective wage floor, by reducing statutory minimum wages and the power of unions, lowering access to or generosity of unemployment benefits, and loosening employment protections would increase employment in European services by allowing employers to hire less-skilled workers at wages that match their lower productivity. Substitution effects in production (more "baggers" employed in supermarkets) or in consumption (greater demand for cheaper meals in restaurants as labor costs were reduced) would result in higher employment.

A second possible explanation for the service-sector employment gap is that productivity levels and growth rates in European services are "too high" to absorb workers. In many respects, this argument flows from the first. Since firms in Europe face high wages for less-skilled workers, employers there substitute capital for labor, raising the productivity level in services. If the effective wage floor rises over time, this will drive further investments in labor-saving technology and work organization, and the resulting productivity growth will slow employment expansion even as overall demand for services rises. A closely related possibility is that firms facing high effective wage floors will skimp on the quality of services in ways that are difficult to measure. This will give the appearance of high productivity levels or growth rates in services (hotel nights per hour worked, for example), but only because aspects of quality (sheets not turned down before bedtime) or labor inputs (self-service breakfasts) are not properly measured.

A third explanation for lower service-sector employment in Europe points to features of European product markets rather than labor markets. In particular, restricted opening hours and local zoning laws may limit retailers' demand for workers. According to estimates produced by the McKinsey Global Institute, modern food stores are open an average of about 130 hours per week in the United States, compared to just 72 hours in France and 65 hours in Germany (McKinsey 2002, 14). Obviously stores with longer opening hours will tend to require more staff. Local zoning laws have also often been cited as an obstacle to employment creation in retail in France in particular (compare Gordon, this volume). Zoning laws restrict the ability of large general merchandise retailers to locate large stores on the outskirts of cities and towns, which would in turn create jobs. However, such arguments focus on just one side of the matter. New supermarkets will also knock out of business small shops in city centers, and the same will sometimes be true also for longer opening hours. The shops which are displaced will tend to have lower productivity and thus more employment per unit of sales than the supermarkets. Thus the overall effect of product market restrictions may well be to limit average productivity and thereby *increase* employment. Unless it is argued that the deregulation of retailing expands total consumption, by reducing propensities to save, a pretty far-fetched hypothesis, it is very unlikely that it could markedly raise retailing employment.[2] Of course it is conceivable that deregulation throughout the economy will, as supporters argue, install greater dynamism and thus push up economic growth. This would increase demand for distribution as for other goods and services, with repercussions for employment in that sector. But this is a completely different proposition from the suggestion that regulation specifically of the distribution sector itself is significantly restricting employment in that sector in Europe.

A final potential explanation for the employment gap in services is that the lower per capita incomes in Europe lead to lower demand for services and service employment. This works through two channels. The first is a pure income effect. At its simplest, with per capita incomes only 70–75 percent of the U.S. level, the demand for services, and thus ceteris paribus employment in services, will be correspondingly less. Furthermore, a large body of research has demonstrated over time and across countries that many services are "luxury" goods whose share in consumption rises faster than total income. The consumption part of the DEMPATEM project provides detailed confirmation of this pattern (see chapter 5). Thus the lower level of per capita incomes suggests that Europe should consume a significantly smaller share of service-sector output. Much higher savings rates in Europe reinforce this tendency for there to be a lower share of consumer services output and thus employment.

---

[2] Higher productivity in retailing does contribute to average productivity and thus average real incomes. But because distribution is only a modest proportion of the economy, high productivity growth in distribution leads to a much smaller rise in average productivity growth and thus consumer spending on distribution services. The McKinsey analyses of retailing note that liberalized opening hours would probably have a "small net effect" on employment (McKinsey 2002, 29).

The parallel channel linking per capita GDP to service-sector consumption operates through home production. The most important factor contributing to lower GDP per capita in Europe, as shown in chapter 1, is European workers' tendency to work far fewer hours than their American counterparts. Productivity levels per hour worked in many European country (Belgium, France, the Netherlands, Norway, and Germany, for example) are similar to that of the United States, but GDP per capita levels are much lower because workers in these countries work many fewer hours. With smaller incomes and more time on their hands, European households may engage in household production of many services that would be marketed in the richer, more time-harried, United States (cf. Freeman and Schettkat 2002, and chapter 8 in this book). While not linked to the labor market specifically, the lower level of hours worked in Europe is often linked to the relatively high average rates of taxation (see, for example, OECD 2003).

It should be noted that the hypotheses about wages and productivity to be examined below relate specifically to services rather than to the economy as a whole. At the macroeconomic level, rapid productivity growth would only tend to be reflected in lower employment rates if the economy was subject to constraints on the growth of aggregate demand—for example, if slow growth of world trade and thus exports acted as an effective fetter on macroeconomic expansion. This is certainly possible—indeed the OECD has noted that "the cross-country correlation between the increase in the employment-population ratio during the 1990s and the increase in labor productivity is weakly negative suggesting that a weak trade off may exist between gains in employment and productivity" (2003, 4). Of course to the extent that this pattern applies, services employment would take its share of the lower employment overall, but the problem would not be specific to services. Similarly, our discussion of wages focuses on relative wages in services and at the bottom end of the labor market that impinge especially on the services sector, leaving aside the issue of overall wage restraint that may affect employment in aggregate.

Given the discussion of the evolution of the employment gap in chapter 1 and the contending hypotheses discussed above, the rest of this chapter will focus on the distribution sector. This is based on the following considerations.

1. Distribution is a major contributor to the gap between European and U.S. employment rates.
2. Distribution is the major services sector most clearly related to household consumption. Community and personal services are differentially supplied

by the market and state sectors across countries, which makes a comparative analysis extremely difficult. Distribution is purely private sector and thus reflects market pressures more directly.

3. Distribution is the most important site of low-skill employment. If European rigidities inhibit employment at the lower end of the labor market, then distribution should exemplify this problem. Institutions such as the minimum wage or collective labor agreements may be found across the economy, but their "bite" will be stronger in low-wage industries. The OECD (2001, table 3.8) has shown that more than one-half of the employment gap between the EU and United States for low-wage jobs (lowest third of the U.S. wage distribution) is located in distribution, and this accounts for over one-quarter of the total jobs deficit.

4. Finally, it is possible—as we will see—to make plausible attempts at measuring both productivity growth in distribution over time within an economy and, a far more difficult task, productivity *levels* across countries. This is much more problematic for many service sectors but is very important for understanding employment differences between countries,

2. Employment in Distribution

This section engages with the labor market explanations for the employment gap between Europe and the United States discussed in the previous section; the demand argument will be considered in the next section. The first part describes pay and employment in the retail sector and reports on a detailed econometric analysis of these national data sets covering pay and employee characteristics. The object is to pin down the extent to which these employment and pay patterns are consistent with the notion that employment in this sector in Europe is substantially constrained by labor market rigidities. We then widen the analysis to compare productivity and capital accumulation in distribution in the United States and our group of European economies to verify whether these patterns support the rapid wage increase, capital intensification, fast productivity growth, low employment growth pattern for European services.

The Employment and Wage Structure

In this section we evaluate the claim that European labor market rigidities are responsible for the employment gap, taking the case of distribution as a sector that should best demonstrate the effects of lack of flexibility. To assess this claim, we have compared the patterns of employment and wages for the United States and four European countries using microdata sets.[3] Distribution comprises wholesale trade, retail trade, and hotels and catering.[4] Wholesale has a character very different from the other two subsectors, being closer to manufacturing in terms of wages and employment patterns. To focus as sharply as possible on the segment of the labor market where the impact of rigidities should be most apparent, wholesale is left out of the detailed analysis that follows when data allow. To keep the task manageable, we will present the results mainly for retailing, which is the larger sector in terms of employment and which has also been the object of a number of important internationally comparative studies.

The national microdata cover three individual years, chosen at the end of the 1970s and the middle to late 1990s.[5] These microdata sets are either establishment-based (West Germany, Netherlands) or household-based, and the variables (measures of wages for example) are not always exactly comparable across countries, as we note below. Accordingly the detailed results are presented for the individual countries without attempts at aggregation.

In chapter 1 it was shown that distribution plays an important role in the employment gap between the United States and Europe on the basis of Labour Force Survey (LFS) data. According to the microdata evidence that we used, the share of retail in distribution employment was some 45 percent in Europe[6] in the mid-1990s, being somewhat larger than in the United States (41 percent). It had declined since the end of the 1970s on both sides of the Atlantic, mainly to the advantage of hotels and catering. European employment in retail was relatively steady as a proportion of the population of working age, whereas it continued to expand in the United States (table 6.1). Thus the employment gap in retail, already considerable at the end of the 1970s, grew over the period.[7] In

[3] The data sets are Current Population Survey (CPS), Beschäftigtenstichprobe, Enquête Emploi (EE), General Household Survey (GHS), and Loonstructuuronderzoek (LSO). It has proved impossible to carry out a comparable analysis of Spain because of limitations in the available data.

[4] LFS, STAN, and the National Accounts do not have systematic long runs of data for the components of the distribution sector.

[5] The end of the 1980s was also considered but not reported here. More detail can be found in the underlying working paper.

[6] There are international differences, with wholesale trade playing a more important role in Germany and the Netherlands, countries that are geared to goods exports and imports.

[7] Part of this gap is compensated for by a higher level of self-employment in European retailing, 1.8 percent (of the working population) as against 1.0 percent for the United States in 2001. However, the stronger decline in self-employment, particularly in France and the Netherlands, meant that the employment gap including the self-employed grew over the period even more than the employee gap.

TABLE 6.1
Employment Rates for Employees in Retail (percentage of population
of working age)

	EU4	US	US – EU4
End of 1970s[a]	4.5	5.8	1.3
Middle of 1990s[b]	4.5	6.1	1.6

Source: OECD Labour Market Statistics database for population and employment in distributive services combined with national sources for shares of retail in distribution (see table 6.2).

[a]United Kingdom, United States, and Netherlands, 1979; Germany, 1978; France, 1982.

[b]France and Germany, 1995; Netherlands, 1996; United States, 1997; United Kingdom, 1998.

the mid-1990s the U.S. employment rate exceeded the European by more than one-third.

Table 6.2 shows how employment in retail in each country differs in composition—gender, age, part-time work, and skill levels—from the rest of the economy, based on full-time equivalents to correct for varying degrees of part-time work. The three skill levels are measured using the international ISCED classification's levels 0–2, 3–4, and 5–7 respectively. Skills are notoriously difficult to compare across countries since the educational systems from which they are derived differ so widely; however, these problems are less severe when comparing retail to the national average.

As a broad generalization, the specific characteristics of retail employment tend to be more consistent within a country over time than between countries. For example, in every country women are overrepresented in retail employment as compared to the average for the other industries, and the extent to which this is true in a particular country tends to be pretty stable. However, in the United States this overrepresentation is minor (about one-tenth in terms of ratio of shares), whereas in the Netherlands and Germany the proportion of women employed in retail is nearly twice that in the economy as a whole. In Germany there is much less than average overrepresentation of young people in retail in contrast to other countries where the level is high and increasing. The Netherlands has extreme underrepresentation of older workers. In France there is significantly less overrepresentation of part-timers; elsewhere levels are much higher though slightly declining.

The percentage of employees who are paid in the bottom third of the distribution of hourly earnings is around twice as high in retailing compared to the rest of the economy. Indeed, retail shows a greater concentration of low-paid workers in France and the Netherlands than

TABLE 6.2
Employment Characteristics in Retail (full-time equivalent employees, percentage of national average)

	Women	Youth 15–24	Older 51+	Part-time <35 hrs.	Pay in bottom 1/3	Skills		
						Low	Middle	High
United States								
1979	113	181	88	284	188	110	116	46
1997	109	226	84	230	194	131	122	49
West Germany								
1978	188	155	87	267	184	65	123	26
1995	171	143	98	229	167	67	116	25
France								
1982	120	195	76	123	160	94	122	29
1995	117	257	67	118	209	73	128	39
United Kingdom[a]								
1989	185	159	89	191	203	139	117	21
1998	126	197	85	182	182	131	137	37
Netherlands								
1979	229	200	52	247	239	131	64	8
1996	171	285	54	176	228	135	121	26

Source: Current Population Survey, Beschäftigtenstichprobe, Enquête Emploi, New Earnings Survey and General Household Survey, Loonstructuuronderzoek.
Note: FTE except Germany, where data are for head count.
[a]UK estimations are for the end of the 1980s as data for retailing were lacking in 1979. Data were pooled: 1989/1990 and 1998/2001. 2001 national average excludes retail.

in the United States, and the proportion has risen much more strongly in France than in the United States. Indeed, U.S. retailing does not seem to be an extreme case in respect of any of the employment characteristics—for most characteristics shown in the table, one or more of the European countries, including France or Germany (often taken to exemplify "old Europe's" excessive regulation), is not so dissimilar to the United States.

When it comes to skills, however, there *is* a striking difference. In the United States, together with the United Kingdom and the Netherlands, the least skilled are overrepresented in retail, while in Germany and France there is a smaller proportion of the least qualified than in other industries. The United States and France present a striking contrast over the 20-year period—the United States moving towards increasing *over*-representation of the least qualified, whereas in France there was increasing *under*-representation. As the proportions of least qualified were declining in the economy, retail seems to have been one of their last U.S. strongholds, whereas in France their share in retail jobs was already low in 1979 and declined faster than in the economy as a whole. This seems consistent with the notion that regulation was increasingly holding back the employment of the low skilled in this industry, which, at least in the less regulated economies, appears as archetypically low skilled. In Germany, also, the least skilled were strongly underrepresented in retail, but in this case without a trend.

Table 6.3 presents a similar analysis of the comparative position of retail for some key dimensions of the wage structure. The simplest comparison—average wages—gives the most striking result. Here there seems remarkable uniformity across our five countries—workers in retailing are on average paid around two-thirds to four-fifths of the national average, and these ratios are rather stable across time. The United States is far from being an outlier. Despite the fact that the U.S. retail

TABLE 6.3
Pay Characteristics in Retail (full-time equivalent employees, percentage of national average)

		All Workers		Low-Skill Workers	
		Average Wage	D1 Wage	Average Wage	D1 Wage
United States	1979	76	96	80	97
	1997	71	86	84	95
West Germany	1978	73	63	73	62
	1995	78	72	82	72
France	1982	79	93	93	99
	1995	75	91	96	103
United Kingdom[a]	1989	72	78	71	80
	1998	71	83	69	88
Netherlands	1979	71	63	77	69
	1996	68	64	75	60

Source: see table 6.2.

Note: FTE and hourly wages, except Germany: head count and monthly wage (median instead of average). No correction for hours worked was possible; consequently wages in retail may be substantially underestimated in comparison with the national average relative to other countries, particularly for D1.

[a]UK estimations are for the end of the 1980s as data for retailing were lacking in 1979. Data were pooled: 1989/1990 and 1998/2001.

shows a much higher concentration of unskilled workers than France or Germany, and unskilled workers' wages are low in the United States, French and German retailers evidently find alternative methods of holding down wage costs. This seems quite inconsistent with the overregulation/wage-compression view of European labor markets, where employers should have less opportunity to pay below the national average.

A fuller picture of wages in retail can be gained by looking at different points in the wage distribution as compared to the national pattern. For a number of countries the retail wage at the first decile (10 percent from the bottom) is a considerably higher proportion of the first-decile (D1) wage in the rest of the economy than is the case for the analogous ratio of average wages. This would seem to suggest an effective wage floor even in retail, and so it is not surprising to find France in this position. However, the same pattern is apparent for the United States, where retailers would be expected to take advantage of a high level of flexibility to pay very low wages.

The right-hand panel of table 6.3 focuses on the low skilled (ISCED 0–2) in retailing. In France their wages are pretty close to the national average for the low skilled, whereas in the United States they have been considerably below, and this is the one indicator that seems consistent with the picture of retail business benefiting in the United States from greater flexibility. However, this pattern also applies to Germany, the United Kingdom, and the Netherlands. Surprisingly, the worst paid amongst the low skilled (final column, D1) do not display the same pattern, for in both France and the United States they were no worse off in retail than elsewhere. Overall, therefore, the comparison of France and the United States provides scant evidence of U.S. retail having a major advantage in terms of pay flexibility. This impression is reinforced by the evidence from Germany, where the low paid are much worse off in retail than in the economy generally, and the same is true for the Netherlands.[8]

The picture of retailing employment emerging from this analysis is far from straightforward. Retail in France and Germany does not have the concentration of low-skill workers that is typical of the sector in the United States and United Kingdom; however, wages are well below the average in the economy on both sides of the Atlantic, and the least skilled seem to be much worse off in retail than elsewhere in most European economies as well as in the United States. These patterns are at

---

[8] The fact that the German pay data is monthly and does not include hours worked limits the value of the comparisons involving Germany as it must exaggerate the width of the distribution since many of the worst paid also work shorter hours. This problem can be sidestepped more effectively in the regression analysis that follows.

odds with the common portrait of wage compression in Europe and deregulated markets in the United States. If retail employed a larger share of workers in the United States than in Europe because it can exploit flexible labor markets, then we would expect retail wages to be much lower compared to the national average wage than in Europe. This is not the case, despite the greater concentration of the low skilled in U.S. retail than in France and Germany. To probe these differences further, we turn to a more detailed analysis of employment and wage structures in retail.

ECONOMETRIC ANALYSIS OF WAGE AND EMPLOYMENT STRUCTURES

If retailing were severely inhibited by labor-market rigidities in Europe, we would anticipate that it would be paying wages that were on average much closer to those in the rest of the economy than in the United States. This would be because higher relative wages for the unskilled in general would push up wage costs in this low-skill sector. Minimum wages or welfare-state floors would prevent employers in this sector from taking advantage of slack labor markets at the bottom end of the pay scale to further economize on wage costs by paying below the going rate for given skill categories (a wage "penalty" for working in retail). Wage compression could also lead to "employment-structure compression." As the pay for typically low-paid groups, youth for example, moves closer to the average, there is less advantage to employing them.

To try to disentangle the wage and employment patterns presented briefly above, we have estimated the wage structure of retail trade relative to the rest of the economy. Quantile regressions for retailing and the rest of the economy, based at different points of the earnings distribution, allow a detailed analysis of the contribution of different factors to the wage gap. We present the results in three successive steps. The appendix to this chapter presents the decomposition technique. The results are summarized here for the ease of presentation; full detail can be found in Glyn et al. 2005.[9] It is clear, however, from the part-time re-

---

[9] The basic equation for the estimation was

$$\ln w_i^\theta = \alpha_0 + \alpha_1 EXP_i + \alpha_2 EXP_i^2 + \alpha_3 PT_{1i} + \alpha_4 PT_{2i} + \alpha_5 \sum_{n=2}^{6} DSKILL_{n,i}$$

+ interactions of part-time with gender and skills
+ interactions of experience and experience squared with gender and skills + error.

Here w^θ stands for earnings at quantile θ and EXP for potential experience. $DSKILL_n$ ($n = 1, \ldots, 3$) are (0,1)-dummy variables for male workers with low, intermediate, and high skills, respectively, while $DSKILL_n$ ($n = 4, \ldots, 6$) denote corresponding variables for the three skill categories of female workers. The above equation was estimated by quantile regressions. Since the German data are top-coded at the social contribution ceiling, we

sults (see table 6.2) that the international variation in the level and evolution of part-time employment in the retail workforce plays a significant role.[10] It has little to do, however, with the regulation of low wages, which is our prime interest

Estimates from a wage equation allow a split of the raw wage differential of retail compared to the rest of the economy into two parts: the retail penalty and the effect of the pattern or composition of the workforce in the industry. The retail penalty reflects the ability of companies in retailing to pay their employees less than companies in the economy as a whole pay employees with the same characteristics, for example, levels of experience or educational attainment. The composition effect reflects the possible overrepresentation in the retail workforce of groups who are paid less across the economy, for example women. The distinction reflects the two options employers in retail may use to achieve lower labor costs: first, pay workers of a given category less than in other sectors, and, second, hire more people from categories of workers who are low paid. The pay penalty reflects the degree of wage flexibility available to retail employers, while the composition effect shows how their hiring policies can take advantage of the wage structure.

Figure 6.1 introduces the results, splitting the raw differential for the median wage into the two components.[11] First it shows that the pure wage penalty for working in retail ("retail penalty") is substantial (10–20 percent) and does not differ much between the countries or over time. There was a slight increase in the penalty in France, the Netherlands, and the United States and a decrease for Germany and the United Kingdom. The figure also shows the impact on the wage bill of the composition of the workforce. This makes a further contribution to lower wage costs in retail—usually reducing them by 5–10 percent. French and German retailers benefited rather less from such workforce concentration. The main point, however, is that U.S. retail does not appear as

---

used Powell's method of censored least absolute deviations instead of the normal quantile regression approach.

[10] The lack of hourly wage data for Germany hampers the proper determination of the part-time pay penalty but not the composition effect. The latter is substantially lower in France and Germany compared to the other three countries; it grew considerably in the United Kingdom and the Netherlands.

[11] Quantile regression can be used for analyzing the differential at different levels of the wage distribution. Ordinary least squares regression, by contrast, analyzes the differential at the means. Figure 6.1 shows the fifth-decile or median results, which are close but not identical to the means. The splits rests on a Blinder-Oaxaca type of decomposition. This also comprises interaction effects, which turned out to be small and are left aside here. See the appendix to the chapter for more detail. It should be noted that we could not uniformly control for characteristics such as firm size. For Germany and the Netherlands we could establish that this still has a considerable effect.

Fig. 6.1. Retail Wage Differentials Compared to the Rest of the Economy Estimated at the Median Wage
Source: For calculation, see appendix; for data sources and notes see table 6.2.
Note: Hotels and catering are excluded from the total economy. The estimates exclude (small) interaction effects. UK estimates refer to the end of the 1980s, as data for retailing were lacking in 1979. Data were pooled: 1989/1990 and 1998/2001.

a real outlier in respect of either the retail pay penalty or concentration on low-paid categories of workers.

These estimates apply to the median-wage level only. However, the lack of labor market flexibility is supposed to bolster wages, and thus discourage employment, particularly at the bottom end of the wage distribution. Quantile regression allows an exploration of whether the impact on pay of factors such as industry varies at different points in the wage distribution. If U.S. retailers were really able to take advantage of greater flexibility at the bottom end of the pay scale to pay very low wages, one would expect the "retail penalty" to be greater at the second decile in the United States than in Europe even if the average penalty over the distribution was similar. Figure 6.2 adds the results for the other two deciles to those for the median shown in figure 6.1.

Three features are striking. First, the penalties are mostly smaller at the bottom of the pay distribution, the second decile (D2), than they are higher up. The fact that they are more modest at D2 than at the median shows that in fact the disadvantage to working in retail is greater in the middle than at the bottom of the distribution. In the same vein, it also seems that workers really high up the organization, at the eighth decile (D8), often take a larger pay hit by working in the retail sector, as compared to those similarly qualified in other sectors, than do those at the bottom and in the middle. This applies in particular to Germany and

Fig. 6.2. Retail Wage Differentials Compared to the Rest of the Economy Estimated at the Second and Eighth Wage Decile.
Source: For calculation, see appendix; for data sources and notes, see table 6.2.
Note: See figure 6.1. Quantile estimation at D8 for France 1982 did not converge.

France, but in all countries the penalty at D8 has increased over time.[12] Second, the size of the pay penalties in U.S. retail, even for those at the bottom of the distribution, is not much greater than in Europe. There is no uniform trend in the evolution of the retail penalty for the lowest paid. The D2 penalty grew in France, Netherlands, and United States and fell in Germany—but from a higher level than in any other country. Third, workforce composition effects do matter, especially in the United Kingdom and the Netherlands, but they show little change over the years. All in all, the U.S. wage structure is not markedly unlike that in the other countries; therefore it can only have minor effects on costs.

There is no reason to suppose that the retail penalty will be the same for all types of workers. In fact, retail employers may be able to pay less than other employers for certain characteristics, and this effect may also vary at different levels of the wage distribution. As a third step we therefore consider the contribution of individual characteristics to both the pay penalty and the impact of workforce composition on the wage bill. The lack of labor market flexibility may be expected to affect the low skilled most. A Blinder-Oaxaca decomposition of the wage differential between retail and the rest of the economy can establish the contributions to the wage differentials shown in figure 6.2 that are made by the

---

[12] Dutch retailing in 1996 seems an exception, but it also had a particularly low share of high skilled workers, according to table 6.2.

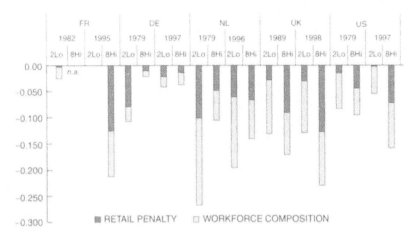

Fig. 6.3. Retail Wage Differentials Compared to the Rest of the Economy: Contribution of Low Skills at the Second Wage Decile and High Skills at the Eighth Wage Decile
Source: For calculation, see appendix; for data sources and notes, see table 6.2.
Note: See fig. 6.1.

pay penalties for specific worker characteristics, on the one hand, and the workforce composition of these same characteristics, on the other hand. In particular we are interested in the role of skills, as it may be that the low skilled at the bottom of the distribution are the most vulnerable to very low pay and suffer more from a lack of protective institutions.

The surprising picture arising from this analysis, shown in figure 6.3 for the second decile (D2Low), is that neither the excess employment of *low*-skilled workers nor paying them less than elsewhere in the economy had much effect on the retail wage bill[13] in any of the countries. Both penalty and composition effects for the low skilled at the bottom of the earnings distribution are negligible in France and United States and small but stable in the United Kingdom. They significantly declined in the Netherlands and Germany to a level comparable to the United Kingdom. By contrast, employing fewer high-skilled workers than the average and paying them less than elsewhere make a substantial and rapidly growing contribution to reducing the wage bill at the high end of the wage dispersion (D8High).

These results contrast strongly with what is implied by the hypothesis of wage inflexibility in Europe. According to this view, one would have

[13] Aggregated over gender and experience.

expected a substantial retail penalty for the low skilled in the United States, with relatively little protection by unions and with a low minimum wage, as they are sorted into those with low ability and employed in low-productivity tasks in that sector. But it turns out that the low skilled, even those at the bottom of the wage distribution, hardly suffer a retail penalty in the United States. The retail penalty is higher in some EU countries than in the United States and is certainly less important in holding down wage costs than the penalty for the better skilled.

This section has sought to discover whether retailing has been inhibited in Europe, as compared to the United States, by not being able to employ a workforce at relatively low wages as compared to the rest of the economy. This does not appear to be the case in general. We are not suggesting that labor market regulations play no role,[14] but the employment and wage patterns analyzed here suggest that they cannot have been the dominant influence on employment differences.

Productivity and Capital Accumulation

If distribution employment was being inhibited by labor market inflexibilities, this should be reflected in labor productivity being too high or having grown too fast. More flexible wages should have resulted in less substitution of capital for labor and less substitution of skilled labor for unskilled labor. Both of these results would have reduced the growth of labor productivity and increased employment. Comparing such trends in Europe and the United States can provide evidence for what is constraining employment.

Changes in the volume of distribution output within countries are typically measured by deflating measures of current-price sales by retail-price indices to obtain sales volumes. Indices for different types of stores are then weighted by the average gross margin (assuming that differences in margin at a point in time reflect differences in the output produced by the store). The index for total real sales is linked to base-year current-price value added to obtain value added at constant prices as

---

[14] The very informative McKinsey report on retailing notes, "US retailers provide services with a low value-added (such as checkout baggers), which are not provided in Europe. . . . the input required for these extra services accounts for 8 percent of the labor volume. . . . The checkout baggers in the US are paid less than the French minimum wage. Although data availability for Germany is limited, we believe that the minimum wage has the same effect as in France. The minimum wage, therefore, may restrict the kind of services provided. If French retailers were to provide bag-packing services compensated at the current minimum wage, the increase in cost would outweigh customers' willingness to pay for the service. . . . Europeans are expected to be less willing to pay for low value-added services due to their lower income levels" (McKinsey 2002, 17–30).

published in National Accounts. This in turn is used with employment data to construct labor productivity. The underlying assumption (Fuchs 1968, chap. 5) is that the quantity and quality of service per real dollar of sales remains constant over time, which is controversial (24-hour shops, lack of informed assistants, time spent queuing, and so forth). A more recent refinement in measurement (in the United States at least) has been to apply double deflation to this sector, so that changes in the real use of intermediate inputs (but still not quality changes) are taken into account. This adjustment increased measured productivity growth in American retailing in the 1980s very slightly (Mohr 1992).

Table 6.4 reports the data for the growth of labor productivity in distribution as calculated from the National Institute Sectoral Productivity dataset, together with some more disaggregated data from various sources.

In the 1970s continental Europe appeared to have distinctly higher productivity growth in distribution than did the United States. This was true also for the economy as a whole and included the final burst of "catch-up" of productivity to American levels. This was also the era of wage pressure, rising unemployment, and a profit squeeze throughout Europe. These developments may very well have put pressure on employment in distribution as in other sectors.

This pattern did not persist into the 1980s when productivity in distribution grew at very comparable rates in Europe and United States. So there is no suggestion that distribution employment in Europe was being inhibited by "excessive" productivity growth as compared to the United States. In the 1990s the contrast is even stronger. Productivity in U.S. distribution steamed ahead, two to three percentage points per year faster than in France, Germany, and the Netherlands. The contrast is very strong in retailing, where productivity has been growing at more than 5 percent per year in the United States, double the previous rate, and double the rate in Europe. Competitive pressure from Wal-Mart aided by the introduction of new technologies appears to account for the remarkable U.S. increase (see Nordhaus 2002; McKinsey 2002; Basker 2005; Triplett and Bosworth 2003). French and German productivity growth was also distinctly *slower* than in the United Kingdom, where labor market deregulation had proceeded far down the American road. In Europe labor productivity growth in distribution has also been distinctly slower than in manufacturing, which is not the case in the United States (or in the United Kingdom in the 1990s). If inflexible labor markets were preventing the employment of low-wage labor in Europe, this would be expected to have a stronger impact in distribution than manufacturing. This should then show up in distribution productivity performing *more* strongly in Europe relative to manufacturing than was

TABLE 6.4
Hourly Labor Productivity Growth (annual average, %)

| | Manu-facturing | Distribution | | | | Market Sector | Whole Economy |
		Total	Wholesale Trade	Retail Trade	Hotels and Catering		
United States							
1970–79	2.2	1.5	2.5	2.3	−1.6	1.1	1.3
1979–90	2.3	2.1	3.4	2.5	−1.8	1.0	1.2
1990–99	3.7	3.7	6.5	5.2	0.2	1.5	2.3
United Kingdom							
1970–79	3.0	1.5		1.9	−1.4	2.7	3.1
1979–90	4.5	2.0		2.3	−0.2	2.2	2.6
1990–99	2.3	1.9	3.9	2.7	0.2	2.1	2.1
France							
1970–79	5.3	3.2				4.4	4.6
1979–90	3.3	1.9	4.7	4.0	−2.1	2.9	3.1
1990–99	2.9	0.6	2.3	1.8	−0.2	1.3	1.1
W. Germany/ Germany							
1970–79	4.8	3.4	3.7	4.2	1.4	3.4	3.8
1979–90	2.2	1.8	1.5	1.4	−0.8	1.7	1.9
1990–99	3.5	0.5	2.7	2.1	−3.5	2.4	2.5
Netherlands							
1970–79	4.5	3.7					3.0
1979–90	3.7	1.7	3.0	3.0	−0.3		1.9
1990–99	2.8	1.4	2.1	1.2	−0.5	1.4	1.1

Source: National Institute Sectoral Productivity Dataset. Figures for the Netherlands are the authors' calculations from STAN 2003 (Market sector excluding agriculture). Wholesale, Retail, and Hotels refer to 1990–2002, and data for that period and 1979–90 come from Groningen Growth and Development Centre 60 Industry Database.

the case in the more flexible United States and United Kingdom—the opposite of the observed pattern. Obviously many other factors influence productivity, but this data set does not conform to the picture of rigid labor markets seriously inhibiting employment growth in European distribution in the 1980s and 1990s.[15]

[15] The qualification about the data set is important. The O'Mahony data set is very carefully constructed from national and OECD sources (including STAN) and is specifically designed for productivity analysis. However, the latest version of OECD's STAN database yields a different pattern for productivity growth in distribution over the last two decades. The productivity data we have constructed based on goods consumption (see

TABLE 6.5
Growth Rate of Capital/Labor Ratio (annual average, %)

			Distribution				
	Manu-facturing	Total	Wholesale Trade	Retail Trade	Hotels and Catering	Market Sector	Whole Economy
United States							
1970–79	2.3	1.5	4.5	1.9	−2.1	1.3	0.4
1979–90	2.3	2.3	4.5	1.7	0.8	1.1	0.3
1990–99	2.9	3.1	4.8	2.8	1.6	1.6	1.1
United Kingdom							
1970–79	2.2	3.9	2.8	5.0	2.1	2.6	2.5
1979–90	3.8	4.1	3.5	5.1	2.6	2.7	2.4
1990–99	2.3	4.2	4.3	4.3	3.5	2.4	2.6
France							
1970–79	4.2	3.9	4.0	3.3	3.7	4.5	3.1
1979–90	5.4	3.2	2.9	3.5	3.0	3.6	2.4
1990–99	3.1	2.1	2.3	2.0	1.1	2.0	1.6
W. Germany/ Germany							
1970–79	3.4	3.0	2.9	3.2	2.8	4.9	3.7
1979–90	1.8	1.3	1.7	1.7	−0.4	1.6	1.7
1990–99	4.3	2.2	3.1	2.5	0.2	3.3	2.8

Source: As table 6.4.

Inflexible labor markets, by raising labor costs, could encourage capital/labor substitution and therefore labor-productivity growth. Was capital/labor substitution stronger in the low-paid service sectors in Europe than in the United States? The O'Mahony data set provides disaggregated capital series constructed around a common set of assumptions, and we derive from these the growth of the capital/labor ratio (table 6.5).

In the 1970s the capital/labor ratio grew distinctly faster in distribution in Europe than in the United States (a pattern similar to that for labor productivity noted above). This trend continued in France in the 1980s, but not in Germany; even in France the rate of capital intensification was less than in the United Kingdom, where deregulation was proceeding apace. In the 1990s the growth of capital intensity was less

next section) shows the same pattern of acceleration in the United States and deceleration in France as O'Mahony (though it shows faster productivity growth in France in the 1980s). This variability of results across data sets underlines how tentative conclusions should be.

TABLE 6.6
Capital/Labor Ratios Levels in 1999 (×1000 per person employed, 1996 $)

	United States	Germany	France	United Kingdom
Distribution	40	32	55	23
Retail	29	28	54	19
Retail capital/labor relative to manufacturing capital/labor	0.34	0.43	0.56	0.31

Source: As table 6.4.

in France and Germany than in the United States and much less than in the United Kingdom.[16]

Comparisons of changes in capital intensity will typically be more robust than comparisons of levels, since levels are more dependent on assumptions about asset lives and there is the additional complication of calculating purchasing power parities for capital stocks. Bearing these provisos in mind, the O'Mahony data set allows the comparisons shown in table 6.6 for levels of capital intensity in distribution in total and in retail.

According to these data the capital/labor ratio is no higher in German distribution and retail than it is in the United States, contrary to what one would expect if a lack of wage flexibility pushed up wages and stimulated investment in higher productivity. The United Kingdom has lower capital intensity, as would be expected from its low-wage/low-investment reputation (and despite apparently heavy increases in capital intensity over the past 25 years). These data suggest very high capital intensity indeed in France. But if this were mainly a reflection of European-style labor market inflexibilities, then a similar pattern would be expected for Germany. Overall there is no consistent picture of higher capital intensities in continental Europe, nor (as we have seen earlier) the higher or faster-growing labor productivity that should be associated with it.

[16] Labor input is measured in terms of employment rather than total hours worked because the former is probably the better measure of the capital intensity of the production process. This will be true to the extent that the utilization of capital is correlated with average hours worked per employee (so that a declining working week is associated with declining hours of utilization). Given the faster decline in hours of work in Europe, measuring capital intensity in relation to total hours worked increased the sharpness of the rise in Europe in the 1970s especially. But by the 1990s, adjusting for average hours makes little difference to these international comparisons and the conclusion stands that capital intensity in distribution increased no faster in continental Europe than in the United States.

TABLE 6.7
Growth of Hourly Product Wages (annual average, %)

| | | Distribution | | | | | |
	Manu-facturing	Total	Wholesale Trade	Retail Trade	Hotels and Catering	Market Sector	Whole Economy
United States							
1970–79	2.3	1.3	2.0	2.2	−1.7	0.9	1.1
1979–90	1.6	2.1	4.3	1.9	−0.5	0.8	0.9
1990–99	2.9	2.7	4.0	2.2	−1.3	1.0	2.1
United Kingdom							
1970–79	3.8	1.7				2.7	3.1
1979–90	4.0	1.7				2.2	2.6
1990–99	2.4	2.1	4.4	1.8	−1.3	1.8	2.0
France							
1970–79	5.7	4.6			2.7	5.1	5.4
1979–90	2.0	1.2			−0.2	2.0	2.2
1990–99	2.5	0.4			−1.8	1.6	1.3
W. Germany/ Germany							
1970–79	5.8	4.6	3.7	4.2	1.4	4.1	3.6
1979–90	2.6	2.5	2.2	3.6	0.8	1.6	1.6
1990–99	3.7	0.1	0.9	−0.5	−3.9	2.1	1.9

Source: As table 6.4, calculated as the sum of the growth rate of hourly labor productivity and the growth rate of labor's share in value added (adjusted for self-employment).

Finally we examine the pattern of increases in real labor costs (table 6.7). These are measured in terms of "product wages," that is, money wages deflated by the price index for value added in the sector concerned. In parallel to the results for productivity and capital intensity, product wages in distribution rose rapidly in France and Germany in the 1970s and represented a substantial squeeze on profits as labor's share rose strongly (in the United Kingdom and Netherlands as well). However, in the 1980s European product wage growth slowed down to the U.S. rate and in 1990s hardly grew at all, compared to steady growth in the United States and United Kingdom.

This section has examined the pattern of employment, wages, capital intensification, and productivity within distribution. The patterns for the 1980s and 1990s are not as one would expect if labor market inflexibilities had been the fundamental restraint on the employment growth of European services.

3. Employment in Distribution and the Growth of Consumption

This section examines the role of the lower level and slower growth of consumption demand in limiting employment in distribution in Europe as compared to the United States.

In comparing the evolution of employment across countries it is most helpful to have an internationally comparable measure of production. The national measures of productivity growth used in the previous section do not readily lend themselves to international comparison of levels. Attempts to measure sectoral productivity by value added deflated by a PPP for appropriate expenditure categories (see Barnard and Jones 1996; Dollar and Wolff 1993) are very seriously flawed, as they reflect productivity in the whole economy rather than measuring efficiency in the sector concerned (Glyn et al. 2005). Sales of goods are the fundamental "throughput" into distribution, suggesting a natural if crude measure of productivity in distribution across countries—consumers expenditure on goods at international PPP prices, per person employed (or hour worked) in distribution. Moreover, measuring productivity by "goods consumption per hour" facilitates a very simple decomposition of the determinants of employment in distribution into goods consumption on the one hand and labor productivity in distribution on the other:

$$\frac{\text{Hours Worked in Distribution}}{\text{Population of Working Age}} = \frac{\text{Consumption of Goods}}{\text{Population of Working Age}} \times \frac{\text{Hours in Distribution}}{\text{Consumption of Goods}}$$

Consumption of goods per head of the working population can be thought of as representing the demand for distribution, in turn reflecting per capita incomes, taxation, savings, and choices between goods and services. Consumption of goods per hour worked in distribution is a gross-output measure of labor productivity. It does not cope with the subtleties of different types of distribution. However, this decomposition does allow us to see whether the "employment deficit" in European distribution is mainly due to low throughput (low consumption of goods) or to high productivity and how these factors have influenced comparative employment trends over time.

Before we look at the results of the analysis, a word is in order about data construction. Our estimate of consumption of goods starts from the OECD's 1999 figures at PPPs—we include consumption of goods strictly defined plus expenditure on hotels and restaurants (a procedure that is partly anticipated in the U.S. National Accounts, which include expenditure on restaurants in goods sales, not services). Of course part

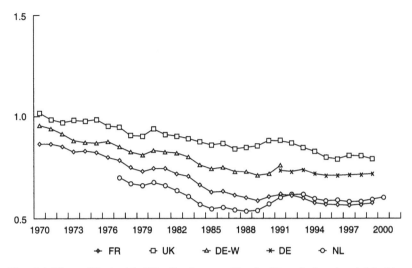

Fig. 6.4. Hours Worked in Distribution per Head of Population Aged 15–64 Relative to U.S., U.S. = 1

of wholesale business is concerned with capital goods and exports, but consumption of goods still appears to be a pretty comprehensive indicator of distribution output.[17] The 1999 data at PPPs are then linked to constant-price National Accounts series for goods consumption to derive time series at 1999 international prices (and the same is done for total consumption and GDP). The population measure is restricted to ages 15–64 to reflect our primary focus on employment, so that per capita consumption as used here differs from the conventional measure based on total population. Series for employment in distribution and hours worked are far from unproblematic, and in this section we have relied primarily on the National Accounts series comparisons (the caveat entered above about variation across data sources applies here also).

Figure 6.4 shows the number of hours worked in distribution in a year per person aged 15–64 expressed as a ratio to the U.S. level. The United States already had more employment in distribution 30 years ago, but the differences have subsequently increased dramatically as work in distribution in the United States has grown rather steadily, while there has been little overall trend in Europe except in France, where distribution work has declined. By 1999 work in distribution per head

[17] Annual changes in consumption of goods is actually more closely correlated over time with total hours worked in U.S. distribution than is the official series for constant-price value added.

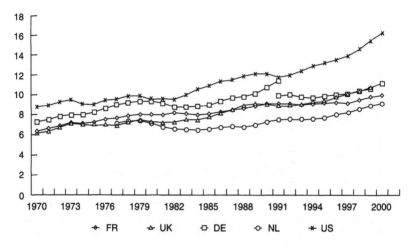

Fig. 6.5. Consumer Spending on Goods per Head of the Population Aged 15–64 × 1000, international prices PPP

was 304 hours in the United States, 239 in the United Kingdom, 217 in Germany, and 175–80 in France and the Netherlands. So the United States has around at least 25 percent more distribution work per head of the population than the United Kingdom and nearly 75 percent more than France and Netherlands—truly enormous differences.[18]

The decomposition above focuses on goods consumption per capita, representing demand for retail work, and productivity in distribution. Figure 6.5 shows that American goods consumption per capita was around one-half greater than the European level in 1970, and if anything the gap has increased. There was some catching up by Europe in the 1970s and again in the boom at the end of the 1980s, but Europe fell further behind when the United States boomed in the 1990s. Differences between the four European countries are comparatively small, while differences between the United States and Europe in per capita consumption of goods are really dramatic. If productivity in distribution in 1999 was the same in the United States and Europe, there would have still have been 50–60 percent more hours worked in U.S. distribution than in Europe to service the higher throughput of goods.

Our internationally comparable measures of labor productivity, consumption of goods in PPP prices per distribution-hour worked, are shown relative to the American level in figure 6.6. After some catching

---

[18] By 1999 average annual hours worked by each worker in distribution were 1,500–1,600 other than in the Netherlands, where the greater incidence of part-time work apparently pushed the figure down as low as 1,200.

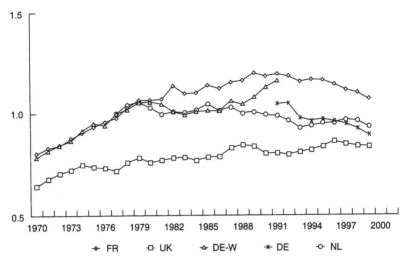

Fig. 6.6. Labor Productivity in Distribution Relative to U.S., U.S. = 1
Goods consumption (volume, PPP) per hour worked

up in the 1970s, it seems that productivity levels in continental Europe were close to those in the United States by 1980, though still well below in the United Kingdom.[19] French productivity then rose somewhat above the American level, but Europe fell back relatively in the 1990s as productivity in distribution boomed in the United States.[20] German and Dutch labor productivity in distribution was similar to the American level by 1999: this implies that for these countries differences with the United States in work done in distribution must mainly reflect differences in consumption per head. High French productivity exacerbates the employment gap with the United States, whereas lower productivity in the United Kingdom offsets the impact of lower consumption per head.

Figure 6.7 shows distribution employment, productivity and goods consumption relative to U.S. levels for France, chosen as one obvious example of a regulated labor market (the pattern for Germany is very

[19] The broad pattern of productivity trends over time is consistent with that shown in table 6.6 based on the standard measures of national productivity, which are not internationally comparable in terms of levels.

[20] Nordhaus (2002) shows that about one-half of the acceleration in American labor productivity growth in the "New Economy" period of 1995–2000 took place in wholesale and retail. Part of the explanation lies in the boom in the "volume" of computer sales (measured using hedonic price indices), but part probably does reflect "genuine" productivity gains reflecting very heavy IT spending in that sector.

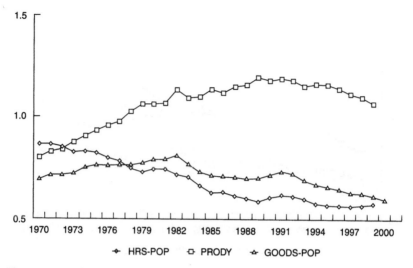

Fig. 6.7. Distribution in France, Relative to U.S., U.S. = 1

similar). In 1970 much lower consumption per head was only partly offset by lower productivity, and employment in distribution was lower. In the 1970s productivity caught up much faster than did consumption, increasing the gap. In the 1980s employment in France fell further behind as productivity grew faster and consumption grew slower. In the 1990s consumption grew far slower in France and only slower growth of productivity in France prevented a further widening of the gap.

Across the four European countries as a whole it is clear that goods consumption per capita is now the most important proximate factor behind lower employment in distribution. Does this just reflect lower per capita GDP, a smaller consumption share, or a bias within consumption against goods? The latter possibility can be dismissed immediately.

Figure 6.8 shows a consistent tendency for goods to constitute a *higher* proportion of total consumption in Europe than in the United States. One likely explanation of the higher goods share in Europe is the greater provision of services by the state (which means that expenditure on such services is not part of National Accounts household consumption). Some convergence towards the American level means that by the end of the period the impact of goods bias was pretty small. Turning to the second influence on goods consumption, the ratio of total consumption to GDP is distinctly smaller in Europe (figure 6.9), and here the differences have fanned out, with the United Kingdom moving towards the United States during the consumer boom of the second half of the 1990s, while the Dutch share fell further.

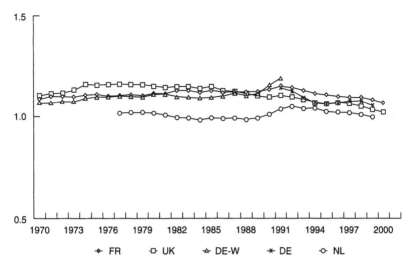

Fig. 6.8. Share of Goods in Personal Consumption, Relative to the U.S., U.S. = 1

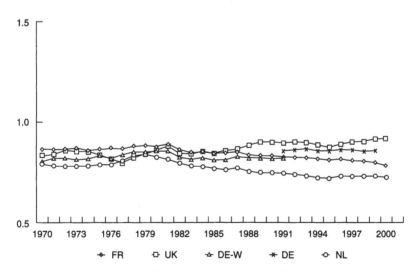

Fig. 6.9. Consumption out of GDP (volume, PPP), Relative to U.S., U.S. = 1

The twin influences of the consumption share and goods share of consumption can be helpfully combined into consumption of goods as a ratio of GDP; this combined measure makes sense since a high share of state provision of services will tend to both reduce the share of consumption in GDP and (as a partial offset) increase the share of goods in personal consumption (as some services are now financed by the tax system). Goods consumption in the United Kingdom is only a little lower as share of GDP than in the United States, while for continental European countries, and especially the Netherlands, the differences are large and contribute materially to low employment in distribution.

This leaves per capita GDP as the final, and most important, influence on goods consumption and therefore distribution employment. The decline in German GDP per capita with unification contributed to a convergence within Europe, and by the end of the period American GDP per capita was about one-third above all the European countries (figure 6.10). This was the dominant factor behind lower consumption of goods per head in Germany and United Kingdom. Obviously GDP per capita reflects many factors, but the most significant influences are low employment rates and hours of work in Europe (with economy-wide productivity levels being fairly similar—see Gordon in this volume for more discussion).

A simple way of summarizing these results is to tabulate (table 6.8) a decomposition of differences in distribution employment compared to

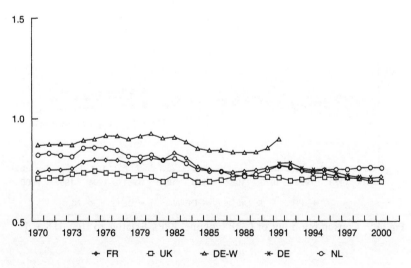

Fig. 6.10. GDP per Capita, Relative to U.S.
Constant PPP prices per head of population 15–64, U.S. = 1

Table 6.8
Summary Table on Distribution Work per Head of Population, Compared
to United States, 1999

	Hours Worked in Distribution ÷ Population	GDP/ Population	Goods Consumption ÷ GDP	Distribution Productivity (US compared to country)
Germany	0.717	0.709	0.903	1.121
France	0.574	0.710	0.863	0.937
United Kingdom	0.790	0.698	0.945	1.197
Netherlands	0.594	0.762	0.728	1.074

the United States into differences in per capita GDP, goods consumption as a share of GDP, and labor productivity. Distribution work particularly in Netherlands and France is held back by the low ratio of goods consumption, in France also by high productivity and throughout Europe by low per capita GDP, much the most important factor overall.[21]

The analysis thus far has been directed to the question: why are so many more people employed in distribution in the United States than in Europe? Basically, the simple answer is that consumption of goods is so much higher in the United States because of high per capita GDP, with productivity differences in distribution appearing to play a subsidiary role. But there is a slightly different question concerning the *proportion* of work in the economy that is carried out in distribution. Do European countries have a smaller share of work carried out in distribution, and what are the proximate factors influencing it?

The first two columns of table 6.9 show that shortfalls between the European economies and the United States in the *proportion* of work done in distribution are quite small compared to the gaps in the absolute level of distribution work per head of the population. A lower *share* would result either from a smaller share of goods consumption in GDP than in the United States or from productivity in distribution in the country being higher relative to the American level than is productivity in the whole economy. Shares of goods consumption are indeed typically lower in Europe, as noted already, and in France and Germany produc-

---

[21] We noted earlier that our measure of labor productivity as goods consumption or "throughput" per hour worked is a rough one. More sophisticated measures, most of which have severe conceptual limitations, can give rather different answers, as the background working paper shows. They typically give France a bigger productivity lead over the United States in distribution than that shown above, but it is hard believe that they are accurate, and so it seems clearer to stick with the simpler analysis presented here.

TABLE 6.9
Summary Table on Distribution Work as Share of Total Work Done 1999

	Share of Distribution in Total Hours (%)	Share of Distribution in Total Hours (rel. to US = 1)	Share of Goods Consumption in GDP (rel. to US = 1)	Productivity Compared to US in Distribution/ Productivity Compared to US in Whole Economy
United States	21.9	1	1	1
United Kingdom	19.7	0.90	0.90	1.0
France	17.8	0.81	0.86	1.06
Germany	19.3	0.88	0.94	1.07
Netherlands	19.2	0.88	0.73	0.83

tivity relative to U.S. levels is a little higher in distribution than in the economy as a whole. In the Netherlands, by contrast, relative productivity in distribution seems particularly low, and this has maintained jobs in distribution despite exceptionally low goods consumption.

It is clear that Europe had a somewhat smaller *proportion* of work done in distribution than the United States well before there was talk of inflexible labor markets (see figure 6.11) and that the shortfall has *not*

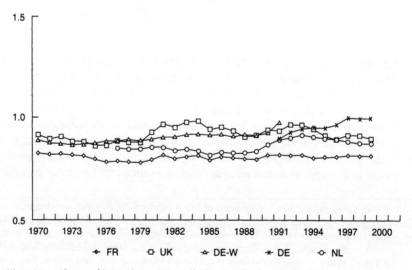

Fig. 6.11. Share of Distribution in All Hours Worked Relative to U.S., U.S. = 1

grown over time. A structural tendency in Europe towards a somewhat *lower* share of goods consumption in GDP would seem to be an important contributory explanation. The contrast to the growing discrepancy between Europe and the United States in the volume of work done in distribution (see figure 6.4) is very striking. It underlines the central importance of the growing difference in aggregate work done in Europe and the United States, expressed in terms of GDP per capita, in explaining differences in employment in distribution in Europe and the United States.

This section highlighted the central importance of the level of consumption in shaping differences in distribution employment between the United States and Europe. The total volume of work in distribution per capita is much higher in the United States because per capita consumption is much higher (compare Gordon 2004). This discrepancy has grown as European productivity in distribution (as best we can measure it) caught up to American levels in the 1970s and then as consumption per capita in the United States drew further ahead in the 1990s. By contrast the gap in the share of employment in distribution was both smaller and much more stable and appears to reflect systematic structural features making for a low share of goods consumption in Europe, with productivity levels in distribution relative to the national average playing a relatively minor role.

4. Conclusions

The services-employment gap has been concentrated in distribution and community and personal services and particular attention has been focused on the role of labor market rigidities in inhibiting the growth of the low-wage services. We have directed attention to the distribution sector as a major employer of low-wage labor. Our detailed examination in section 2 of the wages and employment in retailing suggests that differences between the United States and Europe are not consistently in the direction anticipated by the rigidities/wage-compression hypothesis. For all countries we find substantial wage penalties for workers in retail compared to workers in other sectors of the economy. The United States is not markedly out of line with other countries. This also applies to the low skilled at the lower end of the earnings distribution, where one might expect differences between economies with rigid and economies with flexible labor markets to be strongest. As indicated by the comparatively small retail wage penalties for these groups, there is some support for wage compression at the very low end of the wage distribution as a ubiquitous phenomenon, rather than one specific to allegedly less flexible European labor markets. In contrast to the only moderate wage differentials at the bottom of the retail pay distribution, there is a significant and increasing wage penalty for the high skilled and highly paid in this sector in all five countries.

At the more macroeconomic level, European distribution did suffer from a rapid growth in product wages and a profit squeeze in the 1970s, and this may have held back employment growth in France in particular, but in the 1990s productivity grew considerably faster in U.S. distribution and European product wages grew relatively slowly. This provides no support for the idea that high wages have forced productivity improvement and harmed job creation in services. Finally we showed that the much lower European level of goods consumption per head of the population was the dominating influence in explaining the much lower levels of employment than in U.S. distribution. Even in France, where it appears that, at least until the turn of the century, labor productivity in distribution was somewhat higher than in the United States, this factor is much less important in explaining low employment than is low goods consumption. This suggests that the lower *level* of services employment in Europe may be more importantly explained by the economy-wide influences restraining aggregate hours worked and thus aggregate consumption, rather than specific labor-market constraints on the service sector itself. In similar vein, it is the low share of goods consumption in GDP that is the main explanation of the lower European *share* of retailing in total work.

Appendix: Decomposition of Quantile-Regression Wage Differentials between Sectors

We are interested in the industry wage differential of retail services relative to the aggregate economy. The raw sector differential can partly be explained by specific characteristics of workers in this sector compared to the aggregate and partly by the fact that workers' (observed) characteristics are priced differently in different sectors of the economy. In order to shed some light on the relative magnitude of these alternative explanatory factors, a decomposition technique in the spirit of the well-known Blinder (1973) and Oaxaca (1973) approach is employed. In what follows, the raw retail differential is spread into three components: a rewards, a characteristics, and an interaction effect.

Let the usual wage-equation model be described for a specific sector of the economy as

$$y = x'\beta + \varepsilon \tag{1}$$

and correspondingly for the aggregate as

$$Y = X'B + E. \tag{2}$$

Then define

$$\Delta\hat\beta := \hat\beta - \hat B \quad and \quad \Delta\bar x := \bar x - \bar X, \tag{3}$$

where the vectors $\bar x$ and $\bar X$ contain average values of the regressor in the sector and in the aggregate, respectively. A sensible decomposition of the raw earnings differential is given by

$$\bar y - \bar Y := \bar x\hat\beta - \bar X\hat B$$
$$= \underbrace{\bar X \cdot \Delta\hat\beta}_{\text{rewards effect}} + \underbrace{\Delta\bar x \cdot \hat B}_{\substack{\text{characteristics}\\\text{effect}}} + \underbrace{\Delta\bar x \cdot \Delta\hat\beta}_{\substack{\text{interaction}\\\text{effect}}} \tag{4}$$

To illustrate the decomposition consider the simple case, where earnings are explained by a qualification dummy variable only, which takes a 0 value for low skilled and 1 for skilled workers. Assume that remuneration of low-skilled workers is identical across sectors, so that the regression constant can be disregarded for the ease of exposition. Assume further that, compared to the aggregate, the average worker in the sector is more qualified and the skill premium is higher in the sector, hence $\bar x > \bar X > 0$ and $\beta > B > 0$, respectively. It is evident that under these circumstances the wage differential is favorable to the sector. The situation is depicted in figure 6.A1.

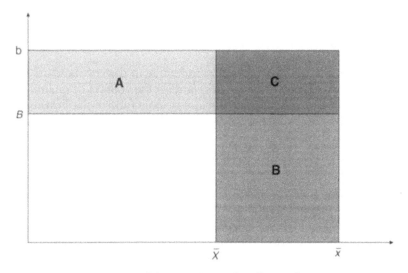

Fig. 6.A1. Decomposition of the Raw Sectoral Differential

The total wage bonus of the sector is equivalent to the sum of the shaded areas. The total effect can be divided into

- the rewards effect (area A) or $\bar{X} \cdot \Delta\beta$; given our assumptions, the rewards effect here indicates a pay bonus for the sector even if the share of qualified workers is the same as in the aggregate economy;
- the characteristics effect (area B) or $\Delta x \cdot B$; even if the group of qualified workers were paid the same as in the aggregate, there would be an advantage to the sector because of its favorable skill structure;
- the interaction effect (area C) or $\Delta x \cdot \Delta\beta$; in the context here, this effect indicates an earnings advantage for the sector because there are relatively more high-paid qualified workers in the sector and these workers are doing especially well compared to the aggregate.

In contrast to the example given here, the negative rewards and/or the characteristics effect could lead to a negative wage differential, or a "wage penalty" for a specific sector. This is what can be expected for retail services.

Note that the sign of the rewards (characteristics) effect is determined by $\Delta\beta$ (or Δx, respectively) given that $\bar{X} > 0$ and $B > 0$, which has been assumed here. If the rewards and characteristics effects have the same signs, the interaction effect is positive. Consider the case where both are negative; hence the sector has a relatively low educated workforce and the skill premium is less than in the aggregate. Clearly this would lead to a wage penalty for the sector. The interaction effect, however, would be positive, since the sector penalty is "reduced" by the fact that the sector has a relatively low share of workers in the category with a negative differential compared to the aggregate. In other words, the interaction effects correct for a double counting of the sector's disadvantage that would otherwise occur.

Application of the decomposition technique in case of standard OLS (or TOBIT) estimation is straightforward. In the context of quantile regressions, however, the approach requires some further clarifications.

Consider the quantile regression model

$$y_i = x_i'B^\theta + \varepsilon_i^\theta \quad with \quad Q_\theta(\varepsilon_i^\theta | x_i) = 0 \tag{5}$$
$$and \quad Y_i = X_i'B^\theta + E_i^\theta \quad with \quad Q_\theta(\varepsilon_i^\theta | x_i) = 0,$$

where Q_θ is the θ-th quantile function, β^θ and B^θ are the quantile-specific vector of coefficients, and ε^θ and E^θ denote error terms.[22] Replacing the vector of explanatory variables in equation (5) by the corresponding

---

[22] In case of median regression ($\theta = 0.5$), the estimates $\hat{\beta}$ and $\hat{B}$ are obtained by minimizing $\Sigma_j |\varepsilon_j|$ and $\Sigma_i |E_i|$, respectively.

sample means gives the expectation for the θ-quantile of dependent variable y_i conditional to average characteristics

$$Q_\theta(y_i|x_i = \bar{x}) = \bar{x}'\beta^\theta \quad and \quad Q_\theta(Y_i|X_i = \bar{X}) = \bar{X}'B^\theta. \tag{6}$$

As an example consider the case with log wages as dependent variable and years of schooling as the only regressor. Assume that the average duration of schooling is $\bar{x}$ in the sector and $\bar{X}$ in the aggregate. Inserting these values into equation (5) yields the expected median for workers *with average years of schooling* as $\bar{x}\hat{\beta}^{0.5}$ in the sector and $\bar{X}\hat{B}^{0.5}$ in the aggregate economy. Note that in general this expectation is not identical to the unconditional median:

$$Q_\theta(y_i) \neq Q_\theta(y_i|x_i = \bar{x}) \quad and \quad Q_\theta(Y_i) \neq Q_\theta(Y_i|X_i = \bar{X}).$$

By contrast, for standard (mean) regression the following relationship holds: $\bar{y} = E(y_i) = E(y_i|\bar{x}) = \bar{x}'\hat{\beta}_{OLS}$ (and similar for the aggregate).

To summarize these considerations, the decomposition approach can be applied to quantile estimation results as well. However, one has to stress the fact that the results are conditional to average characteristics, a restriction that is not necessary in the context of standard estimation like OLS.[23]

Let us now define the conditional θ-th quantile wages in logs as

$$\bar{y}^\theta := Q_\theta(y_i \mid x_i = \bar{x}) \quad and \quad \bar{Y}^\theta := Q_\theta(Y_i \mid X_i = \bar{X}).$$

Then one can calculate the *conditional sector wage differential* at quantile θ as $CWD^\theta = \bar{y}^\theta - \bar{Y}^\theta$. For example, for θ = 0.5 the indicator $CWD^{0.5}$ compares median wages of workers with typical (average) characteristics in the sector to median wages of a group of workers with typical characteristics in the aggregate.

By applying the same decomposition techniques as for the mean wage differential one obtains the breakdown that is used in our empirical study:

$$CWD^\theta = \bar{y}^\theta - \bar{Y}^\theta := \bar{x}\beta^\theta - \bar{X}\hat{B}^\theta$$

$$= \underbrace{\bar{X}\cdot\Delta\beta^\theta}_{\text{rewards effect}} + \underbrace{\Delta\bar{x}\cdot\hat{B}^\theta}_{\substack{\text{characteristics}\\\text{effect}}} + \underbrace{\Delta\bar{x}\cdot\Delta\beta^\theta}_{\substack{\text{interaction}\\\text{effect}}}. \tag{7}$$

---

[23] In case of only minor differences between the conditional and unconditional quantiles, however, the specific restraints in the interpretation of the quantile regression approach can be neglected.

CHAPTER 7

Why Was Europe Left at the Station When America's Productivity Locomotive Departed?

Robert J. Gordon

INTRODUCTION

AFTER A HALF century following World War II of catching up to the level of U.S. productivity, since 1995 Europe has experienced a productivity growth slowdown while the United States has experienced a marked acceleration. As a result, just in the past eight years, Europe has already lost about one-fifth of its previous 1950–95 gain in output per hour relative to the United States. Starting from 71 percent of the U.S. level of productivity in 1870, Europe fell back to 44 percent in 1950, caught up to 94 percent in 1995, and has now fallen back to 85 percent. What were the causes of this stunning setback?

This chapter argues that the focus on policy reform in Europe has been too narrowly on the deregulation of product and labor markets. A broader set of social choices matters for productivity, and some of these differences between the United States and Europe may be irreversible. Much of the surprising acceleration of U.S. productivity growth since 1995 originates in the trade sector, particularly retail trade, and goes far beyond the use of information and communication technology (ICT). The retail sector in the United States has been revolutionized by the "big box" format epitomized by Wal-Mart, and perhaps the most important factor of production in making this format possible is a large plot of virgin land that is much more widely available in the sprawling American metropolitan areas than in the tightly regulated European environment of land-use planning and protection of old central-city retail zones. The American explosion of productivity growth in retailing calls attention to basic lifestyle choices that constitute yet another form of "American exceptionalism." While the American form of metropolitan organization may promote productivity growth, Europeans are rightly skeptical of unmeasured costs of low urban density in America as promoted by explicit government policies. Europeans decry side effects of the American system that may promote productivity without creating consumer welfare, including excess energy use, pollution, and time spent in traffic congestion.

A second set of major differences originates in what could be called "European exceptionalism." As Phelps has argued, European growth is still retarded by corporatist institutions that are designed to protect incumbent producers and inhibit new entry. European cultural attitudes inhibit the development of ambition and independence of teenagers and young adults, who are cradled in subsides such as free tuition for higher education, while American teenagers are expected to get out into the marketplace, work, and contribute real money to their own college education. The differing behavior of productivity growth since 1995 helps to call attention to differences between Europe and the United States that have long been present but seemed unimportant during the five decades prior to 1995 when Europe was rapidly catching up to the American level of productivity.

A third issue raised by the U.S. post-1995 productivity revival has been an explosion of innovation in the production and use of ICT. The past decade has witnessed a growing concentration of innovative activity in the United States, not only in computer hardware and software, but also in pharmaceuticals and biotech research. The sources of this innovative advantage call attention to European shortcomings that cannot be easily cured by deregulation. These include the continuing U.S. advantage of a unified market unincumbered by differences in customs, language, or electric plugs; the competitive U.S. system of private and public universities; the system of peer review that guides U.S. government support of research; well-enforced patent protection; a dynamic capital market able to fund promising start-ups; and the welcome extended by the United States to foreign graduate students in all fields and especially to highly skilled immigrant engineers.

It is important at the outset not only to set out the topic issues discussed in this chapter, but also those that are outside its purview. We have nothing to say here about the well-trodden issues in the functioning of the European labor market, deregulation of labor markets past, present, or future, and specific issues involving product market regulations. Also, while this chapter highlights lifestyle and cultural differences, it does not attempt a comprehensive comparisons of standards of living, and its several dimensions of praise for the American system should not be interpreted as an endorsement for well-known failures such as the lack of universal government-financed health care in the United States.

The chapter begins with basic data on productivity growth in Europe and the United States over selected intervals since 1870 and displays the

Table 7.1

Growth Rate and GDP per Hour Worked, United States versus Europe, 1870–2003

	Annual Average Growth Rate			Europe Level (US = 100)	
	US	Europe	US – Europe		
				1870	71
1870–1913	1.92	1.55	0.37	1913	61
1913–1950	2.48	1.56	0.92	1950	44
1950–1973	2.77	4.77	–2.00	1973	79
1973–1995	1.48	2.25	–0.77	1995	94
1995–2003	2.33	1.15	1.18	2003	85

Source: 1870–1990, Maddison 2001, tables E-8 and E-9, pp. 352–53; 1990–2003, OECD 2003; table 13.

relative *level* of European productivity, falling behind until 1950, catching up until 1995, and then falling behind since then. Data on differences at the sectoral level are then displayed, highlighting the role in the U.S. revival of ICT-using industries, especially retailing. The chapter then continues with a comparison of the retailing environment in the United States versus Europe, followed by attention to broader cultural issues. It concludes with a multipart comparison of the stimuli and barriers to technical change and innovation on the two sides of the Atlantic.

Data on Transatlantic Productivity Differences:
  Growth Rates and Levels

The long history of productivity growth and levels is displayed in table 7.1. The data from 1870 to 1990 come from Maddison (2001) and refer to the total economy, that is, real GDP per hour. These data are updated for 1990–2003 with OECD data on the private economy. While productivity growth in the private economy is usually slightly faster than in the total economy, this is true both in the United States and in Europe, and so the break in coverage at 1990 should not affect our main point of concern, that is, transatlantic differences in growth rates and their implications for relative levels.[1]

[1] The Maddison data refer to 12 countries weighted by relative GDP; these are the 15 members of the EU minus Greece, Portugal, and Spain. The post-1990 OECD data refer to all 15 EU members. While the Maddison data are available through 1998, he provides no intermediate data between 1990 and 1998, and we choose 1995 as a preferable break date that highlights the starting point of the transatlantic productivity growth divergence.

TABLE 7.2

Annual Rate of Change of Output, Hours, and Output per Hour, United States versus Europe, 1990–2002

	1990–95	1995–2000	2000–2002	1995–2002	1995–2002 vs. 1990–95
United States					
Output	2.43	4.01	1.34	3.25	0.82
Hours	1.24	2.03	−1.00	1.17	−0.07
Output					
per hour	1.14	1.97	2.33	2.07	0.93
European Union					
Output	1.61	2.63	1.28	2.24	0.63
Hours	−0.85	1.21	0.40	0.98	1.83
Output					
per hour	2.46	1.42	0.89	1.27	−1.19

Source: McGuckin and van Ark 2003, 5. U.S. hours 2000–2002 revised by author as discussed in text. U.S. GDP figures 1990–2002 were revised in December 2003, and were taken from the BEA web site in February 2004.

The left section of table 7.1 shows average annual percentage growth rates of productivity in the United States, Europe, and the U.S.-European difference, for selected intervals since 1870. The familiar story is that Europe fell behind from 1870 to 1950, then caught up after 1950. Less familiar is the extent to which Europe has fallen behind again after 1995. As shown in the right section of table 7.1, Europe had almost closed the gap in productivity *levels* by 1995, but its slow growth since then has caused its relative productivity level to slip back from 94 to 85 percent, eroding nine points of its 50-point catch-up between 1950 and 1995.

A closer look at the divergence is provided by table 7.2, which contrasts the 1990–95 period with 1995–2002 and provides a uniform treatment of the total economy.[2] All the data in table 7.2 are taken from a recent Conference Board pamphlet by McGuckin and van Ark (2003) except for the incorporation of the latest revised U.S. real GDP data, and also an improved approximation of U.S. hours growth over the last two years, 2000–2002.[3] The initial European slowdown evident in data

[2] Table 7.1 could have been based on post-1990 data from table 7.2, but this would have prevented us from using 2003 data that further extends the period of U.S. divergence.

[3] The McGuckin and van Ark data show a decline in hours at a rate of only −0.31 percent per annum during 2000–2002 and do not reflect the historical revisions to working hours released by the Bureau of Labor Statistics on August 7, 2003. Unfortunately, the annual series on total domestic hours of work compiled by the BEA has not been

for 1995–2000 worsened with data for 2000–2002, whereas the United States experienced accelerating productivity growth at the cost of declining hours of work during 2000–2002.

The right-hand column of table 7.2 displays the *change* in output, hours, and output per hour between 1990–95 and 1995–2002. Surprisingly, the post-1995 acceleration in output growth was almost the same in Europe as in the United States, 0.63 versus 0.82 percentage points, respectively. Most of the literature on the failure of Europe to achieve a post-1995 productivity growth acceleration treats Europe as overregulated and stuck in the mud. On the contrary, Europe's performance in hours of work was the diametric opposite of the United States, accelerating by almost two percentage points compared to pre-1995, whereas there was a slight deceleration of hours growth in the United States. As a result, the productivity change between 1990–95 and 1995–2002 was the mirror image of the hours change, with an acceleration of almost 1 percent per annum for the United States and a deceleration of more than 1 percent for Europe.

Understanding Europe: Distinguishing the Stars from the Basket Cases

If the decomposition of growth sources is a booming academic industry on the west side of the Atlantic, laments about Europe's performance are the corresponding concern of academics on the east side of the Atlantic. While the United States enjoyed a productivity growth revival after 1995, as we have seen in tables 7.1 and 7.2, a growth *deceleration* occurred in numerous European countries as well as in the European Union as a whole. This Europe–United States contrast seems to fly in the face of the widespread evidence (Oliner and Sichel 2000, 2002; Jorgenson and Stiroh 2000) that investment in information and communications technology (ICT) was the basic source of the U.S. achievement. How could ICT be the main source of the U.S. growth revival, while Europe fell behind? Business firms, not to mention university professors, use the same PCs and Microsoft software everywhere in Europe, and Europe is widely acknowledged to be ahead in the use of mobile telephones.

Part of the European puzzle is resolved when we recognize that heterogeneity among European countries is more pronounced than the difference between the European Union and the United States. Numerous

---

released for 2002. Our estimate of total hours of work is based on multiplying together two series. The first, from the BEA web site, is total domestic persons engaged (NIPA table 6.10), and the second, from the BLS web site, is weekly hours per production employee.

studies have shown a relatively strong positive correlation between MFP growth and measures of ICT intensity, for example, the ratio of ICT expenditure to GDP or the change in PC intensity per 100 inhabitants over the 1990s. In such comparisons, numerous countries achieve higher MFP growth rates than the United States over the 1990s, including Ireland, Finland, Sweden, Denmark, Norway, Canada, and Australia. Some, but not all, of these countries surpass the United States in PC intensity or in the share of ICT expenditure. What differs most between Europe and the United States is the low level of PC adoption and ICT expenditure in the "olive belt" ranging from Portugal and Spain in the west to Italy and Greece in the east.[4] The contrast between the Nordic and olive-belt countries suggests irreverent comments about how Scandinavians in their dark winters find PCs more appealing than do olive-belt residents cavorting on their sunny beaches.

Contrasts within Europe also suggest that perhaps we could try to disaggregate the United States to provide a more appropriate comparison with Europe. Silicon Valley could be compared to Ireland and Finland, New England could be compared to Denmark and Sweden, Texas to Australia, and the midwestern heartland to France and Germany. What stands out in this suggestion is the absence of any U.S. equivalent for the European olive-belt countries. Political borders are a product of history, and perhaps the United States would look more like Europe, which includes the olive belt, if we were to aggregate U.S. data with those for the tequila belt, that is, Mexico.

The Industry Decomposition of the Europe–United States Difference

A comprehensive recent study by O'Mahony and van Ark (2003) provides a few answers at a more formal level. As shown in table 7.3, O'Mahony and van Ark support the widespread impression that, after 1995, America accelerated while Europe fell behind. The top line in table 7.3 shows that U.S. productivity growth accelerated by 1.1 percent in the late 1990s while European growth decelerated by 0.9 percent, a mirror-image performance. An initial caveat is that Europe looks much better when the entire decade of the 1990s is aggregated into a single 1990–2000 period; European productivity growth averages out to 2.0 percent per year, considerably higher than U.S. growth of 1.6 percent per year.

The O'Mahony and van Ark study allows us to trace the location of productivity growth accelerations and decelerations to particular indus-

---

[4] Scatter plots supporting these correlations between MFP growth and computer intensity are presented in Bartelsman et al. 2002, figs. 8 and 9.

TABLE 7.3

Labor Productivity by Industry Group, United States versus Europe, 1990–95 versus 1995–2001 (annual growth rates in percent)

	United States			European Union		
	1990– 1995	1995– 2001	1990– 2001	1990– 1995	1995– 2001	1990– 2001
Total economy	1.1	2.2	1.6	2.3	1.7	2.0
ICT-producing industries	8.1	10.0	8.7	5.9	7.5	6.5
ICT-using industries	1.2	4.7	2.9	2.0	1.9	1.9
Non-ICT industries	0.3	–0.2	0.0	1.2	0.5	0.8

Source: O'Mahony and van Ark 2003, table III.3.

trial sectors, divided into ICT-producing, ICT-using, and non-ICT industries. There has been no productivity revival in U.S. industries that are classified as neither ICT-producing nor ICT-using, and this is confirmed on the bottom line of table 7.3 for the United States. These industries are also the core of the European problem, exhibiting a deceleration in the late 1990s greater than for the European economy as a whole. Surprisingly, ICT-producing industries exhibited both higher productivity growth and a greater acceleration in the late 1990s in Europe than the United States. The core of the U.S. success story appears to have been in *ICT-using* industries, that is, retail, wholesale, and securities trading industries.

A separate analysis by van Ark, Inklaar, and McGuckin (2003, fig. 2a) shows that literally *all* of the productivity growth differential of the United States over Europe in the late 1990s came from these three industries, with retail contributing about 55 percent of the differential, wholesale 24 percent, and securities trade 20 percent. The remaining industries had small positive or negative differentials, netting out to zero. As might have been expected, the U.S.-European differential was negative in telecom services, reflecting U.S. backwardness in mobile phones.

THE RETAILING PHENOMENON

We know that U.S. productivity growth accelerated after 1995, and we can speculate about the aspects of ICT innovation that helped this acceleration to occur. But the simultaneous acceleration in productivity growth and in ICT investment as a share of GDP amounts, at least in part, to circumstantial evidence. Questions can be raised about the link between ICT innovation and the productivity revival, given evidence of a further acceleration of productivity growth in the years after 2000, a period when ICT investment collapsed. Other aspects of innovation beyond ICT may be as important as ICT in explaining the outstanding productivity performance since 1995 of the U.S. retail trade sector.

This performance did not occur evenly across the board in retailing but rather was concentrated in "large stores offering a wide array of goods accompanied by low prices and relatively high use of self-service systems" (Sieling, Friedman, and Dumas 2001, 10). A complementary finding by Foster, Haltiwanger, and Krizan (2002) based on a study of a large set of individual retail establishments shows that *all* of retail productivity growth (not just the revival but the entire measured amount of productivity growth over the decade of the 1990s) can be attributed to more productive entering establishments that displaced much less productive existing establishments. The average establishment that continued in business exhibited zero productivity growth, and this despite the massive investment of the retail industry in ICT equipment that presumably went to both old and new establishments. In the Foster results, productivity growth reflects the greater efficiency of newly opened stores, and the Sieling comment implies that most of these highly efficient new stores were large discount operations, the proverbial "big boxes" like Wal-Mart, Home Depot, Best Buy, Circuit City, and new large supermarkets.

The Sieling and Foster findings seem to conflict with the Oliner and Sichel (2000, 2002) finding that, at least for the period through 1999, all of the productivity revival in retailing was achieved by purchasing new computers, software, and communications equipment.[5] All retailers, whether new establishments of the 1990s or older establishments of the 1980s or prior decades, have adopted ICT technology. Bar-code readers have become universal in new and old stores. It is likely that the productivity revival in retailing associated with newly built big-box stores involves far more than the use of computers, including large size, economies of scale, efficient design to allow large-volume unloading from delivery trucks, stacking of merchandise on tall racks with fork-lift trucks, and large-scale purchases taken by customers to vehicles in large adjacent parking lots.

As we have seen, the van Ark, Inklaar, and McGuckin (2003) results identify the retail sector as a major factor explaining Europe's poor performance in the late 1990s. Just as the U.S. retailing sector has achieved efficiency gains for reasons not directly related to computers, including

---

[5] A concise summary of the Oliner-Sichel findings for 1973–95, contrasted with both 1995–99 and 1995–2002, appears in Gordon 2003, table 10, p. 252.

physical investments in a new type of big-box organization, so we can suggest in parallel that Europe has fallen back because European firms are much less free to develop the big-box retail formats.[6] Impediments include land-use regulations that prevent the carving out of new "greenfield" sites for big-box stores in suburban and exurban locations, shop-closing regulations that restrict the revenue potential of new investments, congestion in central-city locations that are near the nodes of Europe's extensive urban public transit systems, and restrictive labor rules that limit flexibility in organizing the workplace and make it expensive to hire and fire workers with the near-total freedom to which U.S. firms are accustomed.

A complementary interpretation is provided in a cross-country study of productivity differences in the service sector by the McKinsey Global Institute (1992). Their set of policy recommendations (chap. 2-D, pp. 13–14) seem as relevant today as when written a decade ago and echo the previous paragraph by pointing to impediments to the development of modern retailing in some but not all European countries. European policymakers have adopted a set of policies that encourage high density and a concentration of retailing activity in the central city. The development of modern big-box retailing formats has been hindered by these policies and the resulting high cost of real estate and the complex and precarious process of obtaining planning approval for large plots of land.

An issue identified by McKinsey is the role of resale price maintenance policies that in the United States assure new competitors that they will be able to attain the same access to suppliers at roughly the same prices as existing retailers. In contrast, in some European countries producers refuse to discount to new, high-volume, low-cost retailing formats in order to protect smaller high-cost merchants. In some European countries, regulations directly prohibit the entry of large-scale stores or limit store opening days and hours, thus preventing large stores from fully amortizing their investments.

A partial survey of other cross-country studies reveals a disappointing lack of specific conclusions at the level of the van Ark et al. and McKinsey studies. The typical study conducts a growth accounting exercise, concludes that Europe has lagged behind the United States in adopting ICT technology to a greater or lesser degree, does not trace differences in behavior to specific industries, and concludes with a general plea for

---

[6] Any generalizations here about "Europe" must be qualified by differences across countries. The Germans until recently were notorious for restrictive shop-closing hours, while the French firm Carrefour and the Swedish firm Ikea are innovators in "big box" retailing formats.

unspecified structural reforms. Among the studies that fit this characterization are Colecchia and Schreyer (2001), Daveri (2002), Rhine-Westphalia Institute for Economic Research (2002), and Vijselaar and Albers (2002).

ECONOMIC INSTITUTIONS AND CULTURE

A refreshing contrast is provided by Phelps (2003), who takes a broader view of economic institutions that promote economic "dynamism" and those that suppress it. His analysis of dynamism starts from Schumpeter's concept of "creative destruction." He adds to Schumpeter's emphasis on entrepreneurship an equal if not greater emphasis on "financiership," that is, the ability of financial markets to steer finance to worthy innovations. The greater success of the United States in encouraging innovation is attributed in part to its greater emphasis on venture capital and initial public equity offerings (IPO) than in Europe.

Europe: Corporatism and Spoiled Youth

In Phelps's view, the relatively poor economic performance of continental Europe results from *both* the underdevelopment of capitalist institutions like venture capital and equity finance, and the overdevelopment on corporatist institutions that suppress innovation and competition. These corporatist institutions impose "penalties, impediments, prohibitions, and mandates . . . generally intended to damp down creative destruction." Among these impediments are licenses and permissions to set up a new plant or firm, the need to consult with workers on changes in the mix of products or plants, and employment protection legislation. Because these institutions are designed to dampen down the changes inherent in "unbridled capitalism," they also lead to the underdevelopment of the stock market, resulting in lower ratios of stock market valuation to GDP in continental Europe than in the United States and other less corporatist economies like Britain, Canada, and Australia.

Phelps provides a complementary analysis of cultural differences between Europe and the United States. Europeans view with disdain the money-grubbing Americans with their out-sized rewards for CEOs and successful entrepreneurs. American children begin to work earlier than European children, earning babysitting money in their early teens, and working in fast-food outlets while in high school, and are forced to work during college, in contrast to European youth who "free ride" on government-paid college tuition and stipends. Phelps concludes that Europe has developed a culture of "dependency" that "breeds an unduly large share of young people who have little sense of independence and are unwilling to strike out on their own." He might have added that high levels of long-term youth unemployment discourage independence and encourage young adults to live with their parents in their 20s and, in Italy, into their 30s.

Caveats

Europeans do not take these criticisms lying down. Yes, they admit that high youth unemployment, low labor force participation, and a generation of young adults living with their parents represents an economic and social failure. But they are quick to criticize aspects of American economic and political institutions that, while making it easy for Wal-Mart and Home Depot to find the land to build thousands of big-box stores, have offsetting disadvantages.

Europeans find abhorrent the hundreds of billions, or even trillions, that Americans have spent on extra highways and extra energy to support the dispersion of the population into huge metropolitan areas spreading over hundreds or even thousands of square miles, in many cases with few transport options other than the automobile. Productivity data do not give Europe sufficient credit for the convenience benefits of frequent bus, subway, and train (including TGV) public transit. Excessive American dispersion is viewed as a response to misguided public policies, especially subsidies to interstate highways in vast amounts relative to public transport, local zoning measures in some suburbs that prohibit residential land allocations below a fixed size, for example, two acres, and the infamous and politically untouchable deduction of mortgage interest payments from income tax.

Europeans enjoy shopping at small individually owned shops on lively central-city main streets and pedestrian arcades, and recoil with distaste from the ubiquitous and cheerless American strip malls and big-box retailers—although Carrefour, Ikea, and others provide American-like options in some European cities. To counter the effects of American land-use regulations that create overly dispersed metropolitan areas, Europeans counter with their own brand of land-use rules that preserve greenbelts and inhibit growth of suburban and exurban retailing. A more complete consideration of these differences leads to the conclusion that GDP data understate the Europe/United States ratio of both productivity and real GDP per capita (see Gordon 2004).

INCENTIVES FOR INNOVATION IN THE UNITED STATES AND EUROPE

Thus far we have concluded that ICT investment has been exaggerated as the sole source of the U.S. productivity revival of the late 1990s, and it is even more clear that lack of ICT investment has been wrongly cited as the main source of the contrasting productivity performance in Europe. The main U.S. advantage was in retail and wholesale trade, where the expansion of new establishments raised productivity growth for reasons going well beyond ICT investment, and the ability of Europe to expand in tandem was hampered by regulations and institutions that have long been cited as a drag on European economic growth.

Albeit narrowly based in computer hardware, at least in the official statistics, the apparent "rupture" or discontinuity in the rate of technical change in the mid-1990s forces us to inquire as to its sources and lessons for understanding the economic history of the United States and other nations. America is now almost universally believed to have surged to the forefront in most of the ICT industries. But our overview of the stimuli and barriers to technological change and innovation focuses not just on computer hardware but more broadly on software, telecommunications, pharmaceuticals, and biotech. Why did the United States have a comparative or absolute advantage in innovative capacity in the late 1990s, more than a century after its initial leadership in the invention of electricity and its early lead in the exploitation of the internal combustion engine?

National Technological Leadership: General Considerations

The mid-1990s discontinuity of technical change in the United States was not predicted in advance, although its significance was spotted almost immediately by *Business Week* and some other astute observers.[7] A decade earlier it had been "Japan as Number One," and briefly the market value of Japanese equities exceeded that of American equities. Rosenberg (1986, 25) perceptively generalizes about the difficulty of forecasting the consequences of inventions in advance: "A disinterested observer who happened to be passing by at Kitty Hawk on that fateful day in 1903 might surely be excused if he did not walk away with visions of 747s or C-5As in his head." The great success of Japanese firms in dominating many leading technologies in the 1980s did not appear to give them any head start in dominating the new technologies of the 1990s. Rosenberg points to the failure of carriage makers to play any role in the development of the automobile, or even the failure of steam locomotive makers to participate in the development of the diesel locomotive. Thus it is perhaps not surprising that Japanese electronics com-

---

[7] Most notably Edward Yardeni, now the chief economist of Deutsche Bank Alex Brown, who early in the 1990s predicted both the stock market boom and the revival of productivity growth.

panies did not participate to any great extent in the particular interplay of chip-making technology and software development that created the Internet and the post-1995 technical acceleration in computer hardware.

Many inventions initially created to solve a narrow problem (for instance, the steam engine was initially invented to pump water out of flooded mines) turn out to have widespread further uses that are not initially foreseen. Major inventions spawn numerous complementary developments; while the initial motivation for the internal combustion engine was to improve the performance-to-weight ratio of the steam engine, it made possible not only motor transport and air transport, but such complementary developments as the suburb, supermarket, super-highway, and the tropical vacation industry. In turn, the complementary inventions raise the consumer surplus associated with the invention, an effect that may continue for a long time. The invention of the Internet is just one of many by-products of the invention of electricity that raise the consumer surplus of that initial major invention.[8]

The literature on technology distinguishes between the initial invention and its subsequent development and diffusion. A long-standing puzzle in the retardation of British economic growth after the 1870s is the fact that many inventions initially made by British inventors were brought to commercial success in the United States, Japan, and elsewhere. This issue of who captures the fruits of innovation suggests that the British were not alone in losing out. The U.S. invention of videotape was followed by exploitation of the consumer VCR market that was almost entirely achieved by Japanese companies. The Finnish company Nokia took over leadership in mobile phones from Motorola. Within any economy there are winners and losers as upstart companies (Intel, Microsoft) seize the advantage in developing technology while leaving older competitors (IBM, Wang, Digital Equipment, Xerox) behind.

While predicting technological developments in advance is exceedingly difficult, there is an ample literature that points to particular national characteristics that help to explain, at least in retrospect, why particular inventions and industries came to be dominated by particular countries.[9] Perhaps the one generalization that spans most industries is the role of the product cycle. No matter what the causes of initial national leadership, technology eventually diffuses from the leading nations to other nations that may have lower labor costs. It is beyond the scope of this discussion to explain why some nations, for example, Ko-

[8] An explicit analysis of the effect of complementary inventions on the consumer surplus of the initial invention is provided by Bresnahan and Gordon (1997, 7–11).

[9] The generalizations in the next several paragraphs select among the more important points made by Mowery and Nelson (1999a).

rea, Taiwan, and Singapore, seem to have done so much better than other nations, for example, Brazil or Bangladesh, in combining technological duplication with an advantage, at least initially, in labor costs, in industries ranging from automobiles to chip, computer, and disk-drive manufacturing.

The Traditional Sources of U.S. Advantage

According to the standard data compiled by Maddison and others, summarized for Europe (but not individual countries) in table 7.1, the level of output per hour in the United States moved ahead of that in the United Kingdom in the late nineteenth century and has remained in first place among the major developed nations ever since. An extensive literature on the sources of U.S. superiority (e.g., Wright 1990) identifies national advantages both in the supply of resources and in national characteristics of demand. The United States achieved initial leadership in petrochemicals in part because of its abundant supply of cheap domestic petroleum, while its leadership in machine tools was the result of its early adoption of mass production methods, which in turn reflected its relative scarcity of labor and its large internal market. In turn mass production, together with long distances, cheap land, and the low density of urban development help to explain why the United States achieved such an enormous early lead in automobile production and ownership in the 1920s. In turn the mass market for automobiles fed back into a rapidly increasing demand for gasoline and stimulated further developments in petroleum and petrochemical manufacturing.

However, it is less clear that America's large domestic market provided a universal source of advantage throughout the history of technological development over the last two centuries. Between 1870 and 1914 flows of goods, capital, and immigrants were notably free, and trade could create international markets on the scale of the U.S. domestic markets, as demonstrated by German dominance in chemicals. After 1960 Japan rose to prominence and even domination in one industry after another, with export markets providing the scale that was lacking, at least initially, at home. Several small countries, for example, the Netherlands and Sweden, have remained close to the productivity frontier over the past century despite their small relative size.

Educational Attainment and University Research

Close integration of industrial R&D and university research is credited with German domination of the chemical products industry between the 1870s and early 1920s, as well as German and Swiss leadership in the development of pharmaceuticals in the early part of the 20th century. More generally, a rise in educational attainment is one of the sources of rising output per hour. While the first cited role of the education system in technological development is the rise of the German chemical industry after 1870, a set of relatively uncoordinated policies at the state and local level resulted in the United States achieving the first universal secondary education between 1910 and 1940 (Goldin 1998) and the highest rate of participation in college education after World War II.

Even in the dismal days of American pessimism during the years of the 1972–95 productivity slowdown, it was widely recognized that America's private and state-supported research universities were its most successful export industry, at least as measured by its lead over other countries and its appeal for students from the rest of the world. The interplay among these research universities, government research grants, and private industry was instrumental in achieving American leadership in the IT industry, and it was no coincidence that Silicon Valley happened to be located next to Stanford University or that another concentration of IT companies in the hardware, software, and biotech industries was located in the Boston area near MIT and Harvard.

A U.S. educational advantage of possible importance is its early development of the graduate school of business and its continuing near-monopoly in this type of education. The mere existence of business schools did not provide any solution to the productivity slowdown of the 1970s and 1980s, and indeed the ongoing superiority of Japanese firms in automobiles and consumer electronics elicited the cynical joke in those years that "the secret advantage of the Japanese manufacturers is that they have no world-class business schools." While U.S. business schools were indeed weak in teaching such specialties as manufacturing production and quality control, they excelled in finance and general management strategy. These skills came into their own in the 1990s and interacted with the rise of the venture capital industry and Internet start-up companies; in the United States more than elsewhere there was a ready supply of thousands of well-educated MBAs, both knowledgeable about finance and receptive to a culture of innovation and risk-taking. Further, U.S. business schools have provided a wealth of talent to further develop U.S. worldwide dominance in investment banking, accounting, and management-consulting firms.

Government-Funded Military and Civilian Research

Ironically for a country that has been suspicious of government involvement, it is the United States that appears to demonstrate the closest links between government policy and technological leadership. The central role of government subsidies in achieving economic growth in the United States goes back to the last half of the nineteenth century, when free farmland under the Homestead Act encouraged immigration and the settlement of the frontier, while land grants to railroads promoted the building of infrastructure. Efficiency in the development of America's endowment of land and raw materials was fostered by agricultural experiment and research stations and by schools of mining established as part of America's then-new network of state universities and colleges. In the modern era research support from the National Institutes of Health and National Science Foundation are credited with postwar American leadership in pharmaceuticals and biomedical research, as well as basic research in the sciences. Defense-funded research and government-funded grants are credited with the early emergence of American leadership in semiconductors, computers, software, biotech, and the Internet itself. Government antitrust policy is credited with the emergence of a software industry largely independent of computer hardware manufacturers.

There are notable differences between the U.S. method of supporting higher education and research and that found in European countries like France, Germany, and the United Kingdom. First, the U.S. mix of private universities and those financed at the state and local level promotes competition and allows the top tier of the private university sector the budgetary freedom to pay high salaries, fund opulent research labs, and achieve the highest levels of quality, in turn attracting many top faculty members and graduate students from other countries. Second, much of U.S. central government research support is allocated through a peer-review system that favors a meritocracy of young, active researchers and discourages elitism and continuing support for senior professors whose best ideas are in the past. In Europe a much larger share of central government support to universities and research institutes goes to general budgetary support that tends to result in a more equal salary structure less prone to reward academic "stars" and also relies less on the periodic quality hurdle imposed by peer review. This set of differences is in addition to specific national shortcomings, for example, the hierarchical dominance of senior research professors in Germany.

Other Government Policies

Explicit government policies to encourage the development of specific industries by trade protection and financial subsidies may have been successful in helping to accelerate the rise of Japan and Korea to industrial success, but they have been less successful in the United States and Europe and indeed may have backfired in Japan in the past decade. The relevance of particular government policies, from protection to defense spending to antitrust, differs across industries sufficiently to discourage generalizations. In the industries that have received the most credit for the post-1995 productivity revival—semiconductors, computer hardware, and computer software—the most important aspect of public policy appears to have been the relatively unfocused support of research and training by the U.S. government. The literature on the American resurgence in semiconductor production as well as its continuing dominance in software also emphasizes the role of private enforcement of intellectual property rights and regulation of licensing agreements (see Bresnahan and Melerba 1999; Mowery 1999). The U.S. pharmaceutical industry initially gained an advantage through massive government support during World War II, health-related research support during most of the postwar period, and a long tradition of strong U.S. patent protection—patent protection was also strong in parts of Europe, but not in Italy and also not in Japan. U.S. drug companies also were able to make high profits, much of which was reinvested in R&D, as a result of high rents earned in the face of a fragmented health care system with no attempt by the government to place price or profit ceilings on drug companies (see Pisano 2002).

Another set of U.S. policies could be interpreted as "enforcement of benign neglect." The U.S. government took no action to arrest the erosion of state sales tax revenues as Internet e-commerce merchants sold items without charging any sales tax to customers. In effect, the freedom of e-commerce transactions from the burden of sales taxes amounted to government subsidization of shipping charges, since for e-commerce these usually amounted to roughly the same surcharge on listed prices as sales taxes at traditional bricks-and-mortar outlets. The U.S. government also maintained a zero-tariff regime for trade in electronic components, fostering large trade flows in both directions and a large U.S. trade deficit in IT manufacturing.

Capital Markets

In the 1980s American capital markets seemed to be a source of American industrial weakness, with their emphasis on short-run profit maximization, and there was much envy of the access of Japanese firms to low-cost bank capital that played a role in the temporary period of Japanese domination of the semiconductor industry. But the American capital market turned out to be a blessing in disguise. A long tradition of government securities regulation that forced public disclosure and information and of access of equity research analysts to internal company information had fostered a large and active market for public offerings, and this together with the relatively recent emergence of the venture capital industry provided ample finance for start-up companies once the technological groundwork for the Internet was laid in the mid-1990s.[10] Lerner (2002) identifies a critical policy change as fostering the relatively recent rise of the U.S. venture capital industry, namely a ruling that allowed pension funds to invest in venture capital firms. While the stock market collapse in 2000–2002 brought the venture capital industry down with it, the financial infrastructure is still there seeking out the next round of innovation. Only a small part of this endowment of innovation-seeking financial specialists was lost during the 2000–2002 stock market decline.

Language and Immigration

The literature on technological leadership omits two sources of American advantage that are surely not insignificant. While language has little to do with domination in computer hardware (where indeed many of the components are imported), it is surely important for the American software industry that English long ago became the world's leading second language in addition to being spoken as a first language by a critical mass of the world's educated population. Another oft-neglected factor that should be discussed more often is the long-standing openness of the United States to immigration and the role of immigrants from India, East Asia, and elsewhere in providing the skilled labor that has been essential to the rise of Silicon Valley.

Another aspect of American advantage and disadvantage is also perhaps too little discussed. The technology literature summarized above places heavy emphasis on the unique role of American research universities in providing a competitive atmosphere geared to the attraction of the best faculty performing the best research. Yet every year another set of test results is announced in which Americans score far down the league tables in math and science when compared to numerous countries in Europe and Asia. Those who wring their hands about the state of American elementary and secondary education might better spend their energies lobbying Congress to increase the immigration quotas for highly educated individuals with skills in those areas where some Americans are weak, science and engineering. And those who would argue

---

[10] As usual there are interconnections between the various sources of American advantage. For instance, the best U.S. private universities have been a critical source of U.S. technological leadership, and their wealth and power has been further augmented by their recent investments in U.S. venture capital firms. For instance, in 1999 Harvard made roughly a 150 percent return on its venture capital investments and a return of over 40 percent on its entire endowment, which now totals more than $20 billion.

that loosening of high-skilled quotas should occur at the cost of a reduction in low-skilled quotas are urged to consider the many benefits of immigration in general, including the provision of new workers to ease the strain of overly tight labor markets, the revitalization of many central cities, and the postponement forever of any so-called Social Security "crisis."

Comparisons with Other Countries

In most comparisons among the leading industrialized nations, Britain (and sometimes Canada) occupy a central ground between the extremes of American exceptionalism and the opposite tendencies of the continental Europeans and Japanese, whether concerning the level of unemployment, employment protection or the lack thereof, the degree of inequality, or the extent of government spending. Yet in comparing the extent of American technological leadership with other countries, the story is not one of extremes, and the balance of advantage varies widely by industry.

Americans dominate most strongly in microprocessors and in computer software. As documented by Langlois (2002), the extent of Intel's domination of the worldwide market for microprocessors is perhaps unprecedented in industrial history, and the same could be said for Microsoft. However, the U.S. advantage in computer hardware is qualified by the role of Asian countries in providing components like memory chips, hard drives, and laptop screens. In fact the United States runs a large trade deficit in computer hardware and peripherals, both because of component imports from Asia and because a substantial share of production by American companies like Intel and Dell takes place not just at home but also in foreign countries like Malaysia and Ireland. In mobile telephones the United States has been handicapped by regulation that favored too much competition and allowed multiple standards, thus allowing the dominant producers of GSM equipment and infrastructure (Nokia and Ericsson) to run away with the worldwide mobile phone market. The American pharmaceutical industry also faces strong competition from British, German, and Swiss firms, but recent evidence suggests that key research labs are moving from Europe to Boston, the Bay Area, and other U.S. research centers.[11]

Several sources of systemic U.S. advantage stand out, most notably the mixed system of government- and private-funded research universi-

---

[11] A meeting of the Governors for Health Care at the World Economic Forum in Davos, Switzerland, on January 22, 2004, centered on the current "brain drain" of pharmaceutical research from Europe to the United States.

ties, the large role of U.S. government agencies providing research funding based on a criterion of peer review, and the strong position in a worldwide perspective of U.S. business schools and U.S.-owned investment banking, accounting, and management-consulting firms. By comparison Germany seems particularly weak in its failure to reform its old-fashioned hierarchical university system, its bureaucratic rules that inhibit start-up firms, its reliance on bank debt finance, and its weakness in venture capital and equity finance (Siebert and Stolpe 2002). France suffers from overcentralized government control, a system of universities and research institutions that places more emphasis on rewarding those with an elite educational pedigree rather than those currently working on the research frontier, and a culture (with its frequent strikes by farmers and government workers) that is relatively hostile to innovation and change (see Messerlin 2002).

Until its structural reforms and privatizations of the 1980s and 1990s, Britain shared with France and Germany a labor market dominated by strong unions. While the strong unions are gone, Britain continues to suffer from handicaps that date back a century or more, including a shortfall of technical skills among manual workers and a lack of graduate management training and business-oriented culture among highly educated workers. Where Britain does well, as in investment banking or as a destination of inward foreign investment, it relies on a relatively narrow set of advantages, including the traditional role of the City of London as a financial center, and the same advantage that the English language provides—that is, as a comfortable place for Asian firms to build plants—to the United States, Canada, Ireland, Australia, and other parts of the former British Empire.

6. Conclusion

After 50 years of catching up to the U.S. level of productivity, since 1995 Europe has been falling behind. The growth rate in output per hour over 1995–2003 in Europe was just half that in the United States, and this annual growth shortfall caused the *level* of European productivity to fall back from 94 percent of the U.S. level to 85 percent. Fully one-fifth of the European catch-up (from 44 to 94 percent) over the previous half-century has been lost over the period since 1995.

Since Europe uses the same computer hardware and software as the United States, the impediments to European growth must lie elsewhere than inadequate investment in ICT. The new upsurge of U.S. productivity growth during 2000–2003, a period when ICT investment slumped, also suggests that ICT investment has previously been given too much credit for the U.S. productivity achievement, and insufficient attention has been directed to other contributing factors. References to "Europe" disguise a wide variety of performance, with Ireland and Finland exhibiting much faster productivity growth than the United States, but "olive belt" nations like Italy and Greece scoring low on productivity and ICT investment (except for mobile phones). Disaggregated studies of industrial sectors suggest that the main difference between Europe and the United States is in ICT-using industries like wholesale and retail trade and in securities trading. The contrast in retailing calls attention to regulatory barriers and land-use regulations in Europe that inhibit the development of the big-box retailing formats that have created many of the productivity gains in the United States.

For many decades, the United States and Europe have gone in opposite directions in the public policies relevant for metropolitan growth. The United States has promoted highly dispersed low-density metropolitan areas through its policies of building intraurban highways, starving public transit, giving tax subsidies to home ownership, and allowing local governments to maintain low density by maintaining minimum residential lot sizes. Europeans have chosen different policies, including public transit subsidies that seem lavish by American standards, with less generous tax subsidies to home ownership and land-use policies that encourage high-density residential living and retail precincts in the central city while inhibiting the exploitation of "greenfield" suburban and exurban sites suitable for modern big-box retail developments.

Phelps provides a unifying framework in which economic dynamism is promoted by policies that promote competition and flexible equity finance and is retarded by corporatist institutions that are designed to protect incumbent producers and inhibit new entry. He also points to European cultural attributes that inhibit the development of ambition and independence by teenagers and young adults, in contrast to their encouragement in the United States. While competition, corporatism, and culture may help to explain the differing evolution of productivity growth on the two sides of the Atlantic since 1995, they reveal institutional flaws in both continents that are inbred and likely to persist.

The outstanding performance of American productivity growth since 1995 raises the danger of a resurgent American triumphalism, perhaps symbolized by an imaginary Arc de Triomphe erected over Sand Hill Road at the border between Palo Alto and Menlo Park, California, the heart of Silicon Valley. No doubt the growing American dominance of innovation in ICT, biotech, and pharmaceuticals reflects in part the fruitful collaboration of government research funding, world-leading private universities, innovative private firms, and a dynamic capital market. However, we should be cautious. The favorable preconditions that fostered innovation after 1995 did not prevent the United States from experiencing the dismal 1972–95 years of the productivity growth slow-down and near-stagnation of real wages, and they do not give the United States an advantage in many other industries. A quarter century after the invasion of Japanese auto imports, the quality rankings of automo-biles still are characterized by a bimodal distribution in which Japanese nameplates (even those manufactured in the United States) dominate the highest rankings and American nameplates dominate the lowest.[12] The United States shows no sign of regaining leadership in the manufacturing of computer peripherals or machine tools. The U.S. innovation infra-structure remains fertile soil when the right seeds are planted, as after 1995, but fertile soil without the right seeds can lie fallow for decades.

[12] See *Consumer Reports*, April 2003, and the latest J. D. Powers initial quality rankings.

CHAPTER 8

Can Marketization of Household Production Explain the Jobs Gap Puzzle?

Richard B. Freeman

The jobs gap puzzle is simple: why do Americans, with higher GDP per capita and a higher birthrate than Europeans, work more in the market than Europeans? Is it because low-wage workers are paid much less in the United States, generating greater employment at the bottom of the skill distribution? Or because the demand for labor is stronger in the United States as a result of more expansionary macroeconomic policies? Because Americans are workaholics? Or because the European welfare state reduces incentives to work?

In the 1990s, many attributed the United States–Europe employment differential to labor market rigidities that raised the cost of low-wage labor in the EU and purportedly priced many low-skill workers out of jobs, particularly in the service sector. Although this explanation fits broadly with the more compressed distribution of wages in the EU than in the United States, it does not stand up to more detailed investigation. In some periods, United States–Europe employment gaps have been as large among skilled workers as among less-skilled workers (Nickell and Bell 1996). Differences in the employment of workers by industry or occupation are barely related to differences in labor costs by industry or occupation (Freeman and Schettkat 2001b; Card, Kramarz, and Lemieux 1999). Estimated elasticities of demand are too low to explain the observed employment differences by movements along comparable demand curves. Within the United States, the big rise in hours worked has been among the more skilled and among women, whose wages have risen relative to the U.S. average. Finally, studies show that increases in the United States minimum wage had negligible effects on employment, which suggests that low wages are not the cause of the U.S. employment miracle.

On the supply side, many analysts stress that the EU's more extensive welfare state increases lengths of joblessness. Unemployment is much shorter in the United States than in the EU largely because the monthly transition of workers from unemployment to employment is a magnitude higher in the United States than in the EU. Studies find that the long duration of unemployment and related benefits in the EU explain some of this gap, but the estimated elasticities of response accord supply-side incentives only a modest proportion of United States–Europe employment differences. Welfare state benefits aside, Linda Bell and I (Freeman and Bell 2001) have shown that the greater wage inequality in the United States contributes to the greater hours worked by giving workers a greater incentive to work long hours and gain promotions, but we have not sought to account for the jobs gap itself in this manner.

Recent analyses of EU employment problems confirm the difficulty of explaining the United States–Europe employment difference using the inflexible markets interpretation that the OECD embodied as conventional wisdom in its 1994 Jobs Study. Combining time-series studies with country case investigations, David Howell's 2005 edited volume documents that this interpretation neither fits the time-series data nor accounts for the divergent ways in which countries responded to the economic problems of the 1980s and 1990s. In perhaps the key chapter of the book, Dean Baker, Andrew Glyn, Howell, and John Schmitt demonstrate that the statistical evidence on which the labor market inflexibility story hinged is nonrobust. Add a few more years of information, change model specifications slightly, measure key variables in different ways, and the regressions that supporters of the inflexible labor market view treated as reliable scientific evidence turn to mush. Micro labor economists, who invariably distrust aggregate cross-country time-series econometrics, may not be surprised at this, but the documentation is necessary to make it clear to even supporters of the conventional story that the rigidities explanation is an emperor with no clothes.

The European Union's Demand Patterns and Employment Growth (DEMPATEM) research project[1] uses quite different data—information on sectoral consumption, employment, and wages, some derived through input-output tables—to examine the demand-side explanation of the EU joblessness problem from a structural perspective. This analysis also finds the standard story wanting. Comparisons of sectoral employment and wages show that United States–Europe differences in employment cannot be explained by wage differences or structural problems. In particular, wages in the retail sector relative to rest of the economy in the EU are not noticeably different from wages in the retail sector relative to the rest of the economy in the United States. The DEMPATEM team attributes the differences in employment to differences in the level of the demand for services, which result from the approximately 30 percent

[1] http://www.uva-aias.net/lower.asp?id=82&lang=en.

higher GDP per capita in the United States. The argument is that the higher GDP per capita in the United States plus the income elasticity of demand for services produces greater consumption of services, which in turn raises employment in the service sector. What is missing is an explanation of why the most productive EU economies have lower employment and hours worked than the United States despite having U.S. levels of productivity per hour.

The failure of the labor market rigidity explanation of EU employment problems to fit the data has led analysts to move from blaming labor market rigidities to blaming product market rigidities, such as store opening and closing hours, difficulties in starting new businesses, and zoning laws for the jobs gap. As yet there is no compelling evidence that these factors are quantitatively important. Since the country with perhaps the most substantial product market rigidities, Austria, has had one of the lowest unemployment rates in the EU, I doubt that an explanation based on product market rigidity will prove to be any more robust than the explanation based on labor market rigidity. Removing rigidities may be virtuous, but it will not restore full employment.

This chapter proposes a very different explanation of the United States–Europe work difference—the marketization hypothesis that greater employment in the United States is due to the more extensive shift of traditional household production—food preparation, child care, elderly care, cleaning houses—to the market than in Europe. The power of the marketization hypothesis comes from the fact that shifts of activities to the market affect both supply and demand of labor. Marketization increases the labor force participation of women. As long as this comes largely out of household production rather than leisure, it creates demand for less-skilled workers to produce traditional household goods and services in the market. By directing attention at a development that shifts demand and supply schedules at the same time, the hypothesis differs from explanations of employment differences that focus on demand or supply factors separately and the impact of wages/prices on movements along the schedules rather than factors that shift the schedules.

This chapter examines the marketization hypothesis in three stages. Section 1 reviews the key differences in employment and hours per adult between the United States and EU—the phenomenon that defines the jobs gap puzzle. Section 2 develops the marketization hypothesis and lays out a research strategy to test it. Section 3 summarizes evidence on the validity of the hypothesis. Because marketization involves the allocation of time, consumption, and employment of diverse groups within countries as well as across countries, a full investigation of the hypothesis requires analysis of diverse data files in a common framework. The limited evidence currently available shows that the hypothesis fits the data in ways

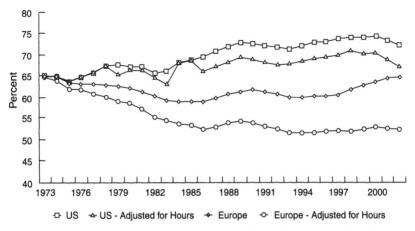

Fig. 8.1. Percentage of Persons 15–64 Years Old Working in the United States and Western Europe, Adjusted for Hours

that contribute to understanding the United States–Europe jobs gap, but does not fully answer the title question of this essay.

1. *CHERCHEZ LES TRAVAILLEURS* . . . IN THE SERVICE SECTOR

There are four facts about U.S. and EU employment patterns that any explanation of the jobs gap must address:

1. The jobs gap developed from the 1970s to the 2000s. In the immediate years after World War II and, as far as we can tell, in earlier periods, the United States had lower employment rates than EU countries, while Americans worked fewer hours than Europeans. The lines labeled employment rate and average hours in figure 8.1 document the historical pattern.

2. Differences in hours worked per employed person add greatly to the gap in time worked between the EU and United States. In 2000 approximately half of the difference in work time per adult was associated with hours worked by the employed and half by differences in the employment rate. In addition, since more-skilled Americans work more hours than less-skilled Americans,[2] the gap is potentially larger at the upper end of the skill distribution. Figure 8.1 shows how the difference in employment rates and the difference in hours worked cumulate to produce a huge total work time difference between the United States and EU.

---

[2] More-skilled Europeans may also work more hours than less-skilled Europeans, but the difference in hours worked is unlikely to be as large in Europe as in the United States.

TABLE 8.1
Employment to Population Rates, European Union versus United States, 2002, by Education for Persons Aged 25–34 and for Persons 15–24 and 55–64

	Men			Women		
	EU	US	Difference	EU	US	Difference
All, aged 15–64	72.9	78.0	−5.1	55.7	66.1	−10.7
Aged 25–64						
Less than secondary	71.0	69.8	1.2	40.5	47.1	−6.6
Secondary	81.7	82.1	−0.4	66.8	70.6	−3.8
Tertiary	88.3	89.9	−1.6	79.8	79.1	0.7
15–24	43.7	57.1	−13.4	37.2	54.3	−17.1
55–64	50.5	66.3	−15.8	31.0	53.2	−22.2

Source: OECD 2003, tables B, C, and D.

3. The gap is greatest among women and nonexistent among prime age male workers. Table 8.1 shows also that the difference in employment rates is negligible for the most educated women. But since highly educated American women work more hours than highly educated EU women, there is still a substantial gap in hours-adjusted employment rates even for that group. The table also shows differences in employment rates among young workers and among workers near retirement.
4. The employment gap is found entirely in services. Table 8.2, based on the DEMPATEM categorization, shows a gap in employment per adult not only in low-wage services, such as distribution, but also in high-wage services, such as education. Similarly, the gap exists in high-paid service occupations as well as low-paid service occupations.

TABLE 8.2
Employment-Population Rates, European Union versus by Sector, 1970 and 2001

	EU	US	Difference
1970			
Low-wage services: distribution	9.8	12.6	2.8
High-wage services: communal	13.0	17.3	4.3
2001			
Low-wage services: distribution	12.0	15.9	3.9
High-wage services: communal	20.5	26.0	5.5

Source: DEMPATEM Project 2003.

On the basis of these facts, any explanation of the employment gap must account for the greater hours worked as well as greater employment per adult in the United States. It must explain why the employment gap occurs among women and the young and those near retirement, but not among prime age males. It must also account for why the United States generates greater employment in high-level services as well as in low-level services than the EU.

2. THE MARKETIZATION HYPOTHESIS

Marketization is the shift from household production to market production. It occurs in less advanced countries as part of industrialization. It also occurs in advanced countries as part of the increased participation of women in the workforce. The marketization hypothesis offers a powerful framework for analyzing the United States–Europe employment gap because the shift from household to market work raises both the supply and the demand for labor, impelling greater employment from both sides of the market. On the supply side, workers who increase their work in the market are supposed to take that time primarily from household production, rather than from leisure or personal time. This reduces the production of household goods and services. On the demand side, the loss of household production increases the demand for market goods and services to replace those goods and services. This increases the derived demand for labor in those activities. By increasing the supply of labor and the demand for labor, marketization moves both blades of Marshall's scissors. This contrasts with standard explanations of employment patterns in terms of movements along either the demand or supply blades in response to changes in wages and benefits.

That time in the market substitutes for time in household production is not a logical necessity. Time in the market could come out of leisure time rather than household production, so that the household would not seek substitutes for household production.[3] If people bought goods and services for leisure activities, the result might be a reduction in market purchases. To take another possibility, increased time in the market could be associated with increased use of household capital, which would allow for the same household production despite less time input. In this case market time would be associated with the purchase of house-

---

[3] If a person equated all margins of time allocation and different time activities were separable, marginal increases in work time would presumably come equally out of leisure and household work. With larger changes in work time, the increases could come out largely from leisure or largely from household work.

hold durables rather than with consumption of goods and services. As another possibility, in households with two or more members, one person could enter the market, raising labor participation and employment, while another reduces work time to produce the traditional household product. In this case, the substitution would be in the time of household members, with no demand for market substitutes. Any of these relations would invalidate the marketization hypothesis that increased labor supply creates demand for market substitutes for household production and thus demand for labor producing those substitutes.

Given the historic concentration of females in household production, the marketization argument applies most readily to differences in employment involving women. In this case, increased labor participation of women generates market demand for goods and services traditionally produced by women in the household. Increased market work by highly educated women whose comparative advantage presumably lies in market activities is, in particular, likely to be accompanied by increased demand for labor of less-educated women or men to do the cooking, cleaning, child rearing, and home care nursing that these women forego by working. As a result, the greater employment by educated women, largely in skilled service sector jobs, will be associated with greater employment of persons in low-skill services. Given that the women who shift into the market presumably do so because they have a comparative advantage in market work, moreover, their household income will increase. Given the high income elasticity of demand for services, this would further increase demand for services, per the DEMPATEM analysis.

Specified in this manner, the marketization hypothesis has the flavor of a comparative statics multiple equilibrium model that traces out the linkages between the household and market sectors that produce different equilibriums in the United States and EU. Diverse exogenous factors could lead the economies to the different equilibriums. Greater female labor supply due to increased education, new opportunities resulting from equal employment opportunity, changes in attitudes toward work, or changes in the tax system could produce higher participation and a corresponding increase in demand for market substitutes for the foregone household production. Alternatively, the influx of low-skilled immigrants or innovative development of fast food restaurants of a particular type could create low-cost market substitutes for household work that would induce women to enter the market. Without specifying the dynamics, the hypothesis is simply that the marketization of household production and the increased employment of women or other groups who traditionally engage in nonmarket activity are duals: you don't get one without the other.

Even at this level, however, the marketization argument has important implications for understanding the United States–Europe employment gap.

First, it suggests that the job outcomes for skilled workers who would otherwise engage in household production are intrinsically related to the employment of less-skilled workers. Policies that affect only the low end of the job market will have a smaller impact on the jobs gap than policies that impact both the low and the high ends of the market. Opening the doors for educated women to work not only increases their employment but also the employment of the less educated. Similarly, policies that affect only the skilled workforce will not raise employment unless accompanied by an expansion of low-wage services. Second, it suggests that measured GDP per capita differences, such as those used in the DEMPATEM analysis, overstate country differences in "true" income since they fail to account for the greater household production in the EU. Pure differences in income are less important in accounting for the United States–Europe jobs gap than that analysis suggests. Third, the high level of dispersion of wages, particularly among women, in the United States could also contribute to the United States–Europe difference in employment by making it more economically sensible for skilled women to work in the market while employing less-skilled workers to undertake household activities.[4] Taking this analysis a step further, the higher dispersion of skills in the United States, found in the OECD International Adult Literacy Surveys for instance (see Devroye and Freeman 2001), could also contribute to the jobs gap: more inequality in skills creates greater incentive for educated persons to work rather than producing household goods, which raises demand for the less educated. The principle of comparative advantage predicts that differences in market productivity associated with differences in literacy and numeracy skills should increase market employment.

Research Strategy for Assessing Marketization

How can we test the impact of the marketization of household production on the employment differences between the EU and the United States?

Investigation of the marketization hypothesis requires three types of data. The first are time use data that identify differences in the allocation of time to household activities. The hypothesis rests on a presumed substitution between time in household production and time at work. If women or others who work more hours in the United States than in the

---

[4] The implicit assumption here is that the greater difference in wages is not matched by comparably greater differences in household productivity.

EU spend the same time in household production as comparable persons in the EU, the hypothesis fails. The second type of data are consumption expenditures that identify the goods and services that households buy in the market as substitutes for household production. The hypothesis requires that households that supply more market work demand additional market goods and services to substitute for the foregone household production—less time spent in meal preparation at home should produce greater expenditures on food in restaurants, for instance. If households that provide more market work have the same consumption expenditures as those that provide less work, the hypothesis fails. The third type of data are employment data that identify the workers producing the goods and services in the market that replace the previous household production. Employment in the restaurant sector, cleaning sector, and related areas should be higher as a result of greater market production in those areas. If sectors that produce traditional household goods and services in the market do not have higher employment in the United States than in the EU (say, because productivity in those sectors in higher in the United States), the marketization hypothesis fails.

Formally, the hypothesis posits three relations. Although each relation should be viewed as depending on other factors as well, for simplicity I write them in linear univariate form linking the main variables of concern:

Time worked in market =
$$-a \text{ Time Worked in Household Production} \qquad (1)$$

Market Expenditures on "Household Goods and Services" =
$$-b \text{ Time Worked in Household Production} \qquad (2)$$

Market Employment of "Household Goods and Services" =
$$c \text{ Market Expenditures on "Household Goods and Services"} \qquad (3)$$

The coefficient a in equation 1 is expected to be close to 1, making market time and household production time complete substitutes. For workers who participate in the labor market, time worked is presumably more productive than time worked in household production, at least for some positive hours in the market. An observed shift from household to market work is thus expected to raise not only measured income (which excludes the value of household production) but also income inclusive of household production. As much U.S. jobs growth has been among educated women, a natural specification would make (1) relate to the market work of educated women, who are largely employed in high-level services.

The second equation focuses on the substitution between household production of goods and services and purchase of those same goods and services in the market. It understates the potential impact of increased market work on spending and employment, since it ignores any increase in spending for nontraditional household goods and services that could also raise market employment. A more general specification would compare diverse consumer expenditures between households with more/less time worked in household production, recognizing that some forms of household production require market expenditures as well, and that increased income from market work would induce greater spending on market goods and services, as the DEMPATEM analysis stresses.

The third equation shows the impact of the additional market spending on employment. In its simplest form this equation relates spending to employment in the affected sectors. A more general specification would follow the effects of spending through input-output tables on final sales and employment. Contrary to my expectation that spending on services would create greater employment than spending on goods, the DEMPATEM project's input-output analyses found that the two forms of spending had similar "final" impacts on employment. As the United States has a job edge in low-skill services, a natural specification would make (3) relate to the market work of less-educated service sector workers. But it could also relate to the work of teenagers and students, who also often work in less-skilled service industries, and who are more likely to be employed in the United States than in the EU.

Ideally, the coefficients in equations (1)–(3) are the same in the United States and the EU, so that we would obtain similar results from comparisons of workers facing different incentives within the two settings and across them. In this case, the natural measure of how differences in marketization of household work contributed to the United States–Europe jobs gap would be the following:

a (Household Time U.S. –Household Time EU) +
$$bc \text{ (Household Time, U.S.—Household Time, EU),} \quad (4)$$

where the first term measures the direct trade-off of work time for household time and the second term measures the indirect effect of that trade-off on the work time of persons producing substitutes for household goods and services.

3. Evidence on the Marketization Hypothesis

Evidence on time spent in household production and time worked across advanced countries, and more importantly within the same country over time (Robinson and Godbey 1999; Freeman and Schettkat 2005), supports the key proposition of the marketization hypothesis: that there is a tight trade-off between the two categories. In addition, data from Germany and the United States support the two other tenets of the marketization hypothesis: that differences in household production induce differences in market purchases and differences in employment (Freeman and Schettkat 2001a). Since Germany is not representative of all EU countries, the ability of the marketization analysis to explain German-U.S. differences may not generalize to the overall United States–Europe difference in consumption spending and employment.

Proposition 1: Household Production versus Market Work

Time use surveys provide the appropriate data to examine the hypothesized relation between time spent in household production and work time. These surveys ask respondents the amount of time they spend doing various activities, such as paid work, child care, preparing meals, cleaning, and so on, whereas standard labor force surveys ask only about hours worked or in some cases time spent looking for work. While sociologists have worked more intensely with time use surveys than economists, the main theory of the allocation of time is an economic theory (Becker 1965), and some economists have examined the empirical evidence as well (Juster and Stafford 1991), albeit sometimes with a critical eye as to what inferences might be drawn from the data (Pollack and Wachter 1975).

To examine differences in the allocation of work time and household production time between the United States and Germany, Schettkat and I analyzed U.S. time use data from the Survey Research Center of the University of Maryland and West German time use data from the scientific use file "Wo bleibt die Zeit?" (Statistiches Budesamt 1999). The U.S. data was collected by telephone interviews, based on a 24-hour diary over the period September 1992 to October 1994. We limited our analysis to 6,062 adults aged 18–64. The German data was collected by diaries covering two days and personal interviews and is representative of German households but not of non-Germans living in Germany. The Wissenschaftszentrum Berlin did the computations for us because we did not have access to the individual data. The analysis covered 17,998 individuals aged 18–64. We compared the allocation of time across four main categories: work, household production time, personal time (largely sleep), and free time. The marketization model holds that differences or changes in work time are associated largely with differences or changes in household production time rather than with the other categories.

Table 8.3 show the hours per week spent on market work and on household work, differentiated between eating and preparing meals,

TABLE 8.3
Comparison, Work Time in 1992, Men and Women, 18–64

	Women			Men		
	US	Germany	Difference	US	Germany	Difference
Hours worked in market	25.4	17.7	7.7	39	35	4
Hours in household production	26.8	36.1	−9.3	14	18	−4
Meals	13.3	19.5	−6.2	9.3	11.6	−2.3
Children, all	4.1	4.8	−0.7	1.3	1.8	−0.5
Those with children <6	11.0	20.1	−9.1			
Shopping	6.7	6.8	−0.1	4.2	4.8	−0.6
Personal travel	2.0	0.5	1.5	2.0	0.4	1.6

Source: Freeman and Schettkat 2001a, tables 5, 6, and 7.

child care, traveling, and shopping time in the United States and Germany for men and women aged 18–64 in 1992 (Freeman and Schettkat 2001a). Consider first the difference between market work (including commuting time) and household work among women in the two countries. American women spend seven hours more per week in market work than do German women but spend nine hours less than German women in household work, so that in total the German women work a bit more. Viewed as a trade-off, U.S. women are trading nine hours per week of household production time for seven hours at the workplace, giving a coefficient of 0.78 (= 7/9) for the parameter a in equation 1. As for men, American men spend four hours more working than German men, but they spend four hours less in household work, giving a one-to-one trade-off of household time and work time. For both genders, the bulk of the difference in household production time is associated with differences in work time rather than differences in personal or leisure time. To put it differently, Americans and Germans spend approximately the same total amount of time working, but Americans devote more to the market, while Germans devote more to the household.

The more detailed categories under the household production line in table 8.3 show that German women spend 2.1 more hours at meals and 4.1 more hours preparing and cleaning up after meals than American women—for a huge difference of 6.2 hours more per week of household production time. By contrast, American and German women spend similar time shopping, while American women spend two more hours per week traveling for personal reasons than do German women, presumably reflecting larger distances and suburban living in the United States. Surprisingly given the higher fertility rate among Americans, the average German woman spends more time taking care of children than the average American woman. As the next line of the table shows, among women who have children less than six years of age, Germans spend nearly twice as much time as Americans in child care (20.4 hours vs 11.0 hours). For men, U.S.-German differences in household production time are similar but generally much more modest. Overall, the principal difference in household production time occurs in eating and meal preparation and clearing after meals, but the difference is large in child care among families with young children.

To what extent do the relationships found in the German-U.S. comparisons generalize to a wider set of countries? To answer this question, Schettkat and I have used the Multinational Time Use Study (MTUS), which provides downloadable data on time use in a variety of countries, harmonized into a 41-activity typology (http://www.iser.essex.ac.uk/mtus/index.php). We calculated time use from the MTUS files for 1992 for six countries, United States, Canada, United Kingdom, Germany, Norway, and Netherlands. Our analysis focused on men and women aged 25–54 (producing slightly different U.S.-German comparisons than those in table 8.3, which treated those aged 18–64).

Table 8.4 presents the average hours worked in the household and the average hours worked in the market for each country by gender. For ease of comparison with the United States, the figures in parentheses show how the relevant statistic deviates from the hours for the United States. The figures show that Germany is an outlier among the countries in time spent on household production. Germans report the highest amount of time in household production of any group, with German women working 5.61 hours a day in household activities. As a result among women, the U.S.-German difference in household time exceeds the difference in market time, whereas for the other three European countries, the difference with the United States is greater in market time than in household time. The Netherlands also shows a distinct pattern, with the fewest hours of market work for both men and women. The unweighted average of hours worked for the four European countries shows that women work 1.02 hours less than American women in the market and 0.85 hours more in the household.

Among men, differences in household work are modest, but in two of the countries, the United Kingdom and the Netherlands, the differences with the United States are inconsistent with the market work/household work trade-off since men give less time to the market and to household

Table 8.4
Comparison, Work Time per Day, 1992, Men and Women, 25–64

	Women	
	Market Work	*Household Work*
United States	3.67	4.26
Germany	2.72 (−0.95)	5.61 (1.35)
Netherlands (1990)	1.72 (−1.95)	4.98 (0.72)
United Kingdom (1995)	2.67 (−1.00)	5.13 (0.87)
Norway	3.02 (−0.65)	4.70 (0.44)
Canada	3.32 (−0.35)	4.83 (0.57)
Europe	2.53 (−1.02)	5.11 (0.85)
	Men	
	Market Work	*Household Work*
United States	5.82	2.43
Germany	5.48 (−0.44)	2.76 (0.33)
Netherlands (1990)	4.88 (−0.94)	2.30 (−.13)
United Kingdom (1995)	4.89 (−0.93)	2.35 (−.08)
Norway	5.29 (−0.53)	2.70 (0.27)
Canada	5.71 (−0.11)	2.60 (0.17)
Europe	5.14 (−0.68)	2.53 (0.10)

Source: Freeman and Schettkat 2004.

work than in the United States. But the differences are small and dwarfed by those found among women.

While the cross-country pattern of household and market time allocation for the six countries is broadly consistent with the marketization hypothesis, the analysis highlights the different levels of marketization among European countries and differences in their divergence from the pattern in the United States. In part, the variation among countries may reflect differences in demographic conditions, particularly the presence of children, which has a massive effect on the household production time of women. Contrasts limited to women with and without young children may better pin down the substitution of market for nonmarket work time. I suspect, however, that much of the variation across countries reflects differences in institutional arrangements, particularly regarding the regulation of work time, and in tax systems. The low work time of women in the Netherlands and the United Kingdom, for instance, must reflect in part at least the Dutch decision to encourage part-time work and the high taxes in the United Kingdom for women who work beyond the hours that exempt them from certain taxes. The data for Canada, which has institutions roughly similar to the United States, show clear trade-offs of work time for household production time for women and men, with rates of substitution close to those for Germany.

One way to control for demographic and institutional differences across countries and better identify the posited trade-off between work time and household time is to look at changes in the allocations of time within a country over time. The MTUS has multiple observations for four of the countries in the sample under investigation for intermittent years from 1965 to 1998; the United States, United Kingdom, Canada, the Netherlands. There are five observations for the United States, Canada, and the Netherlands, and four for the United Kingdom, though not necessarily in the same years. Figure 8.2 provides a simple picture of the patterns of changes within country in these data. The horizontal axis records the change in household hours worked from the earliest year for which I have time use data (1965 for the United States, 1971 for Canada, and 1975 for the United Kingdom and the Netherlands) to the most recent period (1998 for all countries but the United Kingdom, where the data ends at 1995). The vertical axis records the change in hours worked in the market over the same period. The observations identify the country and the gender. The observations for women lie in the bottom right quadrant. They show that women decreased their household work time and increased their market work time. The observations for men lie in the upper left quadrant, save for the Netherlands. They show that men

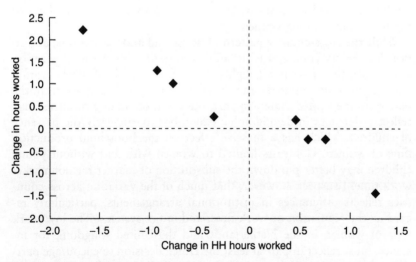

Fig. 8.2. Change in Hours Worked, Market versus Household, 1965–98 (years covered differ by country)

increased their household time and decreased their work time. Taking the two genders together, the observations fit along a well-defined negatively sloped linear curve.

To examine the trade-off more precisely, I pooled the hours data by country, year, and gender and regressed hours of work time on hours of household time, country dummies, and a dummy variable for gender. The regressions included all the years for which data exists for the four countries (not just the first and last year), giving a sample of 36 observations. The results of the calculations are summarized in table 8.5. They yield an estimated coefficient of −1.01 on the household time variable with a standard error of 0.13—stunning support for the hypothesized household time/work time trade-off. Still, there are significant coefficients on the country dummies, indicating that there remain substantial differences in work time beyond those connected with marketization. With the limited number of data points, it is difficult to probe further. For what it is worth, adding a trend variable had no impact on the results, and dividing the sample by gender yielded similar coefficients. In short, the strongest support for proposition 1 of the marketization hypothesis comes from the most sensitive statistical test: the pattern of change in the allocation of hours over time by country.

Propositions 2 and 3: Consumption and Employment

The difference in time use data between the United States and Germany shown in table 8.3 suggests that the United States should substitute mar-

TABLE 8.5
Results for Regression of Hours Worked in the Market on Hours Worked at Home, US, Canada, Netherlands, UK, 1965–1998

Explanatory variable	Dependent Variable Hours Worked in Market
constant	6.70 (.70)
Hours Worked at Home	−1.01 (.13)
Gender Male = 1	0.27 (.28)
Dummy for US	1.52 (.15)
Dummy for Canada	1.26 (.15)
Dummy for UK	.78 (.18)
Dummy for Netherlands	
R^2	.969
SE	.34
No. observations	36

Source: Data tabulated from MTUS time use data files.

ket purchases of food for household preparation and thus that Americans should spend more money on restaurants and related modes of food preparation than Germans. This in turn should generate greater employment in restaurants in the United States than in Germany. Similarly, the lower amount of time spent taking care of children in the United States should generate greater demand for child care in the market, with a corresponding employment difference in the day care industry.

Panel A of table 8.6 uses consumer expenditure data to examine the share of U.S. and German household spending on food and restaurants and on personal care. It shows that while the United States and Germany spend about the same share of household budgets on food, beverages, tobacco, and miscellaneous related items, the United States spends twice as large a share on restaurants as do the Germans. A whopping 16.7 percent of the U.S. consumption budget goes for expenditures in restaurants and related goods and services, compared to 8.3 percent of the German consumption budget. In addition, Americans allocate a larger share of their consumption budget to personal care than do Germans. Freeman and Schettkat (2005) show that Americans spend more on child care as well. Since Americans have higher incomes per capita and consume a larger share of their budgets than Germans, total spending on the relevant sectors differs even more.

To see whether the spending patterns show up in differences in employment in restaurants and other eating and drinking establishments and in private household services, panel B of table 8.6 records the number of persons employed in those sectors relative to the adult population

TABLE 8.6
Shares of Consumer Expenditures and Employment

	United States	Germany
Panel A. Share of consumer spending (%)		
Total food and beverages	30.3	28.6
Nonrestaurant	13.6	20.3
Restaurants and other food establishments	16.7	8.3
Personal care	3.4	1.8
Panel B. Ratio of persons employed to adult population		
In restaurants	5.6	3.5
Private household	0.5	0.3

Source: Freeman and Schettkat 2001a, tables 1 and 4.

in the United States and in Germany. The employment patterns mimic the expenditure patterns. In the United States there are 5.6 persons working in the hotel and restaurant sector per adult and 0.5 persons employed in private households per adult. In Germany there are 3.5 persons working in the hotel and restaurant sector per adult and 0.3 persons employed in private households per adult.

Looking at a broader set of countries, Freeman and Schettkat (2005) report that the ratio of hours spent in restaurants to hours spent cooking and cleaning up at home rose substantially in Canada, the United States, and United Kingdom and rose modestly in the Netherlands in the 1980s and 1990s. Since countries differ in whether they fund child care and some other goods and services through private consumption or through public spending, it is more difficult to link private consumption spending to output and employment for those commodities. Overall, the clearest evidence for marketization comes from the links among time spent providing meals at home, purchases of food from restaurants, and employment in the restaurant sector.

4. Conclusion and Implications

The primary conclusion from this analysis is that changes in time spent in household production are an important component of the United States–Europe jobs gap. The United States has higher employment because Americans produce less goods and services in the household, which generates demand for market products. Since factors that shift the balance from household production to market time create a dynamic toward increases in market production, the marketization argument increases our potential ability to explain the sizable jobs gap.

Thus far, I have not specified the factors that may have moved the United States and EU into different divisions of work time between the market and the household, or that could raise employment in the EU toward the U.S. level. This is not because there are no plausible factors that shift the incentive for market work relative to household work; but rather because we have no evidence on the dynamics that move an economy from one equilibrium to another, and thus of the potential impact of particular factors. In a static model, Schettkat regressed the ln of hours spent in household work/hours spent on market work on estimates of the opportunity cost of household production/market cost across groups of women with different characteristics in the United States and Germany, and obtained an elasticity of household/market work time on the order of −0.80 to −0.95. But the data do not readily permit a test of the impact of the different components of relative costs nor of any time delays in their impacts on time allocation, much less on spending and employment.

This said, the factors that should shift the relative costs and move economies from one equilibrium to another would include several that analysts concerned with market rigidities stress: the wages of the less-skilled workers who provide the labor input for market substitutes for household production; the tax rate on women or other persons who have historically specialized in household work; the dispersion of wages, particularly among women; and others that have not attracted attention: lack of health insurance in the United States for nonemployed persons; regulations of hours worked (such as the French 35-hour work week ruling), which could make it hard for persons who want to work more hours from doing so; equal opportunity or affirmative action policies that increase demand for educated women. Marketization predicts that these factors have larger effects on labor market outcomes than standard demand or supply-side analysis indicates, giving them a potentially greater role in any explanation of the jobs gap. But to assess this prediction requires estimation of all three of the parameters in equations (1)–(3), and analysis of the factors that produced the significant country dummies in table 8.5, all of which remains to be done. Rephrasing the title question to "Can Marketization of Household Production Explain *Some of* the Jobs Gap Puzzle?" allows me to give a strong "yes," but the magnitude of the marketization effect remains to be pinned down.

CHAPTER 9

Service Included? Services and the U.S.-European Employment Gap

Mary Gregory, Wiemer Salverda, and Ronald Schettkat

The contributions to this book have examined a range of dimensions of the role of the service sector in the United States and five leading EU economies (the United Kingdom, Germany, France, the Netherlands, Spain) and their possible implications for employment. In this chapter we conclude by addressing the question, what implications can be drawn from these explorations to contribute to our understanding of the United States–Europe employment gap, to predicting its likely evolution, and to possible policy approaches?

Our focus on the service sector derives from the pervasiveness of its role and its position at the forefront of the process of economic change. It is almost a truism to describe the modern economy as a service economy, but the characterization is nonetheless accurate and important. The "typical" worker in the advanced economies is now a service worker; in many countries the service sector employs 70 percent of the workforce, with this proportion still growing. The importance of the service sector is qualitative as much as quantitative. As early as 1940 Colin Clark noted in his seminal analysis of the process of economic growth that "the most important concomitant of economic progress is the movement of labor from agriculture to manufacture, and from manufacture to commerce and services." The relevance of this insight continues to be confirmed by the experience of subsequent decades.

The research strategy guiding the work was to extend and update our understanding of the growth of services and to probe their role in the selected advanced economies. In particular, have the level and pattern of demand, specifically as they involve services, differed in systematic ways across these economies? What have been the implications for employment and productivity of the patterns of development of the service sector? The contributions assess the role of services from a range of perspectives: household budgets at the microeconomic level, meso-economic analysis of the retail trade sector, and multisector input-output analysis linking industry-level activities and macroeconomic outcomes.

The growing orientation towards services in household consumption patterns is a continuing trend, featuring in each of the selected countries. The study reported by Kalwij and Machin applies standardized expenditure categories to household budget survey data, and confirms that the share of expenditure allocated to services continued to increase markedly during the 1980s and 1990s in each of the six economies. This pattern, already widely observed as a concomitant of economic growth, has evoked two major explanations. The "hierarchy of needs" postulates that services rank as luxuries in consumption, satisfying higher-level needs and therefore coming to the fore once lower-level needs, involving the acquisition of goods, have been met. The "cost disease," on the other hand, attributes the rising share of services to their lower potential for productivity growth, and therefore rising relative costs, where service provision involves an important element of personal and face-to-face contact. In addition recent developments in the major economies, including the emergence of the United States–Europe employment gap, have given rise to further explanations. "Marketization" links the role of services and employment directly; as women increasingly engage in paid employment goods and, particularly, services previously produced in the home are replaced by market purchases, made affordable by the extra incomes earned; these demands in turn generate new paid jobs, again particularly in services and often suited to women.

The detailed microeconometric analysis reported by Kalwij and Machin allows several of these hypotheses to be tested against the recent evidence from the six economies.

Under the "hierarchy of needs" the rising share of services in consumption is brought about by the evolution of demand. As incomes rise and more basic needs are met, preferences increasingly are oriented towards services; the evolving pattern of preferences makes the demand for services income elastic. This demand-side view of evolving preferences receives support from Kalwij and Machin. Their estimates of the budget elasticities of private household expenditures, based on comparable expenditure categories across countries, show services as a luxury commodity, demand for them growing more than proportionally as household expenditure increases, thus raising their budget share. Overall through the 1980s and 1990s rising levels of household expenditure are found to account for about 21 percent of the increase in the budget share of service-related expenditures across the six countries. The role of the level of household demand and the luxury status of services is more strongly characteristic of the European economies. However, the importance of the level of household expenditure for the orientation of the national economy towards services shows considerable variation among the European economies, contributing over 40 percent in Spain and over 30 percent in France and the United Kingdom, through 17 percent in Germany to only 7 percent in the Netherlands. To ensure that their estimates of budget elasticities are comparable across countries and not influenced by differences in national institutional arrangements Kalwij and Machin focus on private expenditures only. Major services, notably in health care, education and housing, often provided through the public or semipublic sector in European economies, are purchased privately in the United States, leading to their inclusion in household consumption in budget surveys. When the comparison is extended to include services publicly provided for private use, the service gap between the United States and Europe narrows, but a substantial difference remains.

The "luxury" role of individual services at a detailed level is confirmed in each country, with expenditure on "food and beverages away from home," "private transport," "communication" and, in some countries, "entertainment" showing marked increases as incomes rise. The increasing budget shares of these services are accompanied by a sharp reduction in the share of "food and nonalcoholic beverages," providing further confirmation of Engels's law of the falling share of food purchases in expenditure as incomes rise. The "luxury" role of services is not, however, universal; their luxury status in some categories represents the displacement of other service categories, as when, for example, privately provided transport services replace use of public facilities.

The "cost disease" takes a different perspective, attributing the rising share of services in expenditure to the excess increase in their cost and price. Where the personal service provided is dependent on the incidence and duration of face-to-face contact the potential for productivity growth is limited, raising its relative cost. Where services are affected by the "cost disease," the shift to services will be visible in nominal expenditure shares and in employment but not in expenditure shares evaluated at constant prices. With shifting preferences as under the hierarchy of needs hypothesis, on the other hand, the increasing share of services in expenditure will be evident at constant as well as at current prices. This differing role for relative prices allows discrimination between the two potential sources. Kalwij and Machin find that in all six countries services have become more expensive over time relative to goods. This is in line with the cost-disease hypothesis that at least parts of the more labor-intensive service sector experience lower productivity gains than goods production. These price effects are found to have a relatively large impact on household expenditure patterns, accounting overall for about 45 percent of the increased share of services, with the effect ranging from 21 percent for the Netherlands to 68 percent for the United Kingdom. These effects are generally proportionately larger than the effects of demand shifts, but again with considerable variation between individual countries.

How far does the rising share of services in consumption demand, whether due to shifting preferences or to the cost disease, impact on employment? And how far does the greater service-orientation in the expenditure patterns of U.S. households explain the higher levels of employment there? Gregory and Russo approach this question from a macroeconomic perspective, using multisector input-output tables for each economy to estimate the output and employment required in each sector of production in order to deliver the goods and services demanded by households. Their estimates show that within each of the six countries, the growing service-orientation of household consumption has been only a minor source of employment growth. However, comparisons between the United States and the European economies confirm that the European consumption patterns, with their lower service shares, are less employment-friendly than the U.S. pattern. If the European economies were notionally to adopt a consumption mix on the U.S. pattern, at an unchanged level of consumption, employment (full-time equivalents) would be higher by 4.5 percent in France, and by around 3 percent in the United Kingdom, Germany, and the Netherlands; only in Spain would it be reduced. This would cut the employment gaps with the United States by one-fifth each for France and Germany, and marginally for the Netherlands; the gap for the United Kingdom, already small, would be halved; but for Spain the gap would widen. Conversely, the consumption mixes of France and Germany applied to the United States would reduce employment there by 5.0 percent and 3.6 percent respectively, narrowing the employment gap by 3.7 and 2.6 percentage points, with correspondingly smaller losses if the other national European patterns were applied. The pattern of consumption expenditures affects the level of employment within and between countries, but its contribution to the employment gap and its potential for eliminating it is limited.

A striking finding from the analysis by Gregory and Russo is of wider significance for views on the role of services: services are no more employment-intensive on average than other activities, including manufacturing. When employment intensity is measured on a "product supply" basis, taking into account jobs generated at each stage of production throughout the supply chain, services and goods production are approximately equal in their employment requirements per unit of final output. Both sectors include outputs of high and low labor-intensity, but on the average, labor intensities are effectively equal. The greater employment-intensity of services of popular wisdom is an illusion, based on the final stage of delivery only. However, services, like goods, are heterogeneous, and some service sectors, such as community, social, and personal services, and wholesale and retail trade, typically show greater employment-intensity than others. Where the more employment-intensive sectors are prominent in consumption, the pattern of demand may well affect employment.

Although the American demand pattern is more employment friendly, the largest part of the employment gap is caused by the higher level of demand. Why do Americans work more and consume more? The "marketization" hypothesis has immediate appeal as an explanation of the United States–Europe employment gap, given that its emergence has been associated with the rising employment rate among women in the United States, after earlier decades in which the employment rate among European women had exceeded the U.S. level. The increase in time supplied to the market, particularly by women, requires market purchases of goods and services in replacement of household production; this additional source of market demand for goods and, particularly, services, in turn generates higher demand for labor for their production. Drawing on household time-use surveys, Freeman finds that Americans, especially women, allocate more time to market work and less time to home production than their European counterparts. Across a group of European countries women work on average 1.02 hours per day less in the market and 0.85 hours more in the household than their American counterparts. This implies a trade-off in hours worked between the market and the home that is fairly close to one-for-one. However, Freeman also finds more striking differences in specific instances, with Germany emerging as an extreme case. On a weekly basis American women spend seven hours more in market work than German women, but nine hours less in household work; American men spend four hours more at work and four hours less in household work than German men. Within the difference in time spent by women in household work, 6.2 hours relates to meals—time taken over the meal itself as well as food preparation and clearing up. In families with preschool children German women allocate nearly twice as much time to child care as American women—20.4 hours against 11.0 hours.

A further implication of marketization is that households that supply more market work should demand additional market goods and services to substitute for forgone household production; for example, less time spent in meal preparation at home should be reflected in greater expenditures on food in restaurants or in purchases of prepared foods in supermarkets (retailing). The rising share of food and beverages away from home in household expenditure reported by Kalwij and Machin aligns prima facie with this substitution. Kalwij and Machin are, however, skeptical that marketization is the reason. They note that two-earner households are also higher-income households, the two being so closely correlated that their respective influences on the services share in expenditure cannot be adequately separated. Rather, Kalwij and Machin take the position that two-earner and higher-income households alike allocate a higher share of their expenditure to the purchase of services from the market, and that household employment patterns explain little of the differences in the services share, once their effect on the household budget has been taken into account.

At the meso-economic level support for the role of marketization is given by Glyn et al. The transfer of household activities to the market should be reflected in higher employment rates in service activities such as catering, day care for children and private services to households. Glyn et al. highlight that the key sectors contributing to the United States–Europe employment gap are community and personal services, and retailing, hotels, and catering. Retail trade, one of the biggest employers in both Europe and the United States, is also of long standing as one of the major areas of employment shortfall for the European economies. Their analysis, focused on retailing, hotels, and catering to avoid issues of the differential role of public provision, shows that this employment difference originates with differences in the level of household demand. Overall consumption of goods per head of population is much higher in the United States, requiring correspondingly higher throughput in the retailing sector. It is the higher level of consumption demand for marketed goods overall in the United States that generates higher employment in retailing relative to the European economies, contributing significantly to the employment gap.

A different perspective on marketization is taken by Fuchs. Rather than seeking to distinguish rising incomes and the growth of two-earner households as separate influences on market demand patterns, he integrates them, pointing out that some of the shift from household to market production will derive from the scale effects and associated productivity gains that are part of the process of economic growth. As demand increases, "It becomes more efficient to produce goods and services in specialized firms instead of unspecialized households." Fuchs thus places marketization by the household in the context of the incentive towards outsourcing more generally. This incentive depends on many factors, notably the level of wages available in the market, but also importantly on household size. The trend towards smaller households is clear in each of the countries. Single-person households are gaining importance everywhere; single-parent households are still a small proportion, but rising rapidly; the number of children per couple is declining (Kalwij and Machin, table 5.1). The smaller the household, the more it suffers from diseconomies of scale in a wide variety of home production tasks, prompting recourse to the market. Furthermore, the skills available within the household are limited, even more so with its smaller size, while the market allows access to a vast range in infinitely varying combinations.

Outsourcing is more typically associated with the activities of firms than with household demands. As the scale of the economy and individual activities within it expand, opportunities emerge for specialist production, generating productivity gains. Business-to-business supply through market transactions replaces previous in-house production. When manufacturing firms outsource parts of the manufacturing process, employment is redistributed across firms and sectors; manufacturing employment overall will be reduced where the productivity gains from outsourcing are labor-saving, but may increase if the cost savings are sufficiently substantial to prompt an overall expansion of output. Similarly, when service producers outsource to other service firms, overall employment in services is likely to be reduced. But where manufacturing firms contract out ancillary service activities to specialist suppliers, employment in services will rise, while employment in manufacturing falls. The extent to which outsourcing by manufacturing and service firms is employment-creating or employment-saving, and how far contemporary patterns are biased towards services, are empirical issues. Gregory and Russo examine this process of structural change in input purchases and the outsourcing of intermediate supplies for the six economies using detailed input-output analysis. Estimating the employment impact of structural change along the supply chain, they find that it is on occasion job-creating, particularly within the service sector, on occasion job-destroying, and on occasion job-transferring between manufacturing and services. The overall contribution to employment change from outsourcing by firms is, however, small. Employers in manufacturing and other nonservice activities can be observed to replace in-house provision by outside purchases of business services, but this shift has made only a minor contribution to the observed growth in service employment across the six economies.

The achievement of productivity gains can be promoted or impeded through many other channels. One that tends to be put forward in the context of the United States–Europe employment gap is that inflexible labor markets in the EU raise labor costs and encourage capital-labor substitution, thus raising productivity but restraining the growth of employment. Glyn et al. assess this process in the context of the retailing sector. They find it to have indeed occurred in the European economies, but only in the 1970s. Subsequently the European productivity advantage has been progressively eroded. Moreover, in recent years the European economies have been showing no consistent pattern of higher capital intensities, while it is U.S. retailing that has experienced strong productivity growth.

Productivity in retailing is a central issue also for Gordon, but he extends his perspective to the national environment for productivity growth. Noting that the retail sector has been a key source of the acceleration of productivity in the United States, contributing more than half of the U.S. advantage over Europe in aggregate productivity growth since the mid-1990s, he attributes this surge to the revolutionizing impact of the "big box" format identified particularly with Wal-Mart. This retailing revolution encompasses but is much more comprehensive and complex than the extended implementation of ICT. Gordon finds the retail sector in the European economies to have been shut out from the benefits of this development by regulatory barriers and land-use restrictions, which in turn reflect the different orientation of public policies towards the growth of urban areas. Further broadening the perspective, he sees productivity growth in the European economies as impeded by a wide set of social choices, going well beyond product or labor market institutions and policies. U.S. superiority in productivity growth, according to Gordon, derives from the much more supportive and effective environment for innovation. The economic dynamism of the United States draws on many well-springs, including education, management training, patent protection, financial infrastructure, and a welcoming environment for skilled immigrants.

However, a warning note on innovation and productivity growth is struck by Baumol. Revisiting his earlier seminal work on the cost disease of low productivity growth, he reminds us that the distinction between progressive and stagnant sectors can apply as much within services as between services and other sectors; while virtually all slow growers are services, not all services are slow growers, with some high-tech service sectors such as communications being productivity leaders. The core reason for stagnant sectors is the "cost disease of personal services," the handicraft attributes of person-to-person contact where quality of service is reduced if the duration of contact is curtailed. This contrasts with manufacturing, where the labor time applied in production is of no concern to the purchaser of the product. Baumol, however, highlights one key set of services, those related to R&D and innovative activities, that are not only subject to cost disease themselves but may be deemed the ultimate source of the cost-disease problem. It is R&D and innovation that, in the final analysis, give rise to the productivity growth in agriculture and manufacturing and therefore to these sectors' continuing fall in employment requirements. However, R&D and innovation are themselves stagnant sectors, subject to cost disease, which will eventually reduce their contribution to productivity growth in the rest of the economy.

How far do the insights from these varying perspectives point towards a reorientation of the way we think about the role the service sector in the modern economy? Traditionally, services have been placed as the third in the trinity of major sectors. The primary group is based on the exploitation of natural resources, in agriculture, mining, and the extraction of natural materials, which secondary processing in the industrial sectors converts into capital and consumer goods. The tertiary service sector, by contrast, produces intangibles. This familiar taxonomy in terms of types of outputs or sequential stages of production seriously underrates the role of services, failing to bring out the pervasiveness and importance of their contribution. The "product supply" approach developed by Gregory and Russo, which takes into account production and employment throughout the product supply chain, shows that the separateness implied in the taxonomy fails to convey the interconnectedness within production. Virtually every sector is involved in the production process for every output in addition to its own. This holds for services as much as for primary products and manufactures. Moreover, structural change in the modern economy, rather than being a linear progression from primary to secondary to tertiary production, increasingly involves a switch into the purchase of services by manufacturers and also by service producers, and a rising role of business-to-business transactions in services. To rephrase Sraffa, contemporary economic activity increasingly comprises not so much "the production of commodities by means of commodities" as "the production of services by means of services."

A major advantage of the product supply approach is that it brings to the fore the potential for achieving productivity growth through efficiency gains within the supply chain. This applies as strongly to services as to the production of goods, and is of particular relevance to the service sector, so often seen as the natural context for the cost disease. Even where supplying the final service requires the time of the provider in an incompressible way, precluding immediate productivity gains, efficiency gains for the service delivery overall can still be achieved through the supply chain. Moreover, the product supply approach highlights productivity gains achieved in the production of services, which are then transmitted throughout the economy through business-to-business transactions.

At the macroeconomic level employment outcomes at any given rate of economic growth can be viewed as determined by the race between demand expansion, which is job-creating, and productivity growth, which is job-destroying. On this perspective the United States–Europe employment gap can be effectively attributed, not to the usual suspects of labor market institutions, but to the differing macroeconomic growth patterns of the U.S. and European economies in terms of the balance between employment and productivity growth. Over the period from the 1970s to the mid-1990s, the European pattern of development can be seen as an "intensive" one, by comparison with the "extensive" pattern characterizing the United States. In the European economies the expansion of labor input was at most limited, reflected in relatively static participation rates in employment and falling hours of work. The counterpart to this pattern was a higher rate of labor productivity growth in the European economies, leading to a substantial narrowing, in some cases elimination, of the productivity gap with the United States. The United States, on the other hand, followed a more extensive pattern, with sharply increasing participation rates, particularly by women, and longer working hours, reflected in lower rates of productivity growth, particularly on a per-hour basis. Hence European concern about the initially rising, subsequently persistent, employment gap could be counterbalanced by its success in reducing the productivity gap. As noted by Gregory and Russo, times may now be changing. The most recent years have seen remarkable recovery in productivity growth in the United States, now sustained for close to a decade. The employment growth that has accompanied this development has been less robust than in earlier decades, with employment rates no longer rising. At the same time employment in the European economies has begun to show the beginnings of a long-awaited recovery, with employment rates edging upwards, although typically still well short of the Lisbon targets or even the U.S. levels of the 1970s.

This perspective on the respective growth process in the United States and Europe in turn prompts another question: The trade-off between productivity growth and jobs emerges for any given rate of economic growth, but what determines the rate of growth? Have there been systematic differences between the United States and Europe in the total growth available, which would change the terms of the trade-off? Growth is often seen as reflecting the supply-side performance of the economy only; innovation, including in the services, is particularly identified by Gordon as giving the U.S. superiority. Salverda and Schettkat, on the other hand, draw attention to the "demand gap" between the United States and the Europe, which has been outstripping the income gap for some years. The high level of household demand in the United States reflects both the low rate of household savings and the high level of labor input. On the European side macroeconomic policies have been a significant influence depressing demand. Through the 1980s and into the 1990s the reduction of inflation was the dominant policy objective; monetary stability, seen as an essential precondition for achieving the goal of monetary union, called for tight monetary policies. In addition, in some countries fiscal considerations reinforced monetary objectives, with the rolling back of the frontiers of the public sector seen as bringing fiscal benefits as well as having political appeal. Tight monetary policies and cutbacks in public payrolls, separately or in combination, depressed employment. This sustained contractionary stance of macroeconomic policy in much of Europe contrasts with the more expansionary orientation of the Fed and the macroeconomic buoyancy of the United States in the Clinton years.

Since the later 1990s, however, this generalization about the roles of employment and productivity growth has swung into reverse. The U.S. economy has been achieving strong productivity gains accompanied by a concern about "jobless growth"; the recovery from the 2001 recession is now identified as the worst recovery for jobs since the Second World War. At the same time productivity growth in the European economies has faltered, putting into reverse the convergence towards U.S. levels achieved over the previous four decades and losing a substantial part of the ground previously won. Is this a pointer towards convergence between the American and European growth patterns, with potential implications for the reduction of the employment gap?

More broadly, what are the likely prospects for the evolution of the employment gap, and how far should this be a source of concern? (We bear in mind that while the United States–Europe divide in employment records is convenient as a broad-brush distinction, substantial variation exists within each grouping.) Salverda and Schettkat point out that the major part of the gap relates to services, where the U.S. employment rate has long exceeded the rate in Europe, a gap masked until recent decades by the higher European employment rates in agriculture and industry. The structural shifts of employment successively out of agriculture and manufacturing (deindustrialization) and the radical restructuring of these sectors are now well advanced in the European economies, and over recent years employment in services has been growing in Europe at rates comparable to the United States. This makes it unlikely that the employment gap will widen further. Indeed, its flattening off has already been evident since the 1990s, and in the early years of the new century employment rates in the United States began to show signs of decline.

Further, the employment gap does not relate to prime age men, among whom employment rates are broadly comparable between Europe and the United States; rather, the jobs gap occurs among women, and the young and those approaching retirement. Although women in the European economies have been entering the labor force later and more slowly than in the United States, the trend towards greater female participation in paid work is already clear. On the evidence of U.S. experience from the 1960s and 1970s the rising educational attainment of women prompts higher employment participation through many channels. By increasing women's reward from market work, it has enabled them to climb the wage hierarchy and improved their career prospects, in turn strengthening a commitment to work even among young mothers. Although European women are catching up in tertiary education everywhere, the educational attainment of American women remains ahead of most European countries. The share of young women with a tertiary degree in many EU countries still only equals the share among older female cohorts in the United States. The trend towards increased labor market participation among European women is likely to be sustained, given the unsatisfied demand for labor market jobs among women in the European economies to which the OECD has drawn attention. The "marketization" process will then cumulatively generate jobs in replacement of home production, many of them jobs for which women are well suited. Europeans still retire from work at earlier ages than their American counterparts, but with ageing populations and rising dependency ratios moves towards later retirement are already on the political agenda in several European countries. In the United States continuation in employment secures continuing medical insurance coverage, typically available by residence in European countries. This is one respect in which part of the jobs shortage in Europe may be generated by, and reflect the conditions of, the European social model.

The employment gap is as much about hours of work as about employment. Hours of work raise two distinct issues: the weekly or annual hours of full-time workers, and the incidence and size of part-time jobs. For full-time workers the trend towards shorter hours in Europe appears to have reversed in the early 2000s. The most notable instance is France with the retreat from the 35-hour week, but in Germany also major private sector firms are bargaining an upwards revision to working hours. The expansion of part-time work, particularly for women, continues to show a small expansion across the European economies. It has the formal endorsement of the Kok Report assessing progress within the EU towards achieving the Lisbon targets for increased employment rates, and a number of policy initiatives within member states, particularly on support for child-raising, are giving support. As with full-time jobs, there appears to be unsatisfied latent demand for more part-time jobs for women in Europe.

The United States–Europe jobs gap can be seen as the outcome of the conjunction of particular historical trends in employment and productivity occurring simultaneously on the two sides of the Atlantic, trends that are now beginning to be reversed. The employment gap began to emerge as American women, responding to the expansion of college education and the progressive social climate that also gave rise to the civil rights movement, moved into the labor market in increasing numbers, responding to and further promoting the development of the service sector. Supported by this growth of female labor supply and further by immigration, the pattern of development in the United States became an extensive one, with rapid employment expansion but sluggish productivity growth. The European economies, on the other hand, badly hit by the recession of the 1980s on top of the structural decline of agricultural and manufacturing employment, experienced largely static employment, achieving output growth through productivity gains and substantially narrowing, in some cases closing, the long-standing productivity gap with the United States. Both of these patterns can now be seen as atypical. In the United States strong productivity growth has reemerged since the mid-1990s, and employment growth has almost disappeared. In Europe employment rates, particularly among women, are increasing but productivity gains have been at best modest. The employment gap is already narrowing in the early years of this century, a trend that seems set to continue.

The continuing development of the service sector and its position as the dominant locus of employment characterizes all industrialized economies. The fundamental force driving this development is nothing less than the process of economic growth itself. The continued search for new advances and enhanced productivity prompts increasing specialization and with it the transfer of more and more economic activities to the market. The process of "marketization" in this wide sense has, from a long-run historical perspective, enabled the transformation from a subsistence existence based on self-sufficient households to the modern economy, supporting the enormous income growth that has been achieved along with a substantial decline in working hours. This process of specialization requires market transactions; supporting the ever-increasing range of market transactions and activities requires services. This process of specialization and marketization is the key to future economic progress, and will continue to sustain a growing role for the service sector.

Bibliography

Alesina, A., E. Glaeser, and B. Sacerdote. 2005. "Work and Leisure in the US and Europe: Why So Different?" In *NBER Macroeconomics Annual, 2005*. Cambridge: MIT Press.

Appelbaum, E., and P. Albin. 1990. "Differential Characteristics of Employment Growth in Service Industries." In *Labor Market Adjustments to Structural Change and Technological Progress*, ed. E. Appelbaum and Ronald Schettkat. New York: Praeger.

Appelbaum, E., and Ronald Schettkat. 2001. "Are Prices Unimportant? The Changing Structure of the Industrialized Economies." In *The Growth of Service Industries: The Paradox of Exploding Costs and Persistent Demand*, ed. Thijs Ten Raa and Ronald Schettkat. Cheltenham: Edward Elgar.

Atkinson Review. 2005. *Final Report: Measurement of Government Output and Productivity for the National Accounts*. London: Office of National Statistics.

Bailey, M. N. 1993. "Competition, Regulation, and Efficiency in Service Industries." *Brookings Papers* 1993, no. 2: 71–130.

Bailey, M. N., and R. M. Solow. 2001. "International Productivity Comparisons Built from the Firm Level." *Journal of Economic Perspectives* 15, no. 3: 151–73.

Baker, D., A. Glyn, D. Howell, and J. Schmitt. 2004. "Labor Market Institutions and Unemployment." In *Questioning Liberalization: Unemployment, Labor Markets, and the Welfare State*, ed. D. Howell. Oxford: Oxford University Press.

Barnard A., and C. Jones. 1996. "Comparing Apples to Oranges: Productivity Measurement and Convergence Across Industries and Countries." *American Economic Review* 86:1216–38.

———. 2000. "Comparing Apples to Oranges: Reply." December 7. http://elsa .berkeley.edu/~chad/sorensen.pdf.

Bartlesman, Eric, Andrea Bassanini, John Haltiwanger, Ron Jarmin, Stefano Scarpetta, and Thorsten Schank. 2002. "The Spread of ICT and Productivity Growth: Is Europe Really Lagging Behind in the New Economy?" OECD draft report presented at the conference "The Information Economy: Productivity Gains and the Digital Divide," Catania, Sicily, June 15.

Basker, E. 2005. "Job Creation or Destruction? Labor-Market Effects of Wal-Mart Expansion." *Review of Economics and Statistics* 87, no 1: 174–83.

Baumol, William J. 1967. "The Macroeconomics of Unbalanced Growth: The Anatomy of Urban Crisis." *American Economic Review* 62:415–26.

———. 2001. "Paradox of the Services: Exploding Costs, Persistent Demand." In *The Growth of Service Industries: The Paradox of Exploding Costs and Persistent Demand*, ed. Thijs Ten Raa and Ronald Schettkat. Cheltenham: Edward Elgar.

Baumol, William J. 2002. *The Free-Market Innovation Machine: Analyzing the Growth Miracle of Capitalism*. Princeton: Princeton University Press.

Baumol, William J., Sue Anne Batey Blackman, and Edward N. Wolff. 1989. *Productivity and American Leadership: The Long View*. Cambridge: MIT Press.

Baumol, William J., and Edward N. Wolff. 1984. "On Interindustry Differences in Absolute Productivity." *Journal of Political Economy* 92, no. 6: 1017–34.

Becker, G. S. 1965. "A Theory of the Allocation of Time." *Economic Journal* 75 (September): 493–517.

Benston, George. 1964. "The Cost of Bank Operations." Ph.D. diss., University of Chicago.

Bertola, G. 1999. "Microeconomic Perspectives on Aggregate Labor Markets." In *Handbook of Labor Economics*, ed. O. Ashenfelter and D. Card, vol. 3C. Amsterdam: North Holland.

Bibow, J. 2003. "On the "Burden" of German Unification." *Banca Nazionale del Lavoro Quarterly Review* 56:137–69.

Blanchard, O. 2004. "The Economic Future of Europe." *Journal of Economic Perspectives* 18:3–26.

Blanchard, O., and J. Wolfers. 2000. "The Role of Shocks and Institutions in the Rise of European Unemployment." *Economic Journal* 110:1–33.

Blinder, Alan S. 1973. "Wage Discrimination: Reduced Form and Structural Estimates." *Journal of Human Resources* 8:436–55.

Blow, L. 2004. "Household Expenditures Patterns in the UK." DEMPATEM Working Paper No. 2, February.

Blow, L., A. S. Kalwij, and J. Ruiz-Castillo. 2004. "Methodological Issues on the Analysis of Consumer Demand Patterns over Time and across Countries." DEMPATEM Working Paper No. 9, February.

Bureau of Labor Standards (BLS). 2000. "Comparative Real Gross Domestic Product Per Capita and Per Employed Person." http://www.bls.gov/fls/flsgdp .pdf. Updated June 2006.

Bresnahan, Timothy F., and Robert J. Gordon. 1997. Introduction to *The Economics of New Goods*, ed. Timothy F. Bresnahan and Robert J. Gordon. Chicago: University of Chicago Press.

Bresnahan, Timothy F., and Franco Malerba. 1999. "Industrial Dynamics and the Evolution of Firms' and Nations' Competitive Capabilities in the World Computer Industry." In *Sources of Industrial Leadership: Studies of Seven Industries*, ed. David C. Mowery and Richard R. Nelson. Cambridge: Cambridge University Press.

Bruyère, M., and O. Chagny. 2002. "The Fragility of International Comparisons of Employment and Hours Worked: An Attempt to Reduce Data Heterogeneity." Observatoire Français des Conjonctures Économiques, No. 2002–05. http://www.ofce.sciences-po.fr/pdf/dtravail/wp2002–05.pdf.

Card, D., F. Kramarz, and T. Lemieux. 1999. "Changes in the Relative Structure of Wages and Employment: A Comparison of the United States, Canada, and France." *Canadian Journal of Economics* 32, no. 4: 843–77.

Card, D., and A. B. Krueger. 1997. *Myth and Measurement*. Princeton: Princeton University Press.

Clark, Colin. 1940. *The Conditions of Economic Progress*. London: Macmillan.
———. 1951. *The Conditions of Economic Progress*. 2nd ed. London: Macmillan.
Colecchia, Allessandra, and Paul Schreyer. 2001. "ICT Investment and Economic Growth in the 1990s: Is the United States a Unique Case?" OECD, Paris, draft paper, October 7.
Cox, Harvey. 1965. *The Secular City: Secularization and Urbanization in Theological Perspective*. New York: Macmillan
Daveri, Francesco. 2002. "The *New Economy* in Europe (1992–2001)." IGIER Working Paper No. 213, April.
Deaton, A., and J. Muellbauer. 1980. *Economics and Consumer Behavior*. Cambridge: Cambridge University Press.
Deelen, M., and Ronald Schettkat. 2004. "Household Demand Patterns in West Germany: 1978–1993." DEMPATEM Working Paper No. 5, February.
DEMPATEM Project. 2003. Demand Patterns and Employment Growth: Consumption and Services in France, Germany, The Netherlands, Spain, the United Kingdom, and the United States. http://www.uva-aias.net/lower.asp?id=82& lang=en.
Devroye, D., and R. B. Freeman. 2001. "Does Inequality in Skills Explain Inequality of Earnings across Advanced Countries?" NBER Working Paper No. 8140, February.
Dietzenbacher, E., and B. Los. 1998. "Structural Decomposition Techniques: Sense and Sensitivity." *Economic Systems Research* 10:307–23.
Dollar, D., and E. N. Wolff. 1993. *Competitiveness, Convergence, and International Specialization*. Cambridge: MIT Press.
Fisher, A.G.B. 1935. *The Clash of Progress and Security*. London: Macmillan.
Foster, L., J. Haltiwanger, and C. J. Krizan. 2002. "The Link between Aggregate and Micro Productivity Growth: Evidence from Retail Trade." NBER Working Paper No. 9120, August.
Frank, R. 1999. *Luxury Fever: Why Money Fails to Satisfy in an Era of Excess*. New York: Free Press.
Freeman, Richard B. 1995. "The Limits of Wage Flexibility to Curing Unemployment." *Oxford Review of Economic Policy* 11, no. 1: 63–72.
———. 2005. "Labor Market Institutions without Blinders: The Debate over Flexibility and Labor Market Performance." NBER Working Paper No. 11286.
Freeman, Richard B., and L. Bell. 2001. "The Incentive for Working Hard: Explaining Hours Worked Differences in the US and Germany." *Labour Economics*, special conference volume, 8, no. 2: 181–202.
Freeman, Richard B., and M. Rein. 1988. *The Dutch Choice: A Plea for Social Policy Complementary to Work*. The Hague: HRWP.
Freeman, Richard B., and Ronald Schettkat. 1998. *Differentials in Service Industry Employment Growth: Germany and the US in the Comparable German American Structural Database*. European Commission Report, Brussels.
———. 1999. "The Role of Wage and Skill Differences in US-German Employment Differences." In *Jahrbücher für Nationalökonomie und Statistik*, special edition, ed. W. Franz, 49–66.

Freeman, Richard B., and Ronald Schettkat. 2001a. "Marketization of Production and the US-Europe Employment Gap." *Oxford Bulletin of Economics and Statistics*, special issue, 63:647–70.

———. 2001b. "Skill Compression, Wage Differentials, and Employment: Germany versus the US." *Oxford Economic Papers* 53, no. 3: 582–603.

———. 2002. "Marketization of Production and the US-Europe Employment Gap." NBER Working Paper No. 8797.

———. 2005. "Marketization of Household Production and the EU-US Gap in Work." *Economic Policy* 1:7–50.

Fuchs, Victor R. 1968. *The Service Economy*. New York: National Bureau of Economic Research, distributed by Columbia University Press.

———. 1980. "Economic Growth and the Rise of Service Employment." NBER Working Paper No. 0486.

Gardes, F., and C. Starzec. 2003. "Household Demand Patterns in France, 1980–1995." DEMPATEM, August.

Glyn, A., and E. Erdem. 2001. "Employment Growth, Structural Change, and Capital Accumulation" In *The Growth of Service Industries: The Paradox of Exploding Costs and Persistent Demand*, ed. Thijs Ten Raa and Ronald Schettkat. Northampton, Mass.: Edward Elgar.

Glyn, Andrew, Wiemer Salverda, Joachim Möller, John Schmitt, and Michel Sollogoub. 2005. "Employment Differences in Services: The Role of Wage, Productivity and Demand." DEMPATEM Working Paper No. 12, revised version.

Goldin, Claudia. 1998. "America's Graduation from High School: The Evolution and Spread of Secondary Schooling in the Twentieth Century." *Journal of Economic History* 58 (June): 345–74.

Gordon, Robert J. 1990. *The Measurement of Durable Goods Prices*. Chicago: University of Chicago Press.

———. 1996. "Problems in the Measurement and Performance of Service-Sector Productivity in the United States." NBER Working Paper No. W5519, March.

———. 2003. "Exploding Productivity Growth: Context, Causes, and Implications." *Brookings Papers on Economic Activity* 2003, no. 2: 207–98.

———. 2004. "Two Centuries of Economic Growth: Europe Chasing the American Frontier." NBER Working Paper No. 10662, August.

Greenhalgh, C., and Mary Gregory. 2000. "Labour Productivity and Product Quality: Their Growth and Inter-Industry Transmission in the UK, 1979 to 1990." In *Productivity, Innovation, and Economic Performance*, ed. R. Barrell, G. Mason, and M. O'Mahoney. New York: Cambridge University Press.

———. 2001. "Structural Change and the Emergence of the New Service Economy." *Oxford Bulletin of Economics and Statistics*, special issue "The Labour Market Consequences of Technical and Structural Change," 63:629–46.

Gregori, Tullio. 2000. "Outsourcing and Employment Service Growth in Italy." DiSES Working Paper No. 67, Trieste University.

Gregory, Mary, and Giovanni Russo. 2004. "The Employment Impact of Differences in Demand and Production Structures." DEMPATEM Working Paper No. 10.

Gregory, Mary, B. Zissimos, and C. Greenhalgh. 2001. "Jobs for the Skilled: How Technology, Trade and Domestic Demand Changed the Structure of UK Employment." *Oxford Economic Papers* 53, no. 1: 20–46.

Griliches, Z. 1992. Introduction to *Output Measurement in the Service Sector*, ed. Z. Griliches. Chicago: University of Chicago Press.

Harker, P. T. 1995. "The Service Quality and Productivity Challenge." In *Service Quality and Productivity Challenge*, ed. P. T. Harker. Norwell, Mass.: Kluwer Academic.

Heshmati, A. 2003. "Productivity Growth, Efficiency and Outsourcing in Manufacturing and Service Industries." *Journal of Economic Surveys* 17:79–112.

Heston A., R. Summers, and B. Aten. 2002. *Penn World Table*. Version 6.1. Center for International Comparisons at the University of Pennsylvania.

Howell, David, ed. 2005. *Fighting Unemployment: The Limits of Free Market Orthodoxy*. New York: Oxford University Press.

Ironmonger, D. 2000. "Household Production and the Household Economy." Research paper, Department of Economics, University of Melbourne.

Jorgenson, Dale W., and Kevin J. Stiroh. 2000. "Raising the Speed Limit: U. S. Economic Growth in the Information Age." *Brookings Papers on Economic Activity* 2000, no. 1: 125–211.

Juster, F. T., and F. P. Stafford. 1991. "The Allocation of Time: Empirical Findings, Behavioral Models, and Problems of Measurement." *Journal of Economic Literature* 29, no. 2: 471–522.

Kaldor, N. 1966. *Causes of the Slow Rate of Economic Growth of the United Kingdom*. Cambridge: Cambridge University Press.

Kalwij, Adriaan S., and Wiemer Salverda. 2004. "Changing Household Demand Patterns in the Netherlands: Some Explanations." DEMPATEM Working Paper No. 3, February.

Katz, L. F., G. W. Loveman, and D. G. Blanchflower. 1995. "A Comparison of Changes in the Structure of Wages in Four OECD Countries." In *Differences and Changes in Wage Structures*, ed. Richard B. Freeman and L. F. Katz. Chicago: University of Chicago Press.

Kravis, Irving B., Alan W. Heston, and Robert Summers. 1978. "Real GDP per Capita for More than One Hundred Countries." *Economic Journal* 88:215–41.

Krueger, A., and J.-S. Pischke. 1997. "Observations and Conjectures on the US Employment Miracle." NBER Working Paper No. 6147.

———. 1999. "Observation and Conjectures on the U.S. Employment Miracle." Paper presented to the Meetings of the American Economic Association, January, New York.

Langlois, Richard N. 2002. "Computers and Semiconductors." In *Technological Innovation and Economic Performance*, ed. Benn Steil, David G. Victor, and Richard R. Nelson. Princeton: Princeton University Press.

Lerner, J. 2002. "Venture Capital." In *Technological Innovation and Economic Performance*, ed. Benn Steil, David G. Victor, and Richard R. Nelson. Princeton: Princeton University Press.

Linder, S. B. 1970. *The Harried Leisure Class*. New York: Columbia University Press.

Luengo-Prado, María-José, and Javier Ruiz-Castillo. 2004. "Demand Patterns in Spain." DEMPATEM Working Paper No. 4, February.

Machin, Stephen, and A. Manning. 1999. "The Causes and Consequences of Long-Term Unemployment in Europe." In *Handbook of Labor Economics*, ed. O. Ashenfelter and D. Card, vol. 3C. Amsterdam: North Holland.

Maddison, A. 1991. *Dynamic Forces in Capitalist Development*. Oxford: Oxford University Press.

———. 1996. "Macroeconomic Accounts for European Countries." In *Quantitative Aspects of Postwar European Economic Growth*, ed. Bart van Ark and Nicholas Crafts. Cambridge: Cambridge University Press.

———. 2001. *The World Economy: A Millennial Perspective*. Paris: OECD.

Manning, A. 2003. *Monopsony in Motion: Imperfect Competition in Labor Markets*. Princeton: Princeton University Press.

McGuckin, Robert H., and Bart van Ark. 2003. *Performance 2002: Productivity, Employment, and Income in the World's Economies*. New York: Conference Board.

McKinsey Global Institute. 1992. *Service Sector Productivity*. Washington, D.C., October.

———. 2002. *Reaching Higher Productivity Growth in France and Germany*.

Messerlin, Patrick A. 2002. "France." In *Technological Innovation and Economic Performance*, ed. Benn Steil, David G. Victor, and Richard R. Nelson. Princeton: Princeton University Press.

Mohr, M. 1992. "Recent and Planned Improvements in the Measurement and Deflation of Services Outputs and Inputs." In *Output Measurement in the Service Sector*, ed. Z. Griliches. Chicago: University of Chicago Press.

Möller, J. 2004. "Lohnkompression im Niedriglohnbereich: Eine Ursache für die unterschiedliche Beschäftigungsentwicklung in Deutschland und den USA?" In *Herausforderungen an den Wirtschaftsstandort Deutschland*, ed. B. Fitzenberger, W. Smolny, and P. Winker. Baden-Baden: Nomos, 2004.

Momigliano, F., and D. Siniscalco. 1982. "Note in tema di terziarizzazione e deindustrializzazione." *Moneta e Credito* 26:143–81.

Mowery, David C. 1999. "The Computer Software Industry." In *Sources of Industrial Leadership: Studies of Seven Industries*, ed. David C. Mowery and Richard R. Nelson. Cambridge: Cambridge University Press.

Mowery, David C., and Richard R. Nelson. 1999a. "Explaining Industrial Leadership." In *Sources of Industrial Leadership: Studies of Seven Industries*, ed. David C. Mowery and Richard R. Nelson. Cambridge: Cambridge University Press.

———, eds. 1999b. *Sources of Industrial Leadership: Studies of Seven Industries*. Cambridge: Cambridge University Press.

Multinational Time Use Study (MTUS). N.d. http://www.iser.essex.ac.uk/mtus/index.php.

Nickell, S. J. 1997. "Unemployment and Labor Market Rigidities: Europe versus North America." *Journal of Economic Perspectives* 11, no. 3: 55–74.

———. 2003. "Labour Market Institutions and Unemployment in OECD Countries." *CESifo DICE Report* 1, no. 2: 13–26.

Nickell, S. J., and B. Bell. 1996. "Changes in the Distribution of Wages and

Unemployment in the OECD Countries." *American Economic Review Papers and Proceedings* 86, no. 5: 302–8.

Nickell, S. J., and R. Layard. 1999. "Labour Market Institutions and Economic Performance." In *Handbook of Labor Economics*, ed. O. Ashenfelter and D. Card, vol. 3C. Amsterdam: North Holland.

Nordhaus, W. 2002. "Productivity Growth and the New Economy." *Brookings Papers on Economic Activity* 2002, no. 2: 211–44.

Oaxaca, Ronald. 1973. "Male-Female Wage Differentials in Urban Labor Markets." *International Economic Review* 14:673–709.

Oi, W. Y., and S. Rosen. 1992. "Productivity in the Distributive Trades." In *Output Measurement in the Service Sector*, ed. Z. Griliches. Chicago: University of Chicago Press.

Oliner, Stephen D., and Daniel E. Sichel. 2000. "The Resurgence of Growth in the Late 1990s: Is Information Technology the Story?" *Journal of Economic Perspectives* 14: 3–22.

———. 2002. "Information Technology and Productivity: Where Are We Now and Where Are We Going?" *Economic Review* (Federal Reserve Bank of Atlanta) 87, no. 3:15–44.

O'Mahony, M. 1999. *Britain's Productivity Performance, 1950–1996*. London: National Institute of Economic and Social Research.

O'Mahony, M., and Willem de Boer. 2002. "Britain's Relative Productivity Performance: Updates to 1999." National Institute of Economic and Social Research, March.

O'Mahony, M., N. Oultonand, and J. Vass. 1996. "Productivity in Market Services: International comparisons." National Institute of Economic and Social Research Discussion Paper No. 105.

O'Mahony, M., and B. van Ark. 2003. *EU Productivity and Competitiveness: An Industry Perspective: Can Europe Resume the Catching-up Process?* DG Enterprise, European Union, Luxembourg. http://www.ggdc.net/pub/EU_productivity_and_competitiveness.pdf.

Organization for Economic Cooperation and Development (OECD). 1979. *Labor Force Statistics, 1966–1977*. Paris.

———. 1994. *OECD Jobs Study: Facts, Analysis and Strategy*. Paris: OECD.

———. 1996. *Services, Measuring Real Annual Value Added*. Paris: OECD.

———. 1997. *International Adult Literacy Survey*, Paris: OECD.

———. 2000a. "Employment in the Service Economy :A Reassessment." In *OECD Employment Outlook 2000*. Paris: OECD.

———. 2000b. OECD Statistical Compendium: Edition 02 # 2000. CD-ROM.

———. 2001. "The Characteristics and Quality of Service Sector Jobs." In *OECD Employment Outlook 2001*. Paris: OECD.

———. 2002. *Purchasing Power Parities and Real Expenditures: 1999 Benchmark Year*. Paris: OECD.

———. 2003. *Employment Outlook 2003*. Paris: OECD.

———. *Employment Outlook*, annual. Paris: OECD.

———. Annual Hours Worked per Person Database. http://www1.oecd.org/scripts.

———. Economic Outlook Database. http://new.sourceoecd.org.

Organization for Economic Cooperation and Development (OECD). Input-Output Database. http://www1.oecd.org/dsti/eas/input-output database.

———. Labour Force Surveys Database. http://www1.oecd.org/scripts.

———. STAN Database. http://new.sourceoecd.org/database/stan.

OECD and Statistics Canada. 1998. *International Adult Literacy Survey*. Paris: OECD.

Oulton, N. 2001. "Must the Growth Rate Decline? Baumol's Unbalanced Growth Revisited." *Oxford Economic Papers* 53, no. 4: 605–27.

Pasinetti, L. 1973. "The Notion of Vertical Integration in Economic Analysis." *Metroeconomica* 25:1–4.

Petit, P. 2000. "Europe in the Triad: Growth Pattern and Structural Changes." In *Technology and the Future of European Employment*, ed. P. Petit and L. Soete. Cheltenham: Edward Elgar.

Phelps, Edmund S. 2003. "Economic Underperformance in Continental Europe: A Prospering Economy Runs on the Dynamism from Its Economic Institutions." Lecture, Royal Institute for International Affairs, London, March 18.

Piketty, T. 1998. "L'emploi dans les services en France et aux Etats-Unis: Une analyse structurelle sur la longue period." *Economie et Statistique* 318:73–99.

Pisano, Gary P. 2002. "Pharmaceutical Biotechnology." In *Technological Innovation and Economic Performance*, ed. Benn Steil, David G. Victor, and Richard R. Nelson. Princeton: Princeton University Press.

Pollack, R. A., and M. L. Wachter. 1975. "The Relevance of the Household Production Function and Its Implications for the Allocation of Time." *Journal of Political Economy* 83, no. 2: 255–77.

Prescott, E. C. 2004. "Why Do Americans Work So Much More Than Europeans?" *Federal Reserve Bank of Minnesota Quarterly Review* 28, no. 1: 2–13.

Rhine-Westphalia Institute for Economic Research (RWI). 2002. *New Economy: An Assessment from a German Viewpoint*. Report commissioned by the Ministry of Economics and Technology, Federal Republic of Germany, Essen, February.

Robinson, John P., and Geoffrey Godbey. 1999. *Time for Life: The Surprising Ways Americans Use Their Time*. University Park: Pennsylvania State University Press.

Rosenberg, Nathan. 1986. "The Impact of Technological Innovation: A Historical View." In *The Positive Sum Strategy: Harnessing Technology for Economic Growth*, ed. Ralph Landau and Nathan Rosenberg. Washington, D.C.: National Academy Press.

Russo, Giovanni, and Ronald Schettkat. 1999. "Are Structural Economic Dynamics a Myth? Changing Industrial Structure in the Final Product Concept." *Economia e Lavaro* 3–4:173–88.

Salter, W.E.G. 1960. *Productivity and Technical Change*. Cambridge: Cambridge University Press.

Salverda, Wiemer, S. Bazen, and Mary Gregory. 2001. *The European-American Employment Gap, Wage Inequality, Earnings Mobility, and Skill: A Study for France, Germany, the Netherlands, the United Kingdom and the United States*. Final Report, European Commission, Brussels.

Salverda, Wiemer. Forthcoming. "Does Low Dutch Unemployment Reflect Superior Performance or Labour Market Transformation?" In *A New Architecture for Labor Market Statistics*, ed. Barry Bluestone and Andrew Sharpe. Chicago: University of Chicago Press.

Schelling, T. 1975. *Micromotives and Macrobehavior*. Cambridge: Cambridge University Press.

Schettkat, Ronald. 2003. "Differences in US-German Time-Allocation: Why Do Americans Work Longer Hours Than Germans?" IZA Discussion Paper No. 697, January.

———. 2004. "US-Sclerosis? What Happened to the 'Great American Job Machine'?" *Challenge* 47, no.2: 1–12.

Schettkat, Ronald, and Joep Damen. 2004. "Demand Patterns and Employment Structures: An Aggregate Analysis." DEMPATEM Working Paper No. 11, February.

Schettkat, Ronald, and Giovanni Russo. 2001. "Structural Dynamics in Employment in Highly Industrialized Economies." In *Technology and the Future of European Employment*, ed. P. Petit and L. Soete. Cheltenham: Edward Elgar.

Schettkat, Ronald, and Lara Yocarini. 2003. "State of the Art in the Analysis of Structural Changes: DEMPATEM in Perspective." DEMPATEM paper.

Schmitt, John. 2004. "Estimating Household Consumption Expenditures in the United States Using the Interview and Diary Portions of the 1980, 1990, and 1997 Consumer Expenditure Surveys." DEMPATEM Working Paper No. 1, February.

Siebert, Horst. 1997. "Labor Market Rigidities: At the Root of Unemployment in Europe." *Journal of Economic Perspectives* 11, no. 3: 37–54.

Siebert, Horst, and Michael Stope. 2002. "Germany." In *Technological Innovation and Economic Performance*, ed. Benn Steil, David G. Victor, and Richard R. Nelson. Princeton: Princeton University Press.

Sieling, Mark, Brian Friedman, and Mark Dumas. 2001. "Labor Productivity in the Retail Trade Industry, 1987–99." *Monthly Labor Review*, December, 3–14.

Statistiches Budesamt. 1999. "Wo blieibt die Zeit?" Scientific Use File, Wiesbaden.

Stiel, Benn, David G. Victor, and Richard R. Nelson, eds. 2002. *Technological Innovation and Economic Performance*. Princeton: Princeton University Press.

Summers, Robert. 1985. "Services in the International Economy." In *Managing the Service Economy*, ed. Robert P. Inman. Cambridge: Cambridge University Press.

Ten Raa, Thijs, and Ronald Schettkat, eds. 2001. *The Growth of Service Industries: The Paradox of Exploding Costs and Persistent Demand*. Cheltenham: Edward Elgar.

Ten Raa, Thijs, and Edward N. Wolff. 2001. "Outsourcing of Services and the Productivity Recovery in U.S. Manufacturing in the 1980s and 1990s." *Journal of Productivity Analysis* 16:149–65.

Theil, H. 1967. *Economics and Information Theory*. Chicago: Rand McNally.

Triplett, J. E., and B. P. Bosworth. 2003. "Productivity Measurement Issues in Service Industries: Baumol's Disease Has Been Cured." *FRBNY Economic Policy Review*, September, 23–33.

Triplett, J. E., and B. P. Bosworth. 2004. *Productivity in the U.S. Services Sector: New Sources of Economic Growth*. Washington, D.C.: Brookings Institution Press.

United Nations Statistics Division. 2003. *National Accounts: About the System of National Accounts, 1993. http://unstats.un.org/unsd/sna1993/introduction .asp,* available July 2003.

U.S. Bureau of Labor Statistics. 1978. *Survey of Consumer Expenditures, 1972– 73.* Washington, D.C.

U.S. Bureau of the Census. 1976. *Historical Statistics of the U.S., Colonial Times to 1970.* Washington, D.C.

———. 1979. *Statistical Abstract of the U.S.: 1978.* Washington, D.C.

van Ark, Bart. 2002. "Changing Gear: Productivity, ICT, and Service Industries: Europe and the United States." Paper presented to the Brookings Workshop on Services Industry Productivity, May 17.

van Ark, Bart, and G. de Jong. 2004. *Productiviteit in dienstverlening.* Assen: Koninklijke Van Gorcum, Stichting Management Studies.

van Ark, Bart, Robert Inklaar, and Robert H. McGuckin. 2003. "Changing Gear: Productivity, ICT and Service Industries in Europe and the United States." In *The Industrial Dynamics of the New Digital Economy*, ed. J. F. Christensen and P. Maskell. Cheltenham: Edward Elgar.

van Ark, Bart, and Marcel Timmer. 2001. "PPPs and International Productivity Comparisons: Bottlenecks and New Directions." Prepared for the Joint World Bank–OECD Seminar on Purchasing Power Parties, Washington, D.C., January 30–February 2, 2001.

Vijselaar, Focco, and Ronald Albers. 2002. "New Technologies and Productivity Growth in the Euro Area." European Central Bank Working Paper no. 122, February.

Warren, E., and A. Warren Tyagi. 2003. *The Two Income Trap.* New York: Basic Books.

Wolff, Edward N. 2005. "Measures of Technical Change and Structural Change in Services in the U.S.: Was There a Resurgence of Productivity Growth in Services?" Unpublished manuscript, New York University.

Wright, Gavin. 1990. "The Origins of American Industrial Success: 1879– 1940." *American Economic Review* 80:651–68.

DEMPATEM Working Papers

Index

adult-equivalent expenditures, 119
Adult Literacy Surveys, 205
affirmative action, 206, 216
Albers, 185
Albin, 103n8
Alesina, 3
American exceptionalism, 12, 176, 194
American jobs machine, 4, 15
American way of leisure, 40n
ancillary service activities, 93, 223
annual hours worked, 16n2; average, 164n18
Appelbaum, 103n8
asset income, 116
Atkinson Review, 39

bag-packing services, 156n14
Baily, 4n4
Baker, 18, 199
Barnard and Jones, 162
Bartelsman, et al., 181n
Basker, 41, 157
Baumol, 6, 9–10, 28, 33, 35, 38–39, 53, 72, 75, 79, 110, 112, 125, 141, 224. *See also* cost disease
Bazen, 5
Becker, 208
Bell, 198–199
Benston, 60
big box, 183; formats 176; organization 184; retail formats 12, 184, 184n6, 196, 224; stores 183, 184, 186
biotech, 178, 187, 191, 196; industries 190
Blackman, 72, 75, 75n3
Blanchard, 3, 4n4, 5, 17–19
Blinder, 172. *See also* Blinder-Oaxaca
Blinder-Oaxaca, 152n11, 154, 172
Blow, Kalwij, and Ruiz-Castillo, 131
Bosworth, 33, 39, 39n, 41, 157
bought-in supplies, 8
brain drain, 194n11
Bresnahan, 188n8, 192
Bresnahan and Gordon, 188n8
Bresnahan and Melerba, 192

bricks-and-mortar, 192
Brown, 187n
Budget des Familles, 113. *See also* FBS
budget effects, 110, 112, 131, 132, 136
budget elasticities, 110, 132, 218, 219
budget survey, 7, 115–117, 219; consumer, 11, 36, 109; of households, 11, 109, 111, 216, 218
Bureau of Labor Statistics (BLS), 39n9, 65n1, 115, 179–180n3
business services, 8, 22, 34, 35, 40, 79n4, 82, 90n4, 103, 106, 223
business-sector inputs, 78
business to business, 34, 38, 223, 225

capital accumulation, 145, 156
capital intensification, 145, 159, 160, 160n16, 161, 224
capital market, 177, 192, 196
capital stocks, 160
capital/labor ratio, 52, 159, 160
capital/labor substitution, 12, 38, 156, 159, 223
Card, 36n8, 198
Card, Kramarz, and Lemieux, 36n8, 198
catering sector, 22
censored least absolute deviation, 151–152n9
characteristics effect, 174
child allowances, 116
Clark, 32, 42, 50–51, 217. *See also* service economies
Clark and Fisher, 50–51. *See also* service economies
Colecchia and Schreyer, 185
collective consumption, 8, 27
collective labor agreement, 145. *See also* minimum wages
collective sector, 27
collectivism, 27
communication services, 11, 110, 128, 136
comparative advantage, 13, 204, 205
composition effect, 1, 152, 152n10; workforce, 154. *See also* workforce composition